EAT LIKE A
WILD MAN

EAT LIKE A
WILD MAN

110 YEARS OF GREAT
SPORTS AFIELD RECIPES

Compiled by Rebecca Gray

WILLOW CREEK PRESS
Minocqua, Wisconsin

Published simultaneously in Canada.
Printed in the United States of America.

First Edition

Eat like a wild man: 110 years of great Sports afield recipes
/compiled by Rebecca Gray.
p. cm.
Includes index.
ISBN 1-57223-088-6
1. Cooking. 2. Game and fish cooking—United States. I. Gray, Rebecca.

Willow Creek Press
P.O. Box 147
Minocqua, WI 54548

3 5 7 9 10 8 6 4

C o n t e n t s

FOREWORD XIII

INTRODUCTION XV

FALL COOKING 1
Venison · Bear · Boar · Duck · Goose · Pheasant ·
Quail · Partridge/Grouse · Woodcock · Dove · Steelhead

WINTER COOKING 141
Rabbit · Perch · Pompano · Flounder
Shellfish · Squirrel · Iguana · Frog · Crow

SPRING COOKING 183
Trout · Smelt · Pike · Walleye · Striped Bass · Turkey · Redfish

SUMMER COOKING 225
Bass · Muskie · Salmon · Swordfish · Panfish · Catfish

WILD VEGETABLES 283
Wild Rice · Dandelion and Watercress · Rose Hips

INDEX 299

Author's Note

There are many decided advantages to compiling recipes from 110 years' worth of *Sports Afield* articles: the varied voices, perspectives, attitudes and historical characters lent a personality to this cookbook that simply could not be accomplished in any other way. However, the differences occasionally produced some inconsistencies, too. Some of the authors of the recipes indicated the number of servings their recipe would produce, some did not. Some used ounces, some tablespoons and pounds for measurements. Some are specific about what they mean by "cleaning" a critter (gutted, beheaded, skinned), some are non-specific about cleaning, assuming the readers understand how to prepare fish and game for cooking.

Only very occasionally and when clarity was in jeopardy have I found it necessary to alter a recipe. I believe that the reader has enough foundation in cooking to make his own judgment about how many people two partridge will feed, how to convert ounces to tablespoons or how to fillet a fish. And if that foundation is not all that well founded (or if memory does not always serve, as is the case many times with me), my assumption is that the reader has on hand several tools to assist: measurement conversion tables and a scale; *The L.L. Bean Fish & Game Cookbook* by Angus Cameron, who makes suggestions on serving sizes for each species of bird; or perhaps even an article clipped from *Sports Afield* on a specific technique.

Better yet, I wish for you many opportunities to cook fish and game; to make experience and opinion the basis for decisions on all your creative endeavors in the kitchen.

A c k n o w l e d g m e n t s

With great appreciation to Terry McDonell, Editor-in-Chief and Publisher of *Sports Afield*, whose sterling ability as an editor I have written about at length in other venues. Simply stated, there is no better. Terry has an impeccable sense of when to impose his opinion and when to leave the author to her own devices. Sid Evans, associate editor of *Sports Afield*, who, if he knew how to cook more than antelope chili, could have been the author of this cookbook. His knowledge of "the wild men" and *Sports Afield* history made him an invaluable editor. Plus, his even manner, good humor and facility for dealing with this wild female cook made him a true joy to work with. Steve Bodio for always getting the point, for his exuberance and friendship and for helping to squelch the demons of insecurity that occasionally haunt this writer. Tom Petrie for being a publisher with a heart as well as a brain. And on the *Sports Afield* staff thanks to: Sonje Berg, for her superb copy editing; Carol Cammero, for accomplishing the exhausting job of getting permissions; Michelle Zaffino, for her tireless editing and proofreading; Bethanie Deeney, for her great design and ability to accommodate "design critiquing by committee"; Michael Lawton, for his fabulous design sense, for his efforts to get the cover "right" and, of course, for the good cigars.

Thanks to my children Hope, Sam and Will, for their patience with their sometimes absent and often distracted mother. And there will never be enough words of acknowledgment, thanks, and appreciation for Ed Gray, who not only is my lifetime editor but who gave me the life. I'll simply say it again Ed, thanks.

"Nature is like an enormous restaurant."
Woody Allen, Love and Death, *1975*

F o r e w o r d

Becky Gray just might be the best game cook I know. She is an enthusiastic and skilled shooter and fisher, sets an incredible table, and then writes about it, making it all seem effortless. She taught me, an ethnic North Italian who has been cooking and eating risotto (we call it "risott") since I could reach a stove, a few things about making that staple.

She's also a gracious and tactful hostess. In 1986, after my partner Betsy Huntington died, I spent several months back East, lost, lonely, hurting, and probably impossible for most people to bear for more than ten minutes. Time and time again Becky and her husband Ed (founder and former publisher of *Gray's Sporting Journal*) would invite me over for meals of ducks shot on a local marsh, accompanied by many bottles of good red wine. They'd let me rant or be silent, and quietly hand me another slice of perfectly-done rare duck breast, another glass (or bottle) of wine. Those were among the best and most memorable meals of my life. Afterward, I'd sleep dreamlessly in their guest room, and rise somehow more determined to go on.

Becky can write—and well. She is the author of three (or four, if you count a combined update of two of the earlier volumes) game and fish cookbooks, all of which manage to be informed, illuminating, and funny. I keep them in the food-writing-as-literature section of my library, along with M. F. K. Fisher, John Thorne, Jim Harrison, Patience Gray and Elizabeth David, although the grease spots on their pages betray their many trips to the kitchen. She loves both the wild (Bristol Bay, the Caribbean flats) and the civilized (books, martinis, the already-mentioned good red wines). Hell, I suspect she probably shoots and casts better than I do, as well.

She also has her priorities straight. In her introduction she says that "...food is at the core of hunting and fishing," something that I fear that our civilization, at least in the States, tends to forget. On the one hand, we sometimes carry the laudable practice of catch-and-release to ludicrous lengths: there are now vegetarian fly-fishing groups. On the other, we become obsessed with the numbers of birds shot or the number of points in a trophy rack. These things are all fine in their place, but we should never forget that outdoor sport is an elegant game rooted in our evolutionary past as hunters and gatherers.

None of the people who composed the recipes in this book has forgotten this fact. The files of *Sports Afield* are one of the richest lodes of the hunter-eater tradition in English. They contain everything from classic venison and duck recipes to ones for crow and mountain lion, both of which can be very good. Their authors range from those who describe eating a mouse on a survival course to the formidable A.J. McClane. Becky Gray understands the traditions—when to add something or clarify a detail, when to leave it alone, even when to disagree. (I agree with Becky, not McClane, on woodcock stew, as another writer on food, Guy de la Valdéne, said, if you are going to stew woodcock, "...why not take it a step further and poach the woodcock overnight in equal parts of catsup, pabulum, and Pepto-Bismol?")

But enough talk. Imagine this book to be a meal at the Grays', a meal that embodies the well-lived sportsman's life. There will be wild food, civilized cooking, great stories and conversation. Take it away, Becky.

Steve Bodio
Magdalena, New Mexico 1997

Introduction

Cookbooks, good cookbooks, have a personality. Often the recipes are a straight-forward reflection of the author's character or of a culture or place; but for a cookbook to reach beyond its primary purpose—that of instruction—it must also reveal bias, taste and indeed, the "religion" of the cuisine.

But how was a cookbook that was a compilation of 110 years of fish and game recipes, conceived by no one author, going to have a very distinct personality? This could turn out to be a hodgepodge of recipes produced by a mess of sportsmen who didn't understand or care about good cooking.

Fortunately, my worries were for naught. This book's personality evolved out of the presentation of a bit of history; the history of *Sports Afield*'s outdoor journalism, and of fish and game cooking. It even reflects a bit of the history of cooking in general in the United States. From a spectrum of journalists, all representatives of their time, came the presentation of these overlapping histories; and from that emerged one spirit, one clear philosophy for the cooking of wild food.

In April, 1922, William Perry Brown wrote in *Sports Afield*, "When the hunt was over, the men returned and all of them ready for the fray. There was ground-hog, 'possum and sweet potatoes, baking in round ovens; pumpkins, beans and hominy, stewing in swinging open fire pots; pyramids of pies were being reared on shelf and table; biscuit, bread, scones and flapjacks lay about in smoking hillocks; coffee in boilers and in pots by the gallon was simmering fragrantly; while on the outskirts of this culinary fairyland hovered squads of juvenile Coveites, who begged, pilfered and surreptitiously gorged themselves almost unnoticed."

Many of the food entries in the early issues of *Sports Afield* resemble this one. The writer describes the cooking scene with great gusto, but rarely explains how the food was produced. The game cooking done at home was performed by women and often by women servants; the cooking in the field was usually performed by the guides. And the field meals were simple, probably because the massive procedure of getting ingredients into the wilderness for their multi-week expeditions made an involved meal unthinkable. If the gentlemen did make a meal the cooking was the most basic and minimal, and they described their participation in the preparation as an unusual and exciting event. Even the ladies' magazines considered it unnecessary to devote much space to meal preparation; so not surprisingly, this sporting magazine for gentlemen had virtually no food features.

But food is at the core of hunting and fishing. In a 1943 *Sports Afield* article by Colonel Townsend Whelen he says, "Some of the most valuable things I learned in [the wilderness] had to do with food and its preparation and cooking. In dietetics, prejudice and sentiment take the place of knowledge and common sense almost as much as they do in religion." And by the 1950s there were not only long features in *Sports Afield* about food, but actual recipes. The better articles and recipes were commonly written by food professionals (Duncan Hines, of the flour and cake-mix company; and restaurateurs Vincent Sardi Jr., of Sardi's Restaurant, and Roy L. Alciatore of Antoine's). Or there were very brief recipes accompanied by unappealing photos and incorporating ingredients such as frozen vegetables. Much of the real gourmet cooking was still being done outside of the home and was strongly wedded to time-consuming and complicated French cooking techniques. Although French cuisine did often include fish and game preparation, at home Mr. Birdseye and the age of convenience reigned over any wild cooking.

In the early 1960s the food world began to change, largely due Julia Child, who brought modified and somewhat streamlined French cooking methods into people's homes. This helped stimulate an explosion of interest in fine food and, more importantly, in the preparation of gourmet meals. There was a craving for new and exotic tastes and fish and game fell naturally into that category. *Sports Afield* began carrying at least one and sometimes two articles in each issue about cooking. The beautiful food photography of Arie de Zanger and Amos Chan accompanied the competent writing of well-known sportsmen who wanted to enhance their reputations with examples of their competency as cooks.

Many of these recipes have been included because they are just plain great. No one can dispute the creative and knowledgeable writings of S.G.B. Tennant or A.J. McClane; they are culinary masters. Some recipes have been included because they help paint the historical portrait that gives this book its character. But finally, and really at the soul of why all of these recipes are here, is the fact that they spring from a single spirit, and are defining of a singular type of person. Steve Bodio probably said it better than anyone in a wonderful essay he published last year: "In living my good and reasonable life, I suspect I should sometimes kill some beautiful animal and eat it, to remind myself what I am." Each author in this book is aware of what it means to engage in the adventure of hunting and fishing, to live directly off the fruits of the natural world, to eat like a wild man. Hopefully we haven't forgotten how to do that in the last 110 years, and hopefully every one of these recipes projects the wilderness in what we cook, what we eat, and who we are.

Rebecca Gray
Lyme, New Hampshire 1997

Fall

FOR THE HUNTER, AND OFTEN FOR THE fisherman, fall is the wildest season of the year. It's when a bit of chaos begins to reign—so much sporting opportunity, so little time. First there's the home-base hunting for partridge and deer—and of course late-season trout-fishing. Then it becomes a question of whether to go for the big stripers on Nantucket or hit South Dakota for the opening day of pheasant season. What about the woodcock in New Brunswick or salmon fishing in Nova Scotia? What compounds the confusion for me is my inability to retain the "or" in all these activities; it's always an "and." Dove and sharptail grouse and turkey and steelhead and bluefish and walleye; AND I love to cook and eat the stuff! Oh, how to do it all?

"People who eat strange meat are considered 'primitive' by our culture, whether or not theirs has existed longer than ours, or created better art, and happier villages."

—Steve Bodio, 1996

Certainly one possibility is to give up parenthood and a career or convince myself that McDonald's fish fillet is pretty darn close to my version of Côtelettes de Brochette Purée de Champignons. Or I could just stay out there; make life simpler, dive deep into the world of the wild, and become a nomad

1

Venison

living on a diet of redfish seviche and venison heart. But these are not real solutions, and that's a different kind of life than most of us can lead.

Of course, my father (much before Mrs. Reagan made it a cliché and within a different context for his daughter) always said it was important to learn to "just say no." But I am not well-known for following good advice and Republican first ladies. So I've developed a kind of blurry-eyed demeanor of excitement trying to doing it all in the fall. I think it's pretty great to rise at 4:00 a.m. for a chance at mallards, return for breakfast at 8:00 a.m., then take a quick grouse walk before starting after pheasants at noon. Finally, there's no better way to end the day than with a two-martini cocktail hour and venison chops on the grill. Sandwich a few days like this among the wild goose Christmas dinner and gathering beach plums with the children for the jelly and partridge sauce and yes, it's crazy, but it's fantastic. And, of course, it's key to fine cooking; for without the procurement of good ingredients, there's less chance of producing a great meal.

Many of us get to wallow in and enjoy the immersion and abundance of the fall season and even learn to be happy with its chaotic nature. At one point in Guy de la Valdéne's marvelous book about woodcock, *Making Game*, he talks about the total "immersion" that hunters experience: "I wish I could take a picture that would tell it all, but after years in the woods I have yet to frame it. Perhaps if I could photograph the path of a falling branch, the sound of a drumming grouse, the rhythm of a woodcock's gait, it would tell all, but I doubt it. The boreal forests of fall are impossible to duplicate except in one's soul." Fall is the season to celebrate the wild in our soul…and it's the ideal place to start a cookbook.

COTTAGE PIE

1 lb. venison
2 oz. dried sliced mushrooms
3 tbsps. flour
6 tbsps. olive oil
1 shallot, minced
1 medium onion, sliced
1 ¼ cups game stock
2 tbsps. gin
¼ cup cashews

1 tsp. juniper berries
¼ tsp. salt
½ tsp. pepper
1 tsp. bouquet garni
3 medium potatoes,
    cut into 1-inch-thick slices
¾ cup warm milk
4 tbsps. butter
2 medium carrots, julienned
2 celery stalks, julienned

I n a small bowl cover the mushrooms with warm water
and soak them for 30 minutes. Drain. Cut the venison into
¼-inch cubes. Dust them with flour. In a Dutch oven heat the
oil over medium heat. Fry the meat cubes until they're
browned on all sides. Add the shallot, onion, stock, gin,
cashews, juniper berries, salt, pepper and bouquet garni.
Bring to boil, lower the heat, and simmer for 1 hour. While
the stew cooks, bring 2 quarts of water to a boil in a large
saucepan. Add the potatoes, cook until tender (about 18
minutes), and drain. Mash the potatoes with 1 tablespoon of
butter and the milk. Julienne the carrots and celery (make the
strips ¼-inch thick, 2 inches long). In a skillet melt 2 tablespoons of butter over medium heat and sauté the carrots and
celery for about 3 minutes. Pour the venison mixture into a
2-quart casserole. Add a carrot/celery layer. Cover completely
with mashed potatoes. Dot the top with the remaining butter
and sprinkle with paprika. Bake at 375°F for 30 minutes, or
until lightly browned.—*Annette and Louis Bignami, November 1987*

THE COLONEL'S CROWN

2 sides, or racks, of venison ribs, each at least 16 inches long

2 tsps. salt

½ tsp. dried marjoram

½ tsp. dried thyme, crushed

1 tbsp. black pepper, freshly ground

4 tbsps. lard

8 small potatoes, peeled and halved

8 medium carrots, sliced 2 inches thick

8 small onions, peeled

2 tbsps. fresh parsley, chopped

Watercress garnish to taste

The crown rack is the most dramatic presentation of venison ribs. If a butcher does your processing, tell him the crown is formed the same as for lamb or veal. If you do it yourself, remove the loin, then saw across the ribs at the point where they curve and head south, keeping the ribs intact and including as much meat as possible. The length of the rack depends on the size of the deer, but when you run out of meaty ribs, stop. Place the 2 rib racks on a table, flat, with the meat side down and the racks end to end, the rib tips pointing away from you. Using a skewer and ordinary kitchen twine, tie the adjacent ribs with 2 knots—the first about 1 inch up from the bottom, the second 2 inches above that. Then fold the left rib rack over the right. Tie the outside 2 ribs together in the same manner. Right the crown, rib tips upward. Trim the tips for fancy capping later. Combine the salt, herbs and spices and rub them over the ribs. Place the crown on a roasting rack in a pan, add the lard for basting, and set in a 325°F oven. Allow 25 minutes per pound, basting frequently. Boil the vegetables in salted water for 10 minutes. Twenty minutes before the crown is done, spoon the drained vegetables into the drippings in the roasting pan and allow them to brown. To serve, fill the center of the crown with the vegetables, cover with parsley, and garnish with watercress. Carve it like a cake, straight down, then salute the hunters and the prey. Serves 4.—*S.G.B. Tennant Jr., October 1984*

THE COLONEL'S STORY

For some men the stalking of a particular deer is the apex in sport; nothing else comes close. They are the dedicated hunters who know the land, who have lived there for years. They notice the gradual decay of tree stumps, they remember where the grass is still green after the first frost. They are as much a part of the woods as the deer they stalk, and they come to know their prey. The most dedicated of this tribe of deerslayers I ever knew was old Colonel J.G. Gee. In the Trinity River bottom country around Huntsville, Texas, the Colonel was notorious for passing up bucks when he had a particular animal in mind. The few times I hunted with Gee we always gathered at the small cabin he and his son used as camp. The party would arrive around dusk, and soon the air was full of stories about "the deer of the year." We'd sit around on bunks that lined the walls, staring at a plate of something that looked like canned tomatoes left by Hood's Texas Brigade, while the Colonel waxed on about Mr. Jingles, or Ole Broke Tail, or the Brute of Coley's Cove. Every now and then someone would change the subject by asking about the Colonel's All-American days at Clemson, or maybe try to draw out a war story or two.

All to no avail. "That's dead and gone," he'd snort in exasperation. There simply wasn't enough vanity there to divert him from the most vital and gripping question of the day: How big—and where—is the present objective? The present was always the challenge for the Colonel. Accolades garnered during his long life were just so much excess baggage. He was a man who loved the here and now.

S.G.B. Tennant Jr.
October 1984

Venison

VENISON ROAST

METHOD I

Haunch roast
Black pepper
Flour
Salt pork or bacon strips
Melted butter

The roast can be rubbed with black pepper (no salt; add the salt after the roast is cooked, so it doesn't "draw out" the none-too-plentiful juices of the dry venison) and flour, larded with strips of salt pork or bacon skewered to its top, and shoved into a hot oven to sear for a ½ hour, then cooked at moderate heat until done. This takes 2 to 3 hours as a rule. Baste the roast frequently with drippings from the pan or with melted butter to keep it moist. Save the drippings for a gravy.

THE BEST CUTS

A haunch roast consists of the major meaty portion of a hind leg. A saddle roast comes from across the back. If the deer is small and a king-sized roast is desired, it can be obtained by cutting the haunch and part of the saddle as one piece. Some things are self-evident: A young deer will provide a better roast than an old one. (Regardless of the animal's size, a young deer's toes do not spread wide; those of an old deer splay far apart.) It is assumed that the deer has been properly dressed in the field. The meat of a deer is tender for about 6 hours after it is killed, then it toughens, and must be hung to restore it to tenderness. Hanging is from a week to several weeks, depending upon the temperature, the climate and the altitude. Remove any parts that show spoilage. The best cuts—especially in a young deer—tend to be the chuck, rump and shoulder cuts. A pot roast is always in order, and it is a more certain way of assuring tender meat on some of the tougher cuts than an oven roast. Essentially, a pot roast consists of a piece of meat rubbed with salt, pepper and flour, then seared in hot fat in a heavy pot on top of the stove until well browned, whereupon liquid is added and the meat is allowed to simmer under cover for several hours. Vegetables can be added to the liquid near the end of the cooking. Onions and carrots absorb much of the gamy taste, and lend flavor of their own.

Bill Wolf
November 1955

METHOD II (FRENCH)

Haunch roast	*Oil*
Black pepper	*Paper bag*
Flour and water	*Salt*
Suet, butter or lard	*Butter*

Pepper the meat and coat it with a firm paste made of flour, water and suet. Lacking suet, use butter or lard to make the dough; the object is to keep the meat constantly basted with a grease. Wrap the entire roast in a big oiled brown paper bag, or oiled vegetable parchment paper tied on with string, and roast it in a hot oven. When it's about done (2 to 3 hours, depending upon the size), remove the wrappings, peel off the dough envelope, salt the meat, rub it with flour, dot it generously with butter, and return it to a very hot oven to brown. Gourmets like the small amount of natural fat found on a venison roast; the less sophisticated want it removed, because it does have a somewhat gamy taste, and, when cold, is a bit like tallow. If preferred, 1 clove or 2 of garlic can be inserted in the natural overlap of muscles in the leg before roasting to "kill" some of the gaminess. A gravy can be made from the pan drippings, a bit of flour and water, but many prefer to serve venison with only red currant jelly as a sauce. There are complicated sauces that use red currant jelly as a base, but just the plain jelly will be sufficient.—*Bill Wolf, November 1955*

VENISON SPAGHETTI SAUCE

2 lbs. venison, ground
½ lb. fresh pork or bear meat,
    trimmed of fat and ground
1 can beef broth (10¾ oz.)
2 cups water
2 cans tomatoes (16 oz.)
1 small can tomato paste (2 oz.)
2 medium onions, diced

½ green bell pepper, diced
2 garlic cloves, minced
½ red bell pepper, diced
8 oz. fresh mushrooms, sliced
1 tbsp. parsley
1 tsp. salt
½ tsp. pepper
1 tsp. thyme
¼ cup Worcestershire sauce

Really good spaghetti sauce must cook for a long while, and venison is meat that holds up under a long simmer. Lightly grease a large frying pan and brown the pork. Remove the pork and set it aside. Brown the venison. Add the pork, beef broth and water. Bring to a boil, lower the heat, cover, and simmer for 5 hours. If needed, add a little water from time to time. An hour before it's time to eat, sauté the onions, garlic and bell peppers in a small pan, then add them to the meat sauce. Add the Worcestershire sauce and tomato paste. Mash up the tomatoes and stir them into the meat sauce. Add salt, pepper, thyme and parsley. Stir. Turn up the heat until the sauce bubbles, add mushrooms, then lower the heat, cover, and simmer for 1 hour.—*A.D. Livingston (author of the* Complete Fish and Game Cookbook, *Stackpole Books), February 1992*

AGING VENISON

Venison can be aged to improve the quality of the meat. Aging carcasses for seven to nine days at 34° to 37° F improves tenderness and changes flavor. It's much better than the 24-hour chill, cut-and-freeze method. You should consider the age of the animal; aging older animals improves tenderness. If the animal has run a long distance before death, the meat may have a high pH, and the potential exists for increased bacterial growth during aging. A clean, temperature controlled aging facility is essential. Freezing stops aging, while aging above 40° results in spoilage. Consider aging if your intended use is steaks and roasts.

Tom R. Kovach
December 1991

TO ROAST A VENISON HAUNCH

Cut off the knuckle, trim the flap, remove the thick skin on the flank and nick the joint at the cramp-bone (knee). Split it, rub with butter, sprinkle well with salt, cover it with a sheet of very thin paper, then with a paste of flour and water, and again with paper; tie it up well with a stout string laced across it; baste it all the time it is roasting. Let it cook 4 or 5 hours. A quarter of an hour before serving it, remove the paste, throw a handful of salt on it, dredge it with flour and baste with a little fresh butter. The gravy should be made as follows: cut 2 or 3 pounds of the scrag (the nape of the neck or any lean meat remnants), or the lean of a loin of old mutton, brown it on a gridiron, and put it into a saucepan with a quart of water; cover it closely, and simmer it for an hour. Then uncover it and stew the gravy to a pint. Season only with salt, and strain. Another gravy is made with a pint of port wine, a pint of strong mutton gravy, as above, and a tablespoon of currant jelly. Let these merely boil up.

Pete Byrnes
October 1964
(transcribed from his grandmother's circa 1857 cookbook)

ROAST SADDLE OF VENISON

1 saddle (3 ¾ lbs.) of venison (have the butcher saw through the backbone so that each serving may be carved without difficulty)
Black peppercorns
Dried juniper berries
4 strips of lard or bacon cut ⅛-inch thick

Stud the venison well with peppercorns and juniper berries. Lay strips of the lard or bacon over the meat and secure them with toothpicks. Stand the saddle on a rack in a roasting pan. Roast for 40 minutes in a very hot oven (450°F). Baste frequently. Carve so that each serving is 1 rib thick. Serve with some of the drippings.—*Yeffe Kimbal and Jean Anderson, October 1987 (from their book* The Art of Indian Cooking)

Venison

FILLET OF VENISON WELLINGTON

1 whole fillet, trimmed of
    excess fat to form a firm roll of meat
4 tbsps. butter
Salt and pepper to taste
1 tsp. dry English mustard

In a frypan, sauté the fillet in melted butter until it is browned on all sides—no more than 10 minutes altogether. Season it with salt and pepper, remove it from the pan and brush the surface lightly with dry mustard. Cool to room temperature. Note: Once the venison is sautéed, continue with the recipe on the next page.

—*Jack Denton Scott, October 1967*

HOW TO COOK A ROYAL STAG

I had it in the home of a baronet in Kent who stalked his meal on ancestral acres in Scotland. It was the fillet from a royal stag, well hung, and it easily served 8 drooling guests. I watched his cook, a gentle and skillful Irishwoman, prepare it. She didn't seem to mind my peering over her shoulder. The pastry was made first, then the chicken-liver paté.

PASTRY
4 cups flour
1 stick butter
1 tsp. salt
½ cup canned vegetable shortening
1 whole egg, beaten
½ cup (or more) water

Put the flour, butter, salt and shortening into a bowl and mix well with your fingers. Stir in the beaten egg and slowly blend in just enough water to form a dough. Wrap in wax paper, or place in a covered bowl, and put in the refrigerator.

CHICKEN-LIVER PATÉ
¾ pound chicken livers, finely minced
5 tbsps. butter
4 shallots, finely minced
3 tbsps. Madeira
Salt and pepper to taste

When the livers are minced as finely as a sharp knife can mince them, place them in a frypan with the melted butter in which the shallots have already been sautéed. Cook the liver until pink; then add the Madeira and salt and pepper and blend well. Set aside.

ASSEMBLY: Now carefully spread the paté over the top surface of the cool fillet, and preheat the oven to 425°F. For the pastry, remove the dough from the refrigerator and on flour-dusted wax paper, large pastry board or marble table use a long rolling pin to roll the dough into a rectangle measuring approximately 12x20 inches and a ½-inch thick. Carefully, so that the paté remains in place, set the fillet on one side of the rolled dough. Beat 2 eggs well. Now draw the other side of the pastry over the fillet and overlap it at the bottom. Brush with beaten egg to seal. Cut off overhanging ends of the pastry and make an envelope fold around the fillet, completely encasing it in the dough, and again brush all edges with beaten egg to seal. Carefully place the pastry-fillet roll, seam-side down, on a shallow pastry tin or baking sheet, and brush the entire roll with the remaining egg. Bake at 425°F for half an hour.

Jack Denton Scott
October 1967

SADDLE OF VENISON

Saddle of venison
Bacon
1 ½ bottles Burgundy
½ tsp. black pepper
2 white onions, sliced
1 cup chopped celery and parsley leaves
1 tsp. salt
2 bay leaves, crushed
1 tsp. thyme
4 cloves
3 shallots
2 oz. butter

Lard the saddle with bacon. In a covered pot, marinate it for 36 hours in all of the ingredients but the shallots and butter. Turn often. Roast for 40 minutes per pound at 450°F, basting often. Remove the meat and prepare the gravy from the marinade, adding shallots and butter. Simmer for 5 minutes. Add 1 teaspoon of wine.—*John Weinrich, October 1961*

ROAST

Tender venison roasts are best cooked rare, to take fullest advantage of the natural savor of the meat. If the deer isn't tender, treat it first with one of the unseasoned commercial tenderizers. For best results with venison, use double the ordinarily recommended amount and let it stand half as long. Moderately slow oven temperatures give the best results with large venison roasts. About 12 minutes per pound should do. If one side of the meat is fattier, placing this uppermost promotes natural basting. Laying strips of beef fat over roasts will vastly improve the final results. The venison should be left, uncovered, salted beforehand if you want, but not floured.

Bradford Angier
November 1962

SHOWMANSHIP

Even a rather mundane venison roast can be made into a memorable experience by the right atmosphere, setting and company. Still, old hunting pals and their reluctant spouses may require some showmanship—such as a venison roast cooked inside a mound of rock salt. If you've got a gift for gab, you might invent a story about Henry VIII, or somebody, cooking a royal stag in this manner. I almost always leave the roast encased in the rock salt mound when I put it on the table. The salt is cracked off ceremoniously, usually by tapping it with the blunt end of a table knife. Any remaining salt can be brushed off with the hand. Then the meat is transferred to a serving platter. For some guests, I enjoy flaming a venison roast with brandy. Sometimes I flame the whole roast, but more often I work with slices in a warmed platter. I heat a little brandy in a saucepan, pour it over the meat, and ignite it with a long match. Dim the lights before flaming.

A.D. Livingston
November 1989

ROCK SALT COOKING

1 venison roast (about 3 lbs.)
5 to 6 lbs. rock salt

If you want to try my rock salt method of cooking a roast, buy at least 5 or 6 pounds of ordinary ice-cream salt. Preheat your oven to 450°F. Select a large-enough roasting pan— you'll need plenty of room all around. (I usually use an ovenproof ceramic dish, which is attractive enough to put on the table.) Line the bottom of the pan with 1 inch of rock salt. Pepper the roast all around, then carefully insert the thermometer. Place the roast on top of the salt layer, turning it so the thermometer sticks straight up. Slowly pour salt around the roast. Dip your hand into a little water from time to time to help form the mound. Keep pouring until the entire roast is covered with at least ½ an inch of rock salt. Then put it into the center of the preheated oven. Cook for ½ an hour, then check the thermometer from time to time. When it reads 130°F, remove the roast from the oven. It can sit for a while, but should be served while still hot.—*A.D. Livingston (author of the* Complete Fish and Game Cookbook, *Stackpole Books), November 1989*

ROASTED VENISON

5 or 6 lbs. meat (legs,
    saddle or other large pieces)
MARINADE
2 large onions, thinly sliced
2 whole cloves
2 large carrots, sliced
3 cups red wine
1 stalk celery, sliced
1 cup red wine vinegar
8 sprigs parsley, chopped
½ cup water
2 sprigs fresh thyme,
    or ½ tsp. dried

4 tbsps. vegetable oil
Juice of 2 lemons
1 bay leaf
6 peppercorns
3 cloves garlic, crushed
TO ROAST VENISON
AND MAKE SAUCE
¼ cup melted butter
½ cup brandy, warmed
1 cup brown sauce (a demiglacé)
Beurre manie
3 tbsps. currant jelly
⅓ cup sour cream
Salt and pepper to taste

Remove the skin from the meat and cut out any tough membranes. Rinse in cold water and pat dry. Sprinkle with salt and pepper. Combine all the marinade ingredients in a large saucepan and simmer for 20 minutes. Cool to room temperature. Place the meat in a deep pan, pour the marinade over it, cover and marinate in the refrigerator for 48 hours, turning the meat from time to time. Preheat the oven to 425°F. Remove the venison from the marinade and pour ½ of it into a roasting pan, into which you've also placed all of the vegetables. Put the roast onto this bed of vegetables, brush it with melted butter and roast for 30 minutes. Lower the heat to 325°F and roast about 10 minutes per pound or until the meat is cooked to your preference. Turn the meat from time to time and baste it with the marinade. Remove

KEEPING IT MOIST

No doubt larding will make the meat moister, but it defeats one advantage to eating venison— its low fat content. I often use a moisturizing trick with garlic. With your thinnest fillet knife, make a narrow slit deep into the roast. Peel a clove of garlic and slice it in half, lengthwise. Insert the garlic pieces into the slit. During cooking the garlic seems to keep the meat from drying out, and the flavor it imparts is not too strong.

A.D. Livingston
November 1989

HOW TO USE A MEAT THERMOMETER

Any roast, if cooked too long, is likely to be dry and tough. This is especially true with venison. The key to having a succulent roast is having the right temperature for the right length of time. Unfortunately, this varies from one piece of meat to another; even the position of the meat in the oven can be important. Furthermore, some ovens are not accurate. For all these reasons, use a meat thermometer. When the temperature inside the roast reaches 130°F, your meat is medium-rare; 135°F to 145°F, medium; 150°F, medium-well; over 160°F, well-done. I recommend 130°F. Let the roast sit a few minutes before carving.

A.D. Livingston
November 1989

the meat from the pan and keep it warm. Drain off the pan juices. Strain this liquid, pressing all the vegetables to extract their flavor. Skim off the fat. Add warm brandy to the pan and ignite. Now pour in 2 cups of the strained marinade and boil the mixture for 5 minutes on the stovetop. Lower the heat, add the brown sauce and simmer for 10 minutes. Boil for 2 minutes more and skim off the scum and fat. Gradually add a small amount of *beurre manie* [*Editor's Note: equal amounts of flour and butter made into a paste; 1 tablespoon will thicken about ¾ cup of liquid, stirred until the right thickness is obtained; the sauce should be the consistency of heavy cream*]. Remove the sauce from the heat and add currant jelly, sour cream, salt and pepper. Taste to adjust the seasoning. Serve the venison with the sauce on the side.—*A.J. McClane, November 1981 (from* Dominique's Famous Fish, Game and Meat Recipes *by Dominique D'Ermo)*

Venison

MARINADE
FOR VENISON

1 venison roast

1 bottle good red wine

1 cup wine vinegar

12 peppercorns

1 tsp. salt

18 whole cloves

2 cups onion slices

2 celery stalks with leaves,
    chopped

2 garlic cloves

2 sticks cinnamon (1 tsp. ground)

½ tsp. powdered thyme

4 or 5 bay leaves

Pinch of sage

THE PURPOSE OF A MARINADE

Amarinade makes meat tender and it does change its taste. A marinade is a liquid consisting of wine and/or vinegar with seasonings in which the meat is soaked from 12 hours to a couple of days. It is best used in a deep earthen crock, or use an enamelware pan that is not chipped. Under no circumstances use a metal pot.

Bill Wolf
November 1955

Pour the bottle of red wine and wine vinegar into a nonmetallic container. Bruise the peppercorns, or add a good teaspoon of ground black pepper if whole corns aren't available. Then add the following: salt, cloves, onion slices, 2 handfuls of chopped celery stalks and leaves, garlic cloves, sticks of cinnamon, bay leaves and a pinch of sage. Let the meat marinate in this in a cool place. Pat the meat dry after taking it from the marinade. Strain the marinade and use some of the liquid in basting, or where a stew or pot roast requires moisture. This is a rather mild marinade and although such a marinade does modify the flavor of venison, it does not alter it beyond the point of recognition, as might be expected from the list of ingredients.
—*Bill Wolf, November 1955*

CREDIT WHERE IT'S DUE

I'd like to be able to say I discovered this recipe from some grizzle-faced old deer guide, or even while experimenting in my home kitchen while using up the last of the venison roast from last year's larder, but it just isn't so. Nope, this recipe comes from the <u>Wild Game Cookbook</u> published by Safari Club International. I invited some hunting friends in to share the repast, and collected raves all around.

Dave Bowring
November 1983

VENISON À LA MODE

3 lbs. venison
4 cups dry red wine
2 or 3 peppercorns
Celery leaves—just a few
2 or 3 whole cloves
1 bay leaf
Sprigs of thyme and parsley
Salt to taste
Bacon fat or olive oil
12 tiny onions, peeled
12 baby carrots

Marinate the venison for at least 24 hours, turning occasionally. Three hours before the meat is to be served, remove it from the marinade, pat it dry with paper towel, and dust it lightly with flour. Using bacon or olive oil, brown the meat on all sides. Transfer it to a baking dish; pour the marinade around it and roast, covered, in a 350°F oven for 2½ hours. Add vegetables the last ½ hour.—*Dave Bowring, November 1983 (from the* Wild Game Cookbook, *published by Safari Club International)*

MARINATED VENISON

1 venison roast (about 2 to 3 lbs.)
2 lemons, juiced (or 1 lemon and
    ½ cup tarragon wine vinegar)
2 onions, sliced
1 tsp. chili powder
½ cup water
2 tsps. salt
2 bay leaves
¼ tsp. black pepper
½ cup ketchup
1 garlic clove, minced

Combine all of the ingredients. Pour the marinade over the venison and place the cover on the container. Turn the meat twice daily, marinating it for about 48 hours.—*John Weinrich, October 1961*

PREPARING THE ROAST

Really good meat doesn't require a marinade, unless you are preparing a dish such as sauerbraten, in which the flavor of the marinade is necessary for the recipe's success. I do quite often marinate meat in ordinary milk. When meat seems a little strong to the nose, I use a marinade with 1 tablespoon of ordinary baking soda per quart water. In any case, I am guilty of putting a frozen roast into a marinade and letting it thaw overnight in the refrigerator. One firm rule: Never marinate meat in a metal container. Use glass or crockery.

A.D. Livingston
November 1989

TIPS FOR SAUERBRATEN

The meat is marinated in wine up to 3 days, and the acid in the wine does a fine job of tenderizing even the toughest cuts. I prefer top shoulder roasts for this recipe, though hindquarter roast will do. Marinate the meat longer if you expect it to be tough. I never marinate venison for less than 24 hours when making sauerbraten.

Jerome B. Robinson
November 1983

VENISON SAUERBRATEN

5 lbs. venison roast
2 large onions, sliced
1 qt. red wine
1 pt. water
1 pt. wine vinegar
2 bay leaves
10 black peppercorns
6 whole cloves
1 tbsp. sugar
3 fresh pine twigs or juniper berries
Flour seasoned with salt and pepper
2 tbsps. butter or vegetable oil
1 large carrot, sliced
¾ cup canned tomatoes
Sour cream

Put the roast in a large nonmetal pan or casserole. Slice 1 onion and add it to the meat. Combine the wine, water, vinegar, bay leaves, peppercorns, cloves and sugar. Bring it to a boil and simmer for 5 minutes. Let it cool, then pour it over the meat. Add the twigs or berries. Cover and marinate the meat in a cool place for 24 to 72 hours, turning it occasionally. Remove the meat, let it drain and wipe it dry. Strain the marinade and reserve 2 cups. Rub the meat with flour, salt and pepper. Heat the butter or oil in a casserole and brown the meat well on all sides. Slice and add the second onion, the carrot, tomatoes, strained marinade and 2 cups of water; simmer covered, turning the meat once or twice, for 2½ hours or until the meat is tender. Remove the meat and keep it warm.

SAUCE: Thicken the gravy with roux of equal parts flour and butter and add sour cream to taste. Serve with mashed potatoes, fresh Brussels sprouts and a green salad vinaigrette. A bottle or two of your favorite red wine completes the dinner.—*Jerome B. Robinson, November 1983*

Venison

VENISON STEAK PAILLARD

1 strip sirloin venison steak
1 tbsp. butter
Salt and pepper

After the fat is trimmed from the boneless strip sirloin venison steaks, place them one at a time between sheets of wax paper and flatten them with the side of a cleaver until they're ¼-inch thick. When the frypan is hot (over high heat), add about 1 tablespoon of butter, put in the steaks and lightly salt and pepper them, all the while shaking the frypan. Turn them just once and immediately remove. Serve them each with a dollop of butter melting atop. The entire procedure takes no more than 2 minutes. The steaks are rare but surprisingly tender and delicious. Serve them with potatoes—which have been broiled in their jackets earlier then peeled, sliced and sautéed in butter until crisp and golden—and an unusual salad: orange slices tossed in olive oil and garlic. Wash it all down with cold ale.—*Jack Denton Scott, October 1967*

VENISON LIVER

One time I remember I was in the highlands of Scotland, where hunting the stag is a fine art. One night after a long, tiring stalk, we went back to the cold pile of stone they call a hunting lodge and thawed ourselves out with the tonic of the country: peaty Scotch. One of our party, a French chef employed by a posh London restaurant, prepared dinner. We had the liver first (which is always tender no matter when it's eaten) in a manner that was good enough to rate as another recipe: First the hunter/chef peeled and thinly sliced a large onion, then sautéed it in 1½ tablespoons of olive oil and 1 tablespoon of butter until it was soft. He sliced the deer liver thinly in 6 slices, then again into 6 slivers from each slice, and cooked them with the onion, turning them often and quickly just until the blood stopped running. He then lightly seasoned the liver with salt and pepper, squirted on a little lemon juice, sprinkled on some chopped parsley and served it.

Jack Denton Scott
October 1967

LIVING OFF THE COUNTRY

In the days before our people had sugar and other condiments, and salt was often scarce, we used to judge our meat according to its flavor (whereas now judge it according to its tenderness) and disguise it with condiments to give it flavor. Instead of fat, we almost universally use sugar and starch, and we suffer from decayed teeth, and cancer is on the increase. In really wild country with men who have been away from civilization long enough to regain normal appetites, taste for meats approaches that of our ancestors.

Colonel Townsend Whelen
December 1943

VENISON BRACCIOLA

1 large, boneless piece of round
    steak of venison, 1 inch thick,
    about 2 lbs. (or 2 smaller
    pieces of 1 lb. each)
2 lbs. salt pork
2 tbsps. butter
3 tbsps. raisins, minced
3 tbsps. Italian parsley,
    finely minced

1 garlic clove, minced
3 walnuts, minced
4 tbsps. freshly grated
    Parmesan cheese
3 tbsps. olive oil
2 garlic cloves
2 2-lbs.-35-oz. cans pomodori
    pelati con basilico (Italian
    plum tomatoes with basil)
Salt and pepper to taste

Place the steak (or steaks) between thick layers of wax paper and with a wooden mallet or the side of a cleaver carefully flatten the meat (without tearing holes in it) until it is ¼-inch thick. Mash the salt pork into a paste, place it in a bowl and mix in the butter, raisins, parsley, minced garlic, walnuts and grated cheese, blending them into a smooth paste. Spread this evenly across each flattened steak. Carefully roll the meat into a firm tube, tucking in the ends so that the paste cannot drip out, and tie in several places with heavy thread or light cord. Place the olive oil and garlic cloves in a large fry pan, removing the garlic when it has browned. Over moderate heat, brown the meat roll on all sides. Place the meat and ½ the oil in which it cooked in a large pot. Run the 2 cans of tomatoes through a food mill and pour the purée over the meat and oil; season with salt and freshly milled black pepper, stir well with a wooden spoon, cover the pot and simmer for 1 hour or until the meat is tender, removing the cover at the halfway point to permit the tomato sauce to thicken. Stir frequently, then serve.—*Jack Denton Scott, October 1967*

Venison

VENISON PILAF

1 deer heart
1 set deer kidneys
5 cups water
1 ⅓ cups long-grain rice
1 medium onion, chopped
1 tsp. salt
½ to 1 tsp. red pepper flakes

No matter whether it is called pilaf, pilau or purloo, meat cooked with rice is an ideal way to prepare some tough meats. Trim and chop the heart and kidneys into ¾-inch cubes. Put the meat into a suitable pot and add the water, onion, salt and red pepper flakes. Bring to a boil, lower the heat, cover tightly and simmer for 1½ hours, or until the deer heart is tender. Add the rice, bring to a new boil, lower the heat, cover, and simmer for 20 minutes. Remove the lid and simmer until the mixture of the pilaf is just right for eating with a fork without dripping. (If you want to eat with chopsticks, use short-grain rice, which will be a little stickier.) The liver of the venison can also be used, but it won't require long simmering. Add it after the heart has simmered for an hour or so. Serves 4 to 6.—*A.D. Livingston (author of the* Complete Fish and Game Cookbook, *Stackpole Books), October 1991*

TENDER VENISON

This recipe requires boned-out meat. Cut steak-sized portions ½ to ¾-inch thick. Brown approximately 1½ pounds of them in a skillet and place them in the bottom of an average 3- to 4-quart slow-cooker. Cover the meat with 1 can of cream of mushroom soup thinned with ½ a cup of milk. Top with 2 tablespoons of butter. Scrub well 6 medium potatoes and place them on top. Set the pot on the low heat setting and forget about it for 8 to 10 hours. Before serving, season to taste.

Almanac
October 1991

STEAK DIANE

2 boned 1 ½-inch-thick
   strip sirloins
8 tbsps. butter
½ garlic clove
2 shallots, minced
1 tbsp. chives, minced
1 tbsp. parsley, minced
1 tbsp. Worcestershire sauce

Slice each steak in half horizontally and flatten between sheets of wax paper using a wooden mallet or the side of a cleaver until about ¼-inch thick. In ½ the butter melted in a frypan, quickly sauté the steaks 20 seconds on each side; remove from the heat. Melt the remaining butter in a chafing dish on a sideboard in the dining room and stir in all the remaining ingredients, removing the garlic when it is brown. Stir constantly with a wooden spoon until the sauce is blended and very hot. Now add the steaks and cook them in the sauce, turning constantly, 2 or 3 minutes. They should be pink-rare and served immediately on warm plates. Serves 4.
—*Jack Denton Scott, October 1967*

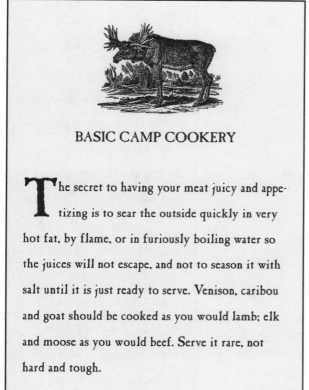

BASIC CAMP COOKERY

The secret to having your meat juicy and appetizing is to sear the outside quickly in very hot fat, by flame, or in furiously boiling water so the juices will not escape, and not to season it with salt until it is just ready to serve. Venison, caribou and goat should be cooked as you would lamb; elk and moose as you would beef. Serve it rare, not hard and tough.

Colonel Townsend Whelen
July 1953

CHICKEN-FRIED VENISON

1 ½ to 2 lbs. venison backstrap,
    cut into steaks
2 cups milk
2 garlic cloves, minced
1 tbsp. red pepper
1 ½ tbsps. black pepper
2 tbsps. salt
1 egg
1 cup flour

Marinate the venison steaks in the milk, garlic and about ½ the red pepper, black pepper and salt for at least 6 hours. When ready to cook, add the egg to the mixture. In a large bowl, mix the remaining salt and pepper in with the flour. Heat about ¼ to ½ inch of oil, preferably in a cast-iron skillet, until almost smoking. Shake the milk off the steaks and dredge them in the flour. Be sure to coat them well. Then drop them 1 or 2 at a time into the oil and cook quickly, 2 to 3 minutes per side, until golden brown.—*Jonathan Miles, April 1996*

COOKING MEAT IN CAMP

If you fry venison, cut it in slices about ¾-inch thick. Have plenty of grease in the pan and be sure it is smoking-hot to sear the pieces immediately and keep the juices in. Put the pieces in slowly, one at a time, so as not to let the sizzling grease cool at all. You don't want the bacon grease or other fat to soak into the meat. When each piece is done, lift it out of the pan with a fork and let it drain a moment. Never take the pan off the fire and pass it around with the meat in it, for just as soon as the grease stops sizzling the meat begins to absorb it. As before, do not use salt until ready to eat.

Colonel Townsend Whelen
March 1958

STEAK

Cooking over open embers is unbeatable. A good trick at the start is to get a glowing bed of coals, then to sprinkle on a few chips and shavings. These will flare up enough both to help seal in the juices and to assure that flavorsome char relished by so many. As you're already aware, the grill should be greased beforehand to prevent sticking. A handy one for wilderness use? One of those lightweight campfire grates. Removing the folding wire legs will make for easier packing. It's a simple matter to lay such a grid between logs or rocks. Individual steaks, of course, can also be very pleasantly grilled merely by holding them over the heat by means of sturdy, forked green sticks. The rest of the time I pan-broil venison steaks, cutting them 2 ½ inches thick, rapidly searing both sides in a hot and preferably heavy frypan, then continuing with somewhat less heat until done to taste. Salt and pepper if you wish and spread butter or margarine after cooking.

Bradford Angier
November 1962

CAJUN BLACKENED VENISON STEAKS

6 venison steaks, cut ½-inch thick, marinated
Cajun blackened meat seasoning (available at specialty food stores; or make your own of equal parts onion powder, garlic powder, black pepper, red cayenne pepper, thyme, oregano and salt)
Vegetable oil or margarine, to coat frying pan
MARINADE
½ cup red wine
2 garlic cloves
Dash low-sodium soy sauce
¼ cup olive oil

Prepare the steaks by tenderizing them with a meat-tenderizing tool until they are well perforated, then marinate them in a shallow dish for several hours or overnight. Turn them at least once while marinating. Remove the steaks from the dish and cover them generously with the seasoning mix. Heat an iron skillet, coated with oil, until searing hot. Do not add any oil at this time! If you think there is not enough oil to keep the meat from sticking, cool the pan, add oil, then reheat. Add the venison to the pan. The meat will cook quickly and will be seared black.—
Thomas McIntyre and Christine N. Glasser, September 1990

VENISON PAPRIKA

2 lbs. boneless venison
    (loin, chuck or shoulder meat
    well trimmed of any fat)
1 tbsp. salt
2 tsps. Hungarian rose paprika (sweet)
4 small onions, coarsely chopped (about 2 cups)
¼ cup butter
8-oz. can tomato sauce
2 tomatoes, peeled, seeded and quartered
¼ to ½ cup sour cream

Sprinkle the venison with salt and paprika. Let it stand while you're chopping the onions. In a heavy 2-quart saucepan heat the butter, add the onions, and cook them until they're transparent. Add the venison, stirring over medium heat until the meat loses its surface color. Lower the heat, add the tomato sauce and tomatoes, cover and simmer until the venison is tender, about 1½ hours. Stir from time to time. When the meat is done, stir in the sour cream and taste to correct the seasoning. Do not let the sauce boil after the sour cream has been added. Serve with broad noodles or rice.—*Melissa Taylor, November 1983*

MOIST VENISON

Common cook's sense told me that dryness might be the problem and adding moisture during the cooking period the answer. My first attempt, a roast haunch larded with fat—I used a knitting needle to insert strips of beef fat—was a tremendous success. [False modesty is not one of Melissa's faults, but the people involved still talk about it.] I basted the roast with tinned bouillon and red wine, cooked it at 350°F for a couple of hours until it was just the other side of pink, and added a bit of currant jelly to the sauce juices. Our guests said it was the best they ever had. I wasn't sure whether it was me or the buck that deserved the praise.

Melissa [and Zack] Taylor
November 1983

PIT COOKING

A friend of mine downed a magnificent buck in the mountains, but the critter—and the meat—was old. I wondered if pit cookery might solve the problem. I cut steaks on the thick side, rubbed every surface with garlic, pounded seasoned flour into them, and cut the steaks into serving portions about the size of a hand. I tossed into the Dutch oven 1 cup of finely diced salt pork, the steak pieces on them, and added 3 sliced onions. The ingredients were covered with milk and the oven sealed in the pit for 10 hours. The slow cookery worked magic, as the meat was so tender it could be cut with a fork.

Harry Botsford
December 1955

CHINESE VENISON PEPPER STEAK

1 lb. boneless venison stew meat, cut across the grain into ¼-inch-thick slices

2 medium green peppers, sliced Chinese style (long, very thin)

3 tbsps. peanut oil (any other cooking oil will burn at the high temperature necessary for this dish)

MARINADE

3 tbsps. dark soy sauce

2 tbsps. dry white wine

2 tbsps. cornstarch

1 tsp. sugar (not to sweeten, but to harmonize the taste)

¼ tsp. pepper

Mix the marinade ingredients in a bowl and add the meat slices; stir to coat the meat well and let it stand for 45 minutes, stirring occasionally to expose all the meat equally to the marinade. Heat a wok or large skillet (cast-iron works well) over high heat until very hot. Pour 2 tablespoons of peanut oil into the wok and immediately add the sliced green peppers. Stir-fry the peppers, turning them constantly, until they become translucent. (The peppers should remain crisp and retain their bright-green color.) Remove the peppers and place them in a bowl nearby. Add 1 tablespoon of peanut oil to the wok and repeat the process with the meat slices, turning them constantly until they are evenly browned but not overcooked. Return the peppers to the wok or skillet and mix them with the meat for 30 seconds. Serve immediately over a bed of steamed white rice. Add soy sauce to suit individual tastes. Serves 3 or 4.

—Dan Small, December 1981

VENISON STIR-FRY

1 to 2 tbsps. peanut oil

2 garlic cloves, sliced

1 tsp. grated ginger

1 ½ lbs. venison steak,
  trimmed and thinly sliced

½ red bell pepper, seeded
  and cut into thin strips

½ green bell pepper,
  seeded and cut into thin strips

4 green onions, sliced the long way

1 cup mushrooms, sliced

2 cups cauliflower florets or
  broccoli tops

1 cup red wine or beef broth

VENISON SMORGASBORD

Some hunters don't consider venison the most edible of game meat. It is lean, dry, sometimes tough. More important is that deer aren't handled properly in the field. Too often the carcass isn't skinned until long after the animal is killed. Then there is the long drive home, with the animal lashed to a fender. Even the best beef might not be fit to eat if treated in the same manner.

Erwin A. Bauer
December 1966

Heat the oil and stir-fry the garlic and ginger for 2 minutes. Add the venison slices and stir-fry them until the meat is no longer pink. Add the vegetables and mix well. Stir-fry them for 5 minutes; lower the heat and stir in the liquid. Cover and simmer for about 10 minutes. The vegetables should still be slightly crunchy. Serve with hot rice. Serves 4 to 6.—*Ferne Holmes, May 1992*

SWISS STEAK

3 lbs. venison flank steak
2 tsps. salt
½ tsp. black pepper
½ to 1 cup flour
5 tbsps. butter, margarine
    or bacon fat
1 large onion, diced
½ cup carrots, diced
1 can tomatoes
6 to 8 small potatoes, peeled

This is good both for a change and for those days when you're confronted with the tougher cuts. Flank handled this way will work into a tasty steak of sorts. Slitting such venison every few inches along the trimmed edges will keep it from curling unduly. Mix the salt and black pepper and season one side of the steak with half of this. Then with the back of a heavy knife or the edge of a saucer, pound all the flour you can into the meat. Turn the steak and repeat both procedures. Quickly

brown the meat all over in the butter in a Dutch oven or in a large skillet that has a cover. Then spread the onion and carrot, diced together, over the steak. Add a can of tomatoes. Cover and simmer over low heat 1 ½ hours. Finally, bank the meat with enough small, peeled potatoes for the meal. Cook for an additional ½ hour or until the potatoes are mealy.—*Bradford Angier, November 1962*

VENISON PASTY
(MEAT PIE)

2 to 3 lbs. venison neck meat,
    sliced into steaks
1 tbsp. basil
1 tbsp. tarragon
1 tbsp. thyme
1 tbsp. grated nutmeg
1 tsp. salt
1 tsp. pepper
5 tbsps. butter
1 lb. pastry dough
1 cup gravy
1 cup port
1 tbsp. lemon juice

ON VENISON CARE

Observe a forequarter; if the vein be bluish, the meat is fresh; if it has a green or yellow cast, it is stale. In the hindquarter, if there is a faint smell under the kidney, and the knuckle is limp, the meat is stale. The haunch is the finest joint; however, the kernel in the fat should be taken out. The neck is the next best joint and merely requires wiping dry with a clean cloth. The shoulder and breast are mostly used pasties.

Pete Byrnes
October 1964
(transcribed from his grandmother's circa 1857 cookbook)

Cut a neck or breast into small steaks, rub them over with a mixture of the sweet herbs, grated nutmeg, salt and pepper, and fry them slightly in butter. Line the sides and edges of a dish with pastry dough, lay in the steaks, and add ½ a pint of rich gravy made with the trimmings of the venison. Then add a glass of port wine, and 1 tablespoon of lemon or 1 teaspoon of vinegar; cover the dish with pastry dough, and bake it for nearly 2 hours. Some more gravy may be poured into the pie before serving it.—*Pete Byrnes, October 1964 (transcribed from his grandmother's circa 1857 cookbook)*

VENISON STEAKS AND CHOPS

From the loin, haunch or chuck steaks and chops are usually cut under an inch thick. If broiled, the steaks should be seared severely and quickly on both sides, and then finished at a slightly reduced heat. If pan-fried, they should likewise be seared in smoking-hot fat, cooked to the desired point, put on a warm plate, and served with some of the pan gravy poured over them. Do not overcook. Even those persons who believe venison roasts should be "tenderized" by immersion in a marinade for a day or more do not advocate a marinade for steaks, since they should be tender enough not to require it; but I use a method that has much to recommend it. I put a thin film of garlic-tarragon vinegar on a large plate and slosh both sides of the steak in it. The vinegar makes the steaks a bit more tender than they would be without it, and the garlic tarragon imparts a faint pleasant taste. It does not make the steak taste like vinegar, tarragon or garlic; but gives it a slight additional flavor. Moist steak will spatter in the hot fat if it is pan-fried, so use a lid as a shield for the first minute or two. The application of pepper is permissible during the cooking, but salt should not be applied until the steak is done.

Chops come only from the saddle and loin. Considered the best part of the deer by many. Handle the same as steaks—and always remember when broiling to baste the meat frequently and well with melted butter or olive oil.

Bill Wolf
November 1955

VENISON CHOPS

Boneless venison chops
Bottled teriyaki sauce
Meat tenderizer (optional)
Butter

Place the chops in a glass baking dish. Pour in enough teriyaki sauce to cover them about halfway. Marinate for 30 to 45 minutes; turn and marinate the other side for an equal time. (If meat tenderizer is needed, use as directed on the package.) Broil as you would any fine steak, topping with a pat of butter when the chops are turned. The final touch is a good bottle of cabernet sauvignon to accompany the chops.
—*George Harrison, November 1983*

Venison

BAKED VENISON CHOPS

4 thick venison chops
1 cup canned tomatoes
1 onion, sliced
Salt and pepper to taste
1 cup water

Arrange the chops in an open baking pan. Measure out 1 cup of canned tomatoes, using the solid portions. Spoon this over the chops, then distribute a sliced onion atop the meat. Salt and pepper to taste. Pour in 1 cup of water and bake in a moderately hot oven for 45 minutes. Turn the chops once after 15 minutes. Another ½ hour should find them tender and ready to serve, perhaps along with mashed potatoes, into each serving of which a spoonful of the juice is depressed. If the group has had this before, you'll have to call them only once for dinner.—*Bradford Angier, November 1962*

GAME COOKING I'VE LIKED

Although a tender and tasty young antelope is my favorite big game, I'll never forget the deer chops I used to eat in old Mexico. The "safari" consisted of two Mexicans who, humanely enough, would rather hunt than work and so were always glad to go off on an expedition. They would take their old rifles and head off into the dry Sonoran hills early in the morning. Usually they were back by nightfall with a deer, which they would exchange for a dollar. Speaking of such game as deer naturally brings the conversation to steaks. Few cuts of meat are as well known. Few can be prepared in so many different ways. One word of warning: Deer, moose, elk, caribou and other such meats have a tendency to be dry and should not be overdone. I prefer my steaks broiled, but that's simply a matter of taste. Here is how I prepare a steak that's 2 ½ inches thick. Rub the steak with salt and black pepper. If you wish, you may also use English mustard. Then rub your grid with suet to prevent sticking. Preheat the oven at high temperature for 15 minutes. Place the steak 5 inches from the flame. Sear quickly on both sides to prevent the loss of the natural juices. You may turn your steak 2 or more times. For rare, cook 10 minutes on each side; for medium, with a pink center, 15 minutes on each side. Do not melt butter over the steak until it is done cooking. Serve sizzling hot.

Duncan Hines (with Bradford Angier)
March 1959

BASIC CAMP COOKERY

All my cooking has been done over the open campfire. Food tastes so much better when it is cooked over the blaze and coals of wildwood, just as a juicy steak broiled over charcoal is superior to one heat-treated in a frypan. It is so easy to regulate the open cooking fire to give quick heat, a bed of coals for broiling, or to find a place over it where foods will just simmer or keep warm. When you want to boil a thing in a hurry, dry balsam, spruce, white and pitch pine, and cedar, particularly when split, roar up into a quick and big blaze. For steady burning, however, jack pine, chestnut, aspen, and particularly maple are more satisfactory, while for long-lasting and for broiling coals, choose ash, oak, hickory, birch and tamarack.

Colonel Townsend Whelen
July 1953

BARBECUED VENISON CHOPS WITH SAVORY BUTTER

6 venison chops
½ cup butter, softened
2 tsps. dry mustard
1 tbsp. onion, minced
1 tbsp. parsley, minced
½ cup chili sauce
⅓ cup lemon juice
1 tsp. salt

Blend the butter, mustard, onion and parsley, and shape the herbed butter into a roll. Chill it hard. Combine the chili sauce, lemon juice and salt, and dip the chops into the mixture. Broil the chops for 45 minutes 12 to 14 inches above glowing coals; turn the chops once, about 20 minutes before they are done. Slice the butter roll; place a slice on top of each hot chop and serve.—*John Weinrich, October 1961*

VENISON RAGOUT—1979

4 lbs. venison shoulder,
    cut into 1 ½ to 2-inch cubes
2 cups red wine
1 cup cider vinegar
4 medium onions, quartered
4 medium carrots, pared and chunked
7 peppercorns
4 whole cloves
1 large bay leaf

2 tsps. salt
½ tsp. crushed dried rosemary
¼ tsp. thyme
½ cup of vegetable oil
1 cup red wine
4 beef bouillon cubes
    (or 4 cups venison broth)
4 cups hot water
2 to 3 tbsps. flour

Place the venison in a large bowl and add the 2 cups of wine, and the vinegar, onions, carrots and all of the spices and herbs. Cover this and let it stand in a cool place for at least 24 hours, turning the meat occasionally so that all the pieces are exposed to the marinade. Venison may marinate up to 5 days. When ready to prepare, remove the meat and pat it dry. Strain the marinade, reserving the vegetables and seasonings and discarding the liquid. In your stew pot, warm up the vegetable oil and quickly brown the venison over high heat. When richly brown on all surfaces, add the remaining cup of red wine, the bouillon cubes dissolved in 4 cups of hot water, and the reserved vegetables and seasoning from the marinade. Use additional hot water to cover. Bring to the boiling point. Lower the heat at once. Cover and simmer for about 1 ½ hours. Remove the meat to a serving dish. Skim the fat from the pot liquid and stir in flour to thicken the gravy if desired. Pour it over the meat to serve.—*A.J. McClane, October 1979*

WHY NOT A STEW?

I have always had a weakness for venison stew—in camp at least. The beauty of venison stew is that you can have it in the pot while the balance of your kill is still quivering. And again: A stew accounts for much meat that is hardly fit for any other use. You can't fry or broil or bake the brisket. The shoulder is poor for steaks and thin for jerking. Besides, if your aim has been true, and your ball has gone in and perhaps come out, you have "spoiled" a good deal of meat for any other use but the pot. A little "mussing up" in that quarter improves, if anything, the flavor of the stew.

R. Ritchie
October 1898

SCHWÄBISCHE SPÄTZLE

2 eggs, slightly beaten
1 cup water
1 tsp. salt
3 cups flour

Mix all ingredients. Beat them until the dough is firm, adding extra flour if necessary. In a large saucepan bring 3 quarts of salted water to a boil. Cut away ¼ x 2 ½-inch strips of dough, dropping them into the boiling water. Do not overcrowd. When the dumplings float, they're done. Remove them, rinse in hot water, drain, and keep them warm until ready to serve. Venison ragout and spätzle make a perfect main dish.

Anthony Acerrano
December 1989

VENISON RAGOUT—1989

2 to 3 lbs. venison,
    cut into 1-inch pieces
3 tbsps. olive oil
¼ lb. mushrooms; left whole if
    small, halved if larger
1 dozen small white onions
    (peeled or diced chunks)
½ cup beef stock or bouillon
    (optional)

5 tbsps. tomato paste
3 tbsps. brandy
1 ½ cups Burgundy
¾ cup dry sherry
¼ cup ruby port
4 tbsps. flour
½ tsp. garlic powder
    (or 1 small clove, bruised)
¼ tsp. black pepper
2 bay leaves

Brown the venison in hot olive oil in a deep skillet or Dutch oven. Remove the meat and replace with mushrooms and onions, browning them slightly while stirring. Remove them from the pan. Shut off the heat under the skillet and stir in beef stock and tomato paste. In a separate bowl, mix the liquors with the flour to form a paste, then add this to the skillet, heating just short of the boiling point. Now add the venison, mushrooms, onions and spices. Cover tightly and bake in a 350°F oven for 1 ½ hours. Spätzle can be found in the gourmet section of grocery stores or in specialty shops, but it is easy to make.—*Anthony Acerrano, December 1989*

Venison

VENISON NECK STEW

4 or 5 lbs. neck of venison
3 medium potatoes
3 medium onions
3 carrots
1 celery stalk
2 cups water
1 beef bouillon cube
1 tbsp. parsley
Salt and pepper to taste

Heat enough water in a Dutch oven to cover the neck bones and dissolve the boullion cube in it. Add the neck bones, bring to a boil, lower the heat, cover, and simmer for 2 hours. While the meat is cooking, peel and quarter the onions, carrots and potatoes. Put all the vegetables and the parsley into the Dutch oven. Bring to a new boil, lower the heat, cover tightly, and simmer for ½ an hour. Remove the neck pieces and pull off the meat with a fork. Discard the bones and put the meat back into the Dutch oven. Stir in a little salt and pepper and simmer for 15 minutes. This stew makes a complete meal when served with sourdough bread.—*A.D. Livingston (author of the* Complete Fish and Game Cookbook, *Stackpole Books), November 1991*

BEGINNER'S STEW

Take your fore-shoulder and brisket and wipe off all hairs with a damp cloth, if particular. With an ax, a hatchet and a dry-barked log for a chopping block, cut your meat and bone it into moderately small pieces, being careful to save all marrow and fat. Then for the kettle and the fire. I prefer a heavy tin kettle to a regular stew kettle with a handle, but everyone to his choice. Do you want venison soup or a stew? A stew. Well, then, have your water at the boiling point and quickly put in your meat and cover over. Be careful to have plenty of meat and water enough to just cover it.

R. Ritchie
October 1898

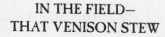

IN THE FIELD—
THAT VENISON STEW

A venison stew, properly seasoned with the proper ingredients, is very satisfying and very filling. It does not lie on the stomach like a fry, nor need scraping like a broil, nor has it the smoky flavor of a roast by an open fire. It is taken in a semi-liquid form and percolates thro' the system from the palate to the diaphragm—or whatever you call it—filling the inner man with joy and gladness. But a venison stew must have for its foundation strong meat with plenty of juices and wild flavor.

R. Ritchie
October 1898

VENISON RAGOUT
WITH ONIONS

*3 lbs. top round of venison cut
   in pieces 4 times the
   size of your thumbnail
2 ½ tbsps. butter
3 tbsps. dry sherry, warmed
36 small white onions
1 tbsp. tomato paste
2 tbsps. meat glaze
3 ½ tbsps. flour*

*1 ½ cups beef stock
   (canned beef broth is excellent
   for this purpose)
2 cups dry red wine
2 small bay leaves
14 small white mushrooms
Salt and pepper to taste
2 tbsps. fresh parsley,
   finely chopped*

Sauté the venison in the hot, melted butter, turning often until brown. Pour the warmed sherry over it and stir well with a wooden spoon; then take the meat from the frypan and reserve. Add the onions to the butter and sherry and brown, turning them often so they do not burn. Stir in the tomato paste, meat glaze and flour, blending until smooth; then add the beef stock and stir until the mixture simmers. Add ½ cup of the red wine, the venison pieces, the bay leaves and the mushrooms, and season with salt and pepper. Stir well with a wooden spoon and simmer slowly for 1 ½ hours, or until the venison is tender. Add the rest of the red wine during the cooking, a small amount at a time. Serve this in small individual casseroles, sprinkled with parsley, over hot buttered noodles. Serves 6.—*Jack Denton Scott, October 1967*

Venison

"BOILED" VENISON

2 to 3 lbs. shoulder or ham roast
2 onions, sliced
2 carrots, sliced
2 to 3 tsps. salt
3 cups hot water

The Dutch oven will conveniently "boil" a big, solid chunk of venison. Place the meat in the bottom of the receptacle along with onions, carrots, and 1 teaspoon of salt per pound of meat. Half cover the venison with simmering water. Cook about 1 hour for every pound, at the end of which time the meat should be tender but not stringy or mushy. If you want to use it in cold sandwiches, let it cool in the broth. Then move it to a flat container that will also hold a little of the fluid. Press the meat into shape with a weighted cover or plate, so that it can later be more handily sliced.—*Bradford Angier, November 1962*

BOILING MEAT

Cut the meat into about 2-inch cubes. Drop them individually into just enough bubbling water to cover. Do not boil. Don't salt until almost ready to serve. Meat so cooked can best be relished after it has been simmering, covered, only 5 minutes or so. However, many get in the habit of letting it cook an hour or more. If you are going to use the meat cold, let it cool in the broth. For a taste treat try sprinkling a little soy sauce over such venison and serving a tart jam or marmalade on the side.

Bradford Angier
November 1962

No discussion of venison cooking would be complete without mentioning stews, since they provide a way to use some of the lesser cuts from the neck, chuck and flanks; but, frankly, there is no mysterious way to make a superior stew. If you have a favorite home recipe for beef stew, it can be applied equally well to venison. Use herbs with discretion exactly as you would with beef. The worst I ate was a mixture of thyme, tarragon, garlic, Tabasco and assorted flavors, dumped in to "kill the wild taste," with no evidence of venison. My friend, who made it, suffered agonies of embarrassment when even his neighbor's dog wouldn't touch it.

Bill Wolf
November 1955

VENISON IN STEWS

Several pounds of venison, cut
*   into cubes, 1-inch or better*
Flour
Salt and pepper to taste
1 lb. mushrooms, sliced
1 cup onion, chopped
1 green pepper, finely chopped
½ cup butter
3 to 4 cups beef broth
½ bottle red wine
2 large potatoes, peeled and cubed
4 carrots, cut into 1-inch lengths
1 small can whole-kernel corn

Dredge the venison cubes in flour that has been seasoned with salt and pepper. Meanwhile, have sautéing in the heaviest metal pot or kettle you possess the cleaned and sliced mushrooms, chopped onion and green pepper. Use the butter to sauté these. When lightly golden brown, remove them from the pot, turn up the heat, and sear the meat in the butter and juices until the cubes are browned on all sides. More butter may be required. Return the sautéed vegetables to the pot with the meat, and add enough beef stock (canned bouillon will serve) to almost cover. Let this simmer for about 2 hours, then add the red wine, potatoes, carrots and corn. Bring this to a boil, turn down the heat, and simmer until the vegetables are done.—*Bill Wolf, November 1955*

SAVORY VENISON STEW

¼ cup bacon drippings

2 lbs. boneless venison stew meat, cut in 1-inch cubes

½ cup flour

2 to 3 medium onions, coarsely chopped

3 to 4 carrots, sliced

2 to 3 stalks celery, coarsely chopped

2 10-oz. cans beef broth

1 to 2 cups dry red wine (enough to cover veggies)

Salt and pepper to taste

2 bay leaves, crushed

Rub the bottom and sides of a Dutch oven or large pot with just enough bacon grease to prevent sticking. Add the vegetables, and salt and pepper to taste; cover and cook slowly over low heat while you prepare the meat. Dredge the meat chunks lightly in flour (an easy way is to shake them in a paper bag) and brown them in bacon drippings in a large skillet. When the meat chunks are browned, add them to the vegetables in the Dutch oven. Pour in the beef broth (or your own homemade venison or other game stock) and add enough red wine to cover all the ingredients. Add crushed bay leaves and other herbs if desired. Stir, cover tightly and let simmer over low heat for 2 hours. Stir occasionally to prevent sticking. Serve over rice or hot biscuits. Serves 4 or 5.—*Dan Small, December 1981*

IN THE FIELD
THAT VENISON STEW

Let me add right here that if you are making a stew to eat, there are other things that you can't do at the same time. You can't hurry the stew for the sake of an evening hunt. You have simply got to make an evening or a morning of it, or else stick to a fry or a boil. Camp stews are the result of time and patience. But the other ingredients? A very edible and filling stew can be made out of plain meat and water with bacon added, properly peppered and salted before serving, with a few baking-powder dumplings on top. But for a savory stew, onions are almost as necessary as meat itself.

R. Ritchie
October 1898

STEWING

Stew meat, which can be the toughest in the deer, is best browned at the outset along with fat, chopped onion and seasonings, in the bottom of the kettle. You can then, if you want, stir in flour and add enough liquid to make a thick, smooth gravy. For liquid, use any fluid in which vegetables have been cooked or canned, broth from boiled meat, or plain water. Season to taste, bring to a boil and then place tightly covered where it will simmer all morning or all afternoon. The preceding is the basis of the stew called mulligan. What the end result of this staple will be depends more or less on ingenuity, imagination and the materials at hand. Available vegetables go well in such a stew. So do odds and ends of steaks and roasts. Cooking vegetables, particularly onion, along with the deer meat make one of the most widely enjoyed mulligans. The addition of any such components, except when included for flavor alone, should be so staggered that everything will be done at the same time. Any extra fluid should be heated before it is added.

Bradford Angier
November 1962

VENISON STEW—1961

1 ½ lbs. venison, cubed
⅓ cup sifted flour, seasoned with:
*   1 ½ tsps. salt*
*   ¼ tsp. pepper*
*   1 tsp. dry mustard*
*   ½ tsp. paprika*
2 tbsps. shortening
1 ½ cups red table wine
8-oz. can whole onions
1 cup frozen peas
1 tsp. cornstarch
½ cup sour cream
½ pkg. pastry mix

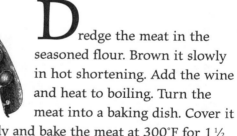

Dredge the meat in the seasoned flour. Brown it slowly in hot shortening. Add the wine and heat to boiling. Turn the meat into a baking dish. Cover it tightly and bake the meat at 300°F for 1 ½ to 2 hours, until tender. Drain the onions and peas (they need not be fully thawed). Stir the cornstarch into the sour cream. Add the onions, peas and sour cream to the meat. Mix well. Prepare the pastry and roll it out to fit the top of the dish, fluting the edges and slashing the top. Brown at 400°F for 20 minutes.—*John Weinrich, October 1961*

41

Venison

VENISON STEW—1995

2 lbs. venison stew-meat,
    cut into bite-size cubes
½ cup flour, mixed with
    1 tsp. seasoned salt
2 oz. butter
1 cup hearty Burgundy
¼ cup dry red wine
1 cup beef bouillon
3 carrots, chopped
1 medium onion, diced

1 garlic clove, crushed
2 bay leaves
1 tbsp. fresh parsley, chopped
¼ tsp. each chervil,
    chives and thyme
½ lb. mushrooms, sliced
½ cup cooked barley (optional)
½ cup sour cream
1 tsp. paprika
Salt and pepper to taste

Pour the flour and seasoned-salt mixture into a bag and add the cubed venison. Shake the bag until the meat is thoroughly coated. Brown the cubes, a few at a time, in a large buttered frying pan and set aside when done. Melt 2 ounces of butter in a 4-quart stew pot over a medium flame. Add the meat cubes, Burgundy, dry wine and beef bouillon and bring to a low boil. Add the carrots, onion, garlic, bay leaves, parsley and chervil/chives/thyme mix. Salt and pepper to taste. Cover and simmer for ½ an hour, then add the mushrooms and barley and simmer for an additional 10 minutes. Stir in the sour cream and paprika and simmer for another 5 minutes. Serve with a warm, crisp loaf of Italian bread and fill up the glasses with hearty Burgundy. Serves 4.—*Donald Seeley, January 1995*

ONIONS

You have been careful to replace the cover to your kettle every time you remove it to skim or stir your stew with the indispensable long-handled spoon; now be doubly careful the onions are in. Onions are too scarce to waste their sweetness on the mountain air. You want all that on the inside of the pot. Now you haven't a few potatoes, have you? They are not the *sine qua non* that onions are, it's true, but they are mighty handy for a stew. Peel and slice up a few and add a ½-hour or so before taking the stew off. I believe this stew is done.

R. Ritchie
October 1898

PRESERVING VENISON

If you're camping in one place and have a quantity of fresh venison you'd like to preserve with a minimum of trouble, cut it into forearm-sized strips, following the membranous divisions among the muscles as far as possible. Pull off as much of this parchment as you reasonably can. Roll the pieces in a mixture made proportionately of 3 pounds of table salt, 4 tablespoons of allspice and 5 tablespoons of black pepper. Rubbing this well into the meat, then shaking off any excess, will give the best results. You can either drape the strips over a wire or similar support, well away from any animals, or you can suspend them there after first piercing an end of each with a knife and looping in a string or wire. The treated meat must be kept dry. If you have to travel, re-hang it after reaching your destination. About 1 month is needed for it to shrink and to absorb the seasoning properly; less in dry country and more in damp regions.

Bradford Angier
November 1962

VENISON STROGANOFF

1 lb. boneless venison stew-meat, cut
      across the grain into ¼-inch-thick slices
Flour and salt
2 tbsps. bacon drippings
8-oz. can sliced mushrooms
      (or ½-lb. fresh mushrooms, sliced)
1 medium onion, finely chopped
1 garlic clove, minced
3 tbsps. butter
10½-oz. can condensed beef broth
1 cup sour cream
2 tbsps. dry white wine

Dredge the meat in the salted flour. Heat a skillet, add the bacon drippings, and brown the meat quickly on both sides. Add the mushrooms, onion and garlic; stir and cook over medium heat for 3 to 4 minutes. Remove the contents from the skillet and place them in the top pan of a medium double boiler whose bottom pan contains water simmering over low heat. Add 2 tablespoons of butter to the drippings in the skillet; stir in 3 tablespoons of flour and the can of beef broth. Stir and cook over medium-high heat until the mixture thickens, then add it to the meat and mushrooms in the double boiler. Stir in the sour cream and wine. At the last minute, stir in the remaining tablespoon of butter.—*Dan Small, December 1981*

Venison

SMOTHERED VENISON

3 lbs. venison,
*   round or rump*
Salt and pepper to taste
Flour
Melted fat
1 tsp. celery seed
2 tbsps. prepared mustard
*   or horseradish*
1 cup strained tomatoes

Season the venison with salt and pepper, then roll it in flour. Place it in a Dutch oven or heavy covered pan and brown on all sides in the melted fat. Add the celery seeds, prepared mustard or horseradish and strained tomatoes. Cover and simmer for about 3 hours.—*John Weinrich, October 1961*

IN THE PINK

It was the least droolable dinner I have ever had. When my friend's wife came smiling into the dining room, bearing the huge, white china platter with the browned meat still bubbling on it, we all sat quietly, reverently, until the master of the house rose to carve and the whole awful truth was revealed: A crime had been committed. The meat was tough, stringy, a sacrilegious serving of what should have been the world's choicest dish. My friend and I just sat and stared, stricken dumb by the horrible deed. Visions rose of the snowy miles we had trudged, the hours we had silently still-hunted, the cost, the days of planning, the three weeks of aging the meat, the care we had given the carcass, hanging it properly, bleeding it well, the expert butcher work—all wasted. What had happened? Well, the dear woman had her own manner of treating and cooking what she called "wild" meat. She had soaked it in wine overnight, salted it heavily and roasted it for five hours! All this presumably to take the "wild, gamy flavor out," as she explained smilingly when my friend had regained his self-control with terrible effort and asked her what she had done to produce such a mess. Over the years I have learned that this is not unusual. Much care, time, money and effort go into bagging the best of game, most of which is quickly, thoughtlessly and foolishly converted into garbage-pail material by the unknowing and the uncaring. The haunch should be cooked juicy. The key word is pink. All good meat should come to the table with a bit of blood oozing, the color of a maiden-blush pink.

Jack Denton Scott
August 1963

COOKING
MEAT IN CAMP

Venison also goes well in stews and mulligans. Cut in small pieces and drop into hard-boiling, unsalted water (slowly, so as not to stop the boiling). Boil the meat for ½ an hour before you drop in the vegetables or dumplings. Again, season at the end with salt and plenty of black pepper; use celery salt if you have it. If you use rice, you can season it with curry powder, and add a little flour to thicken the gravy, which makes a more tasty dish. Incidentally, the best of all meat for stews is that around the head of the animal.

Colonel Townsend Whelen
March 1958

GUIYÁS
(VENISON GOULASH)

3 lbs. stewing venison, cubed
2 lbs. small white onions, sliced
8 oz. fat (lard or canned
 vegetable shortening)
1 tbsp. marjoram
1 ½ tbsps. paprika
2 cans beef broth

Sauté the onion slices in fat until soft; then add the cubed venison and brown it on all sides. Sprinkle in the marjoram and paprika, cover the ingredients with beef broth, cover the pot and simmer slowly for 3 hours or until the meat is tender, stirring often and from time to time adding more warm beef broth; the gravy should be thickish. Broad noodles are excellent with this, the gravy liberally spooned over them; a fresh green vegetable is an eye-appealing accompaniment, and, of course, glasses of cold beer or ale are a must.—*Jack Denton Scott, October 1967*

Venison

MOOSE STEW

¼ cup flour

2 tsps. salt

½ tsp. pepper

1 lb. lean moose meat,
    cut into 1-inch pieces

⅓ cup cooking oil

½ onion, diced

6 carrots, peeled and
    cut into 1-inch chunks

3 ribs celery, cut into 1-inch chunks

3 potatoes, peeled and
    cut into 1-inch chunks

16-oz. can tomato sauce

¹⁄₁₆ tsp. cinnamon

Water

TO STEW COLD VENISON

Cut the meat in slices and put the trimmings and bones into a saucepan with enough water to cover. Let them stew 2 hours. Strain the liquid in a pan, then add some bits of butter rolled in flour and whatever gravy was left of the venison. Stir in some currant jelly, and let it boil ½ an hour. Then put in the meat, and keep it over the fire long enough to heat.

Pete Byrnes
October 1964
(transcribed from his grandmother's circa 1857 cookbook)

In a paper bag mix the flour, salt and pepper. Add the meat and shake the bag until the meat is thoroughly coated. In a heavy skillet preheat the oil. Brown the flour-coated meat in the oil, along with the onion. Add the remaining ingredients, covering them with water. Simmer this mixture, with the cover on, for approximately 1 hour. Serves 4.—*A.J. McClane, November 1981 (from* Collins Backroom Cooking Secrets *by Tom Collins)*

STIFATHO

3 lbs. cubed venison, antelope or elk	4 bay leaves
5 garlic cloves	5 cloves
3 lbs. walnut-sized onions	1 tbsp. honey
6-oz. can tomato paste	1 tsp. freshly ground black pepper (or to taste)
3 tbsps. any red vinegar	1 tsp. salt (or to taste)

Remove all fat from the meat; then, using a cast-iron Dutch oven, braise the meat in a modest amount of butter with the 5 garlic cloves, pressed finely. Remove the meat but conserve the drippings. Sauté the peeled whole onions, turning them constantly until their outer skins are soft to a fork prick—this should take only a few minutes. Remove the onions from the Dutch oven and return the meat. Add the can of tomato paste plus 6 ounces of water. Add all the remaining ingredients, stir well, cover, and cook over very low heat for about 45 minutes. Then add the onions for approximately ½ an hour. (This time is dependent on the size of your onions. No matter what their diameter, they should be firm yet pliant. Test by placing one on a cutting board. Press on its side with the flat of a knife. If its center squeezes easily out the end, it's done.) Serves 6.—*Ted Kerasote, September 1988*

Venison

VENISON AND WILD RICE STEW

*3 ½ lbs. shoulder of venison, cut
  into 2-inch cubes*
2 qts. water
*2 yellow onions, peeled and
  quartered*
2 tsps. salt
⅛ tsp. pepper, freshly ground
*1 ½ cups wild rice,
  washed in cold water*

Place the venison, water and onions in a large, heavy kettle and simmer, uncovered, for 3 hours or until the venison is tender. Mix in the salt, pepper and wild rice, cover, and simmer for 20 minutes. Stir the mixture, then simmer, uncovered, for about 20 minutes more, or until the rice is tender and most of the liquid is absorbed. Serves 6 to 8.—*Yeffe Kimbal and Jean Anderson, October 1987 (from their book* The Art of Indian Cooking)

BASIC CAMP COOKERY

If you are cooking a stew, cut your meat into 1½-inch cubes and drop them one at a time into boiling water. Don't add salt until almost ready to serve. Meat can be eaten when it has been boiling only 5 minutes. The Eskimos prefer it that way and the vitamins are retained, but most people prefer to boil it for 1 hour or more. Usually, however, rice or vegetables are cooked with it in a stew and these dictate the amount of boiling.

Colonel Townsend Whelen
July 1953

MEMORABLE BURGER BUNS

2 packets active dry yeast
¼ cup sugar
1½ cups hot water (120°F to 130°F)
6 cups flour
⅓ cup instant nonfat dry milk
1 tbsp. salt
5 tbsps. softened butter
2 tbsps. sesame seeds

Combine the yeast, sugar and hot water in a small bowl. Set aside. Combine the flour, dry milk and salt in a bowl. Cut in the butter with a knife. Make a well in the flour mixture and pour in the liquid. Beat well enough to make a stiff dough. Turn it onto a floured surface and knead for 10 minutes, until the dough becomes elastic. Return the dough to the cleaned and greased bowl, cover it and leave it in a warm place until it doubles in volume. Punch down the dough and pinch any air bubbles. Let it rest for 10 minutes. Use a sharp knife to divide the dough into 20 equal pieces. Shape each into a ball, place about 2 inches apart on greased baking sheets, and flatten each ball slightly. Cover the buns with wax paper and let them rise again for about 1 hour, until they are doubled in volume. Then brush them with beaten egg and sprinkle generously with sesame seeds. Bake for 15 minutes at 375°F until golden brown.

Jane Tennant
January 1987

MARRAKECH BURGERS

2 lbs. gameburger (deer, moose or elk)
2 tsps. fresh cilantro leaves, chopped
2 tsps. fresh mint, chopped
2 tsps. fresh parsley, chopped
1 tsp. black pepper, freshly ground
½ tsp. cayenne pepper
2 tsps. curry powder
2 tsps. ground cumin
1 tsp. powdered ginger
½ tsp. dry mustard
½ tsp. ground cloves
1 onion, finely chopped, sautéed in butter

Combine all the ingredients and refrigerate for 2 hours. Mold the meat into patties with your hands and cook the patties under the broiler for 10 minutes per side. Serve a cucumber-and-yogurt relish and a sweet mango chutney with the burgers. Serves 4.—*Jane Tennant, January 1987*

FLAMED VENISON BURGERS

2 lbs. ground venison
4 tbsps. shallots, chopped,
*   sautéed in butter*
4 tsps. black pepper, coarsely ground
3 tsps. creamed horseradish
Salt to taste
Dash of Tabasco
1 tbsp. Worcestershire sauce
2 tbsps. cognac, warmed

Mix the shallots and seasonings into the meat with your hands. Form patties and pan-broil them over high heat for about 1 minute per side. Pour the warmed cognac into the skillet and ignite. When the flames subside, quickly put the patties onto toasted and buttered hamburger buns, pouring any juices from the pan over the meat. Serve with a raw red onion and orange salad. Serves 4.—*Jane Tennant, January 1987*

GRINDING VENISON

Most of the recipes that include ground venison are from the more recent decades of <u>Sports Afield</u> articles rather than our grandfathers' time. Nowadays venison burger is used for everything from spaghetti to stuffed peppers to burgers for lunch meat. In the old days, it seems jerky was the venison lunch meat of choice. "Jerking" venison is rather time consuming for what you get; then again, one of the more time-intensive and frustrating things I've ever attempted was to grind my own deer meat. Granted, I was seven months pregnant with my largest and heaviest baby. To add to my tender emotions, I had found it necessary to limit my fall hunting for the baby's sake and was, also upon occasion, a hunting widow. I chose a lonely, fatigued, late-night hour to grind venison. I couldn't get the meat through the grinder without it either mushing out the other side or clogging the grinder. The attempt ended in buckets of tears rather than buckets of burger meat. Since then I have given my venison to a butcher to grind, when I can find one. His bigger-bladed grinder may work just fine, but it's difficult in this age of wild meat regulation to sometimes find a consenting butcher. But if you've got a good butcher or a better temperament than I, venison burger is a great option for the meat that didn't go into the stew.—R.C.G.

LIVING OFF
THE COUNTRY

We rarely cooked the hams unless we had nothing else, but usually turned them into "jerky" as provision against a meatless time, because they were the easiest to cut in broad, thin strips. To prepare jerky or jerky venison, cut the meat into long strips about ³/₄-inch thick and 3 to 5 inches wide. If you have plenty of salt, dip these in very salty water. If not, never mind this. Hang these strips on a scaffold about 5 feet above your campfire where they will get mild heat to dry the meat and keep flies away. Don't let it "cook." When it is completely dried, which will take 2 to 4 days, pack it away for future consumption. It will keep indefinitely, but guard it from pack rats, mice, and dampness. We used it almost exclusively for our lunches. A man can travel a long distance on jerky alone.

Colonel Townsend Whelen
December 1943

VENISON BURGERS

1 lb. venison
1 large onion
¼ lb. bacon,
    salt pork or suet
Salt and pepper
1 egg
5 tbsps. butter

Put through a meat grinder the venison, onion and bacon, salt pork or suet. Grind a second time if fine meat is desired. Then mix it all thoroughly to distribute the onion and the fat, and add salt and pepper. The bacon, salt pork or suet is used to relieve the dryness of the venison. One egg mixed into it will help hold this mixture together when it is formed into patties and fried in butter, or broiled with butter basting, but it is not absolutely necessary. Serve on a hot toasted bun with a slice of mild Bermuda or Texas onion, and provide relish or mustard.—*Bill Wolf, November 1955*

PASTITSIO

1 ½ lbs. linguine

2 lbs. ground venison,
    antelope or elk

1 large onion, finely chopped

2 garlic cloves, pressed

2 tbsps. olive oil

8-oz. can tomato sauce

4 oz. water

½ tsp. basil

½ tsp. oregano

¼ tsp. cinnamon

3 eggs, beaten

1 lb. Parmesan cheese,
    grated

Sauté the onion and garlic in the olive oil. Put in the meat and brown for a few minutes before adding the tomato sauce, water, basil, oregano and cinnamon. Simmer the ingredients for about 15 minutes. While the above is simmering, cook the linguine. (1 ½ pounds of linguine needs 9 quarts of water to cook properly. If you use much less water, it will taste starchy. If you don't have a pot this big, cook the linguine in 2 batches.) Drain the pasta, beat the 3 eggs and add them to the linguine along with ½ cup of Parmesan. Butter the bottom of a 13x9-inch pan; sprinkle some Parmesan over it. Divide the linguine mixture in half. Layer one half into the pan and sprinkle with Parmesan. Place the browned meat mixture on top of this layer and sprinkle on more cheese. Place the other half of the linguine mixture onto the meat, sprinkle Parmesan cheese on and top it with béchamel sauce. Spread the sauce evenly, letting it seep through the layers. Bake at 350°F for 45 minutes to 1 hour.—*Ted Kerasote, September 1988*

BÉCHAMEL TOPPING

3 eggs
4 tbsps. butter
3 tbsps. flour
2 cups whole milk
Dash of nutmeg

To make the béchamel topping, first beat the 3 eggs. Then melt the butter in a deep-sided skillet. Keeping the flame low, add the flour, mixing with a wire whisk for 3 minutes. Slowly add the milk, continuing to stir. Add the beaten eggs along with a ½ cup of grated Parmesan and a dash of nutmeg. Don't let the mixture boil, but do let it thicken.

Ted Kerasote
September 1988

SAUCE

1 can tomato sauce
1 can tomato soup
³/₄ cup water
1 tbsp. Worcestershire sauce
1 medium onion, finely chopped
1 tsp. beef bouillon
Black pepper to taste

Mix everything in a saucepan and simmer
for 10 minutes.

Dave Harbour
November 1983

STUFFED PEPPERS SUPREME

2 lbs. ground venison

2 eggs

4 slices day-old white bread,
    moistened with 1 cup milk

1 large onion, finely chopped

½ tsp. garlic powder (more if desired)

2 tbsps. A-1 Steak Sauce or Worcestershire sauce

1 tbsp. beef bouillon (granulated)

Black pepper to taste

6 to 8 green peppers

P lace all of the ingredients (except the green peppers) in a large bowl and mix them thoroughly with your hands. The secret to preparing moist stuffing is to add sufficient liquid to produce a medium consistency. Add more milk or beef bouillon if necessary. Prepare the green peppers by washing them thoroughly and removing the seeds. If the peppers are large, they may be split lengthwise. Generously fill each half with the meat mixture. Place them in a glass baking dish containing about a ½-inch of water. Bake at 350°F for 45 minutes. Remove them from the oven and cover them with the sauce. Return them to the oven for a final 15 or 20 minutes. Serves 6 hungry hunters.—*Dave Harbour, November 1983*

UVOURILAKIA

*1 ½ lbs. lean ground venison,
    antelope or elk
1 large onion, finely chopped
½ cup brown rice, cooked
½ tsp. oregano
½ tsp. fresh parsley, finely
    chopped
½ tsp. freshly ground black
    pepper (or to taste)
½ tsp. salt (or to taste)
2 vegetable bouillon cubes
2 large carrots, sliced into
    thin rounds
Juice of 1 large lemon
2 eggs*

BASIC CAMP COOKERY

It has been my experience that the trappers, prospectors, and guides of our western mountain country can give most of the Easterners cards and spades when it comes to cooking. For one thing they are more accustomed to "batching" it, doing all their work all the time, while the Easterners, except for the short period they might be in the bush each year, spend their time at home, where they rely on their better halves for the home chores.

Colonel Townsend Whelen
July 1953

Combine all of the above ingredients (except the bouillon cubes, carrots, lemon and eggs), adding a little water. Using your palms, make 1-inch-diameter meatballs from the mixture. Bring 1 quart of water and the bouillon cubes to a boil. Drop in the meatballs and carrots; cover, and cook over low heat for 1 hour. Next, beat the 2 eggs and the juice from the lemon into a froth. Strain off the juice from the meatballs and slowly pour it into the frothed egg and lemon mixture. (If you pour too quickly, the mixture will curdle.) Beat with a wire whisk as you pour. Pour the combined broth back over the meatballs and carrots and serve. Serves 6.—*Ted Kerasote, September 1988*

GREEN PEPPER SEEDS AND OTHER NASTY THINGS

This recipe from <u>The Art of Indian Cooking</u> implies that you use the seeds, as part of the core, in the stuffing of the peppers. I have always understood the seeds of green peppers to be indigestible at best and perhaps even slightly poisonous at worst. Their reputation is not unlike that of bay leaves, and I have religiously avoided getting seeds and leaves into food. Although you'd think that Native Americans would know about seeds and leaves, the seeds probably really aren't that tasty anyway and should be left out.—R.C.G.

GREEN PEPPERS STUFFED WITH VENISON

6 green peppers
2 ½ cups diced leftover
    cooked venison
6 mushrooms, washed and
    coarsely chopped
2 scallions, washed and thinly sliced
5 tbsps. bacon drippings or melted
    butter or margarine
1 tsp. salt
⅛ tsp. black pepper

Wash and core the green peppers; chop the cores. Mix the chopped cores with the venison, chopped mushrooms, sliced scallions, bacon drippings, salt and black pepper. Stuff the peppers with the venison mixture, stand them in a shallow baking pan and bake in a moderate oven (350°F) for 45 minutes. Serves 6.—*Yeffe Kimbal and Jean Anderson, October 1987 (from their book* The Art of Indian Cooking*)*

Venison

CHAMA CHILI VENADO

3 lbs. venison flank,
    neck or trimmings in chunks
¼ cup manteca or pork lard
4 tbsps. ground chili powder,
    or molido
3 dried red peppers, crushed
1 tbsp. dried oregano

1 tsp. whole dried cumin,
    bruised
2 garlic cloves, diced
2 tsps. salt,
        black pepper to taste
3 onions, peeled and
    chopped at fireside

The spices should be combined at home and carried in a can or plastic bag; the lard and garlic should be packaged separately. You can make chili powder from scratch by mixing ground cayenne, oregano, cumin and salt (3:2:1:1). Use a Dutch oven, 3-quart size or better, nestled in a generous bed of coals. Brown the meat in the lard, half at a time. With a slotted spoon, set the browned meat aside, adding more lard as necessary. After all the meat is well browned, pour off any extra grease. Combine the meat, chili powder and all the spices. Dice and add the garlic. Stir the meat vigorously, coating each piece with the spices, and continue cooking over low heat for 10 minutes. It may be necessary to remove the kettle from the coals to prevent burning, but the heat of the pot should be sufficient to allow the herbs and peppers to soften and blend. Add enough water to cover the meat. Return to the fire with enough coals to bring the chili to a boil. Cover and simmer, stirring occasionally, for 1 hour. Grate or chop the onions finely and add them to the chili. Continue cooking for 1 hour, adding more water as necessary until the onion dissolves.—*S.G.B. Tennant Jr., February 1985*

POTATO BREAD

3 medium potatoes or equivalent leftover mashed or boiled
1 cake of yeast
2 ½ cups water
8 cups flour
1 tbsp. salt

Boil and mash the potatoes; let them cool, then add the yeast plus a ½-cup of water and 3 tablespoons of flour to make a sponge. Let it rise for 30 minutes. Add the rest of the water, salt and flour. Knead until it makes a firm dough; add more flour if needed. Cover the dough with a clean dish towel, set it aside and let it rise until double. Punch it down and let it double in size again. Divide it into loaves and place them into greased pans. Let the dough rise in the pans, then bake for 45 minutes at 350°F.

Lee Arten
November 1992

PRESSURE-COOKED VENISON CHILI

2 lbs. venison scraps, cut into small cubes
2 tbsps. oil
1 cup water
2 28-oz. cans whole tomatoes, drained
15-oz. can refried beans
2 15-oz. cans red kidney beans
2 green peppers, chopped
2 large onions, chopped
3 garlic cloves, crushed
2 tbsps. margarine
2 tbsps. hot chili powder
1 tsp. cumin
1 tbsp. hot sauce (or more)
1 tbsp. salt
Cayenne pepper, green chilies or jalapeños (all optional)

With a sharp knife, cut the meat into ½ to ¼-inch cubes. Brown them in oil over high heat in a pressure cooker. Add the water, lock on the lid, and cover the vent. Cook for 20 minutes, vent cover rocking slowly. Remove the cooker from the heat and run it under cold water until the pressure drops. Drain the liquid and reserve it; it can be used in other recipes. To the meat in the cooker add the tomatoes (save the juice) and refried beans. Replace the cover and vent and return the cooker to the heat. Cook for 10 minutes, vent rocking slowly. In a large hot frypan, sauté the green peppers, onions and garlic in margarine until tender. Cool the cooker, add the vegetables, beans and spices, and simmer covered until the desired consistency is reached. If it is too thick, add some of the reserved stock or tomato juice.—*Fred Everson, October 1990*

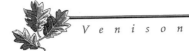

Venison

VENISON MINCEMEAT

1 qt. apple cider
2 cups seedless raisins
1 cup dried currants
3 greening apples; peeled,
    cored and chopped
1 cup suet, chopped
2 lbs. ground venison
2 tsps. salt
2 tsps. cinnamon
2 tsps. ginger
1 tsp. cloves
1 tsp. nutmeg
½ tsp. allspice

Place the cider, raisins, cur-rants, apples and suet in a large, heavy kettle; cover, and simmer for 2 hours. Stir in the remain-ing ingredients and simmer, uncovered, for 2 hours, stirring occasionally. Makes 2 quarts of pie filling.—*Yeffe Kimbal and Jean Anderson, October 1987 (from their book* The Art of Indian Cooking*)*

COOKING MEAT IN CAMP

Nearly all the venison I have eaten has been cooked over an open wood campfire. Only on one trip did we have a sheep-herder stove along, and its oven was too small for a big roast of venison. Almost always we broiled the better cuts of meat. This is the best and tastiest way: You can broil in a regular wire broiler over a bed of hot glowing coals. Don't use pitch pine or you will taste the creosote in the meat. Or if your fold-ing baker has a grill to replace the pan, you can broil it nicely in that. While broiling, baste it more frequently than other meats, using melted butter, bacon grease or vegetable shortening. Also, you can broil on a stick over the coals. We usually preferred to "siwash" broil ours. You cut a dry stick, making a point at each end. Cut the meat in chunks about the size of a baseball, or a tri-fle smaller, and impale a number of these on the stick. Between each chunk, stick a piece of bacon or salt pork a little smaller than a golf ball to do the basting. Use no salt until completely through cooking. Hold this stick close over the coals or flame, and turn it until each piece is seared. Then place one end of the stick in the ground close to the fire, and incline it and the chunks of meat over the coals or alongside the blaze. Turn it from time to time so it will broil evenly all around. When almost burned outside, remove, salt and eat.

Colonel Townsend Whelen
March 1958

SCOTCH-IRISH EGGS

6 large hard-boiled eggs
1 lb. venison breakfast sausage
2 raw eggs
1 tbsp. flour
Salt and pepper to taste
1 cup dry bread crumbs
Oil for deep-frying

Shell the hard-boiled eggs. Combine the flour, salt and pepper into the sausage meat, then roll the mix into 6 equal balls. Press the balls into patties that are just large enough to wrap one cooked egg apiece, distributing the sausage as evenly as possible. When the cooked eggs are wrapped, beat the 2 raw eggs in a bowl and place the cup of bread crumbs on a plate. Dredge each patty in the beaten eggs, then roll them in the bread crumbs, coating evenly all around. Deep-fry the patties in hot oil for 3 or 4 minutes. Remove them with a large slotted spoon and drain on a brown paper bag. Let them cool, then wrap them in foil. They should keep at least half a day. Cook some at night so you'll have one to eat while walking to the deer stand in the morning.

A.D. Livingston
August 1995

BREAKFAST SAUSAGE PATTIES

2 lbs. ground venison
½ medium onion, chopped
½ garlic clove, finely pressed
4 tbsps. fresh parsley, finely chopped
4 tsps. salt
½ tsp. crushed dried red pepper
½ tsp. freshly ground black pepper
¾ tsp. cumin
¾ tsp. ground allspice

Mix all the ingredients, roll the meat into the shape of a log, wrap it in aluminum foil, and store it in the refrigerator or freezer. Increase the pepper if you want hotter sausage. Increase the allspice if you want a nuttier flavor. Depending on the chewiness you want, chop your onions coarse or fine.
—*Ted Kerasote, November 1988*

Venison

VENISON AND POTATO SAUSAGE

10 lbs. ground lean venison

10 lbs. raw potato, ground

3 lbs. raw onion, ground

10 tsps. salt

(1 per lb. of meat)

2 tsps. pepper

(1 per 5 lbs. of meat)

Sausage casings

NOT A STUFFER OR A GRINDER?

Here I'm suggesting that if you are not an experienced venison meat grinder and sausage stuffer that you not attempt this recipe (see the sidebar on meat grinding, p.50, and the story behind trying to get my sausage casing attachment to work should be left only to imagination). Plus without any fat in the recipe the meat would not hold together as sausage patties.—R.C.G.

Grind the meat, potatoes and onions separately first, then mix them all together with salt and pepper and put through the meat grinder a second time. Fill the sausage casings by hand or with a sausage stuffer attachment on your meat grinder. Tie off or twist the sausage into individual links or leave them whole. Do not pack the casings too tightly or they will burst when cooked. Wrap them in meal-size packages and freeze. I prefer sausage with no pork added, as above, but you may add up to 3 pounds of ground pork to this recipe if you wish. Be sure to increase the proportions of all other ingredients accordingly. It is better to go sparingly with salt and pepper—you can always add more later. Sausage will keep only about 3 months in your freezer if pork is added, up to a year otherwise. To serve, simply place the frozen sausage in boiling water and let it simmer for 45 minutes. Punch a few holes in the casing to release pressure as the sausage expands while cooking. Leftover sausage (if your family leaves any!) may be warmed up in the oven or served cold.—*Dan Small, December 1981*

COOKING MEAT IN CAMP

By "venison" I mean the meat of any hoofed North American animal. Deer and caribou meat, if they can be distinguished from beef, taste somewhat like a combination of beef and lamb. Moose meat can hardly be distinguished from beef; the same with elk. Mountain sheep is like the most delicious domestic lamb you ever ate. Young goat is like lamb; older goat like mutton. I have never eaten antelope, but some think it the best of all. There is no strong taste or odor to any of this meat if it is properly cared for. Disagreeably strong meat is from gut-shot animals that have not been gutted quickly, with all the juices promptly wiped off the meat and out of the cavity. A large buck or bull shot in the rutting season sometimes is not very good meat, but the only one I remember that we could not eat with relish was a big bull caribou I shot during the rutting season. After trying it, my companion and I decided that we did not care for it at all. It was very strong, and we ditched the meat, but its head was an exceptionally fine trophy. There is no problem about cooking venison at home. It should be cooked exactly as you would cook beef. Let it be well-done on the outside, and rare within.

Colonel Townsend Whelen
March 1958

SLOW-COOKER VENISON SOUP

2 meaty venison bones
Water, salted to taste
5 carrots, cut into chunks
2 celery stalks, coarsely chopped
2 medium onions, quartered
2 medium potatoes, peeled and quartered
3 leeks, if available
2 bay leaves

Place the bones in a slow-cooker and fill with water to within 1 inch of the top. Add a little salt, cover and set the cooker on low. Allow the bones to cook overnight. Cut up the vegetables and place them in a covered bowl or plastic bag in the refrigerator overnight. Next morning, remove the bones from the broth and discard them after putting any bits of meat that cling to them back into the broth. Skim off any floating fat and add the vegetables. Cover once again, turn the temperature to high and let the soup simmer all day. It will be ready to serve that evening.

—*Dan Small, December 1981*

Venison

SPANISH BEAN SOUP WITH VENISON

1 lb. dried garbanzo beans
1 lb. smoked venison sausage
2 leg shanks or other bony parts
3 large potatoes, peeled and diced
¼ lb. salt pork
3 medium onions, peeled and diced
3 tomatoes, diced
3 celery ribs, chopped
Salt, pepper and mild paprika

In a Dutch oven bring 3 quarts of water to a boil. Add the garbanzo beans and venison sausage and bones. Bring to a boil, lower the heat, cover the pot, and simmer for 12 hours. Remove the venison bones, discarding them after you've pulled off and diced the meat. Add the meat to the pot, along with the potatoes. Dice the salt pork and fry it quickly in a skillet until browned and you have some grease. Sauté the onions in it, then add them and the browned salt pork to the pot. Cover and simmer for 30 minutes. Add the tomatoes and celery, then simmer for 30 minutes. Before serving, sprinkle the top with paprika.—*A.D. Livingston, February 1996*

BROTH AND SOUP

When hunting in canoe or pack-horse country, you sometimes find yourself with more good venison than you can hope to bring out. On occasions like this, why not really splurge on broth and enjoy all you possibly can? What I've done at such times is get the kettle simmering, hang a ladle nearby and let everyone help himself until the pot is exhausted. Then begin another. The liquid will boil down, so don't get it too salty at the start. Just cut the meat into small pieces so that you'll get the most good out of it. Shot portions are fine. So are all the lesser cuts that you haven't time or room to handle otherwise. Marrow bones, split or sawed, are unequaled. Add about 1 cup of cold water for every ½ pound of meat and bone. Cover and simmer for 4 hours. FOR SOUP: Start as you would if making broth. In fact, you can ladle out what broth you need for the liquid part of the soup. Gently sauté, in the bottom of the soup kettle, whatever vegetables you're going to use. Then add the broth and cover. Do not boil or you'll spoil the flavor. Do not season until 5 minutes before you're ready to serve.

Bradford Angier
November 1962

OLD TERMS IN RECIPES

Pete Byrnes was kind enough to make most of the conversions from his grandmother's recipes so they would be useable. However, he did not indicate what the measurement of "3 blades" would be the equivalent of in today's teaspoon world. After some research and with the Oxford English Dictionary as my source, I believe 3 blades converts to 3 leaves, or about 1 teaspoon of mace.—R.C.G.

VENISON SOUP

4 lbs. fresh venison
1 lb. ham
1 onion, minced
Black pepper to taste
Water to cover (approximately
*   4 cups), plus 1 qt.*
*   boiling water*
1 head celery
3 blades (leaves) mace
* (approximately 1 tsp. powdered)*
¼ lb. butter
¼ cup flour
2 cups port or Madeira

Cut the fresh venison from the bones and cut the ham into small slices. Place the meats into a pot and add the onion and black pepper. Put in only as much water as will cover the ingredients and stew them gently for 1 hour, keeping the pot closely covered. Skim it well and pour in 1 quart of boiling water. Add the head of celery, cut small, and 3 blades of mace. Boil the soup gently for 2 ½ hours; then put in the butter, cut small and rolled in flour, and the port or Madeira. Let it simmer for ¼ of an hour longer.—*Pete Byrnes, October 1964 (transcribed from his grandmother's circa 1857 cookbook)*

Venison

DEER LIVER

The sooner you prepare liver, the better the taste. You can even cook it easily in camp over an open fire.

¼ to ½ lb. venison liver per
*   person, sliced very thinly*
Flour, salt and pepper to taste
3 tbsps. butter
2 medium onions, sliced and
*   separated into rings*

Dredge the liver slices in flour seasoned with salt and pepper. Melt butter in a large skillet. Add the onion rings and sauté them until tender over medium heat. Move the onions to one side of the pan and sauté the liver slices in the same butter for 4 minutes, 2 minutes to a side. Serve the liver slices topped with onion rings on a heated platter.

—*Dan Small, December 1981*

IS WILD GAME SAFE TO EAT?

Wild creatures are the first casualties of our chemical manipulation of the environment....[But] big game animals that live in the wilderness areas or on the high, remote plains—elk, sheep, goats and pronghorns—tend to have flesh in which very few or no contaminates can be found. Since the liver serves as the primary detoxifying organ in vertebrates, and these large animals have the most complex livers of all our game creatures, these animals tend to be relatively less contaminated than fish or birds.

While big-game animals are leaner than the leanest steer (for example, 100 grams of beef club contains, on the average, 380 calories, whereas 100 grams of mule deer contains 220), most current evidence indicates that you can't reduce your cholesterol by eating wild meat. Contained within the cell of the membrane of muscle itself and not within fat cells, cholesterol is ingested with every bite.

Concern over our own diet may be narcissistic; what can be forgotten in our concern for our own health is that contaminants in our environment directly affect the wildlife population.

Ted Kerasote
December 1988

FRIED DEER HEART

Deer heart
Salt and pepper to taste
Flour
Butter or grease

Split the heart, removing all the vents and ducts; then slice it thin. Salt and pepper to taste, dredge it in flour, and fry it briefly in a medium-hot skillet lightly coated with butter or grease. Don't over cook it! Enjoy. Try it with a decent cabernet sauvignon, or even a poor one.—*Grits Gresham, November 1983*

LIVER

1 deer liver
½ lb. bacon
2 large onions

Slice the liver about ½-inch thick. Cook the bacon in a heavy frypan until done to taste. Add the liver and onions, browning the liver until done. Liver is best when it is kept on the rare side. Overcooking gives you a tough, dry, tasteless and far less nutritious product.—*Bradford Angier, November 1962*

GRILLED LIVER

Grilled liver beats the frypan product four ways from go. This is the reason why, if you're hungry by the time you've collected Old Tanglehorns, you may choose to emulate the Indian hunter. If so, build a small fire and drape the liver, or slices of it, over a rack made of green wood. Or just shove a pointed stick into the ground and impale the liver on it, turning it occasionally in any event. It will not take long to cook. Fresh liver is delicious without seasoning, although if you want, you can do as many sportsmen do and always carry a small container of salt. Liver sliced 1 inch or so thick and briefly grilled over an open fire until crisp outside and pinkly juicy within is delectable. Cutting into the meat will show you when it is ready. Butter liberally just before serving.

Bradford Angier
November 1962

BRAIN

3 eggs, beaten
1 cup bread crumbs
Salt and pepper to taste
5 tbsps. butter

This one is worth the trouble. It's also a practical way of reminding yourself how small and precisely positioned the brain of a deer actually is. The best way in is with a meat saw, although a battered woodpile bludgeon will get the job done. Remove the outer membrane of the brains. Dip them in beaten egg, roll in cracker or bread crumbs seasoned with salt and pepper and slowly fry uncovered in butter or margarine. These have a delicate flavor and go well with scrambled eggs. If you haven't any fresh eggs in camp, however, dip the brains in melted butter or margarine and then roll them in crumbs. Pan-broil slowly until crisp outside and hot throughout. Serve with buttered toast, boiled potatoes or steaming-hot biscuits.—*Bradford Angier, November 1962*

Venison

BOILED AND SLICED DEER HEART FOR SANDWICHES

1 deer heart
Water
2 bay leaves
1 small onion, quartered
Salt and pepper to taste

Place the heart in a large saucepan and cover it with water. Add the bay leaves, onion and a little salt and pepper. Bring to a boil, then turn the heat down, cover and let simmer for 2 or 3 hours until the heart is tender. Remove the heart, drain it, and allow it to cool. Store it overnight in the refrigerator. Sliced very thinly, deer heart makes excellent meat for sandwiches. Serve it on whole wheat bread with hot mustard or lettuce and mayonnaise.

—*Dan Small,*
December 1981

VENISON COUNTRY PATÉ

2 lbs. deer liver, veins and membranes removed
1 ½ lbs. sliced bacon
1 ½ cups soft bread crumbs
1 cup wine (whatever you have on hand, from muscatel to Bordeaux)
2 tsps. salt
¼ tsp. white pepper
1 ½ cups onion, finely minced
3 small garlic cloves
3 tbsps. unsalted butter
3 eggs, lightly beaten
⅛ tsp. ground cloves
3 bay leaves
½ tsp. dried thyme leaves

Blanch the bacon in boiling water for 10 minutes. Drain it and pat it dry. Set it aside. Mince the liver with a sharp knife. Combine the liver, bread crumbs, wine, salt and pepper in a large bowl. Cover and refrigerate for 1 hour. Heat the oven to 325°F. Sauté the onions and garlic in butter until soft. Combine with the eggs, cloves, thyme and the liver mixture. Line the bottom and sides of a 2-quart terrine with bacon slices. Fill the terrine with the paté. Top with the bay leaves and thyme leaves. Place the paté terrine in a large baking pan and add 2 inches of hot water to the outer pan. Bake for 2 hours, or until a thermometer inserted to the center reads 150°F. Remove the paté terrine from the water. Let it stand 40 minutes. Cover the paté with foil and place weight on top. Refrigerate overnight.

Kit Harrison
November 1983

MULE DEER LIVER

It is for most of us our first memory of venison's taste—the venison of deer camps, wood stoves, cold lucent fall nights.... After you have tagged him, dressed him and hung him well off the ground, slip his heavy liver into a sack and carry it down through new snow to the cabin of weathered logs. Put up your empty rifle, then blow the cobwebs out of the ancient chipped-enamel coffeepot and fill it with icy spring water. Add a fair amount of salt to make the water briny, then place the liver in it. Find a cold shadowed spot, maybe in a snowbank behind the cabin, and let the liver soak, without freezing, for a day. (Make sure the lid is tightly on the pot and it is kept well away from where a badger might wreak havoc on it.) Remove the liver from the water and dry it with a clean yellow towel. Peel all the thin bluish membrane from the organ's surface, and with your sharp skinning knife cut slices ⅓-inch thick. In a heavy iron skillet with a blackened bottom, lightly brown slices of onion in bacon fat, then remove them and set aside. In a plastic bread bag put white flour and salt and pepper to taste, and shake the slices of liver in it, flouring each evenly. Spoon more bacon fat from the red Folger's can and add it to the skillet until the fat is a ¼ deep and very hot, though not smoking. Now, place the slices into the hot fat and fry quickly. Turn the meat when beads of blood begin to appear on the white up side. When the liver is done, the flour coating should be crisp and the meat slightly pink inside, not gray as an aged pronghorn's tongue. Put the meat on a platter of cracked blue china, place the warm onions on top, get the old men to turn the ball game down on the radio, tell the gin rummy players to clear the Bicycle cards off the table, and set the meat before them. Serve with fried potatoes or maybe carrots, a salad of fresh iceberg lettuce and wedges of tomatoes, perhaps some hot garlic bread, cold milk and drop of whiskey. Cut a piece with the same knife you've been using for everything else so far, and lift the fork to your mouth.

Thomas McIntyre
November 1983

Venison

HEART AND KIDNEYS

1 lb. venison kidney and heart,
    cut into walnut-size chunks
1 tsp. salt
2 ½ cups water
2 tbsps. butter
Evaporated milk
2 tbsps. flour
1 cup onions, chopped
½ cup celery
Salt and pepper to taste
Paprika
Parsley

Cut the venison heart and kidney into chunks. Place these in cold water, with a ½ teaspoon of salt. Simmer until the meat is tender, and 2 cups of broth remain. Now get the butter, margarine or other fat melting in a frypan. Gradually add the milk and flour, stirring until it is smooth and thick. Sauté the chopped onion and celery in this over low heat until tender. Add the broth. When it's hot, the heart and kidney go in next. Stir together over low heat. Salt and pepper to taste. Top with paprika and (powdered) parsley.—*Bradford Angier, November 1962*

MOOSE CAMP

Now, moose, it's time you died, and carefully I creep along a hundred yards or so and I come on her lying down. She has not given up yet, as her head is up and ears back. My gun speaks as the poor creature struggles to rise, and her troubles are over. I've a lot to do: The hard work is all ahead of me. It is no easy job to turn an 800-pound moose on its back, but that is the first step toward the skinning and cutting up. My Savage talks and explains how glad I'll be for help: Soon I hear a distant halloo, and my answering shout brings the old boy himself. He was in camp, eating a lonely meal preparatory to the nightly wood getting, when he heard my shot in the distance. Between us, we soon had our disagreeable job finished; but there is something needed for the pot. The tongue, the nose and a kidney, covered with festoons of much rich tallow—that's all for the pot, to be put on the fire early tomorrow. Tonight, though, we'll eat another delicacy—the luscious brisket—the best part of the moose for camp eating.

Percival Nash
April 1905

JUICY BRISKET

Both ribs and brisket are encased in fat. When the venison is done, remove the fat and find moist meat underneath. The broth is strained and served as soup, the venison served with dumplings. The horseradish sauce is a must.

4 tbsps. butter
3 tbsps. flour
1 ½ cups venison stock
⅓ cup milk, heated
½ tsp. white vinegar
⅓ tsp. sugar
Salt and pepper to taste
1 ½ cups fresh horseradish root, grated

Melt the butter in the top of a double boiler over water. Add the flour and blend into a smooth paste. Stir in the venison stock, small amounts at a time; then blend in the heated milk. Stir well and let it remain over simmering water for 15 minutes, adding more stock if the mixture gets too thick. A minute before serving, stir in the vinegar, sugar, salt and pepper and the horseradish, blending into a smooth sauce.

Jack Denton Scott
October 1967

REHFLEISCH
(BOILED VENISON)

2 lbs. venison short ribs
3 white onions, halved
12 celery stalks
3 carrots, halved lengthwise
2 large sprigs Italian parsley
Salt and pepper to taste
3 lbs. brisket of venison (tied with cord)

These are cuts of venison most of us don't know how to cook. Here's the answer: Place the short ribs in a large soup kettle, cover them with cold water and bring to a boil; with a slotted spoon skim the scum that floats to the surface. Add the vegetables and liberally shake in salt and pepper. Put in the brisket, bring to a boil, again remove the floating scum, lower the heat, cover the pot and simmer for 2 hours, or until the meat is tender.—*Jack Denton Scott, October 1967*

JESSE'S
HOMEMADE JERKY

2 lbs. venison sliced ⅛-inch thick,
*   with the grain*
2 tbsps. Worcestershire sauce
2 tbsps. soy sauce
1 tbsp. salt
1 tsp. ground red pepper
2 garlic cloves, sliced
1 cup corn whiskey
1 cup water

A GOOD MARINADE

2 cups water
1 tsp. oregano
1 tsp. cumin
1 tsp. chili powder
1 cup beer
¼ cup brown sugar
¼ cup salt
Dash of Worcestershire

S.G.B. Tennant Jr.
September 1983

It is easiest to slice meat when it is lightly frozen. The cuts should be thin, long and with the grain, although they may be cut as wide as the meat allows. Remove all the fat that you can, as it will not keep and will spoil the jerky. Marinate the strips in a glass container overnight. (You may substitute 2 cups red wine for the whiskey and water.) Pat the strips dry and arrange them side by side on oven roasting racks, without overlap. Cook at minimum heat, say 150°F, for 6 hours. Leave the oven door ajar to allow moisture to escape. The meat should be dark, dry and firm; otherwise, turn the meat and continue drying. Store the jerky in a cool, airtight container. Alternate drying techniques include a "hard cure" in an electric smoker for 12 hours. Crisp jerky means the heat was too high. For sweeter jerky, baste with molasses or honey and water just before drying. When drying outdoors, the meat—whether laid on rocks and turned every few hours or hung from a rack on the porch—must be protected from moisture and creatures at all times. A cool fire keeps the flies at bay, sometimes. An original Pacific Indian procedure included a marinade of seawater reduced to enhance its saltiness. You can vary the marinade given above by adding more salt, sugar or some juniper berries to taste. If the cut and type of meat used produce extremely tough jerky, slice against the grain next time.—*S.G.B. Tennant Jr., September 1983*

JERKY

There's nothing complicated about making jerky. You cut lean venison into long strips about a ¹/₂-inch thick. These you hang apart from one another in the sun, in the attic or some other place where, kept dry, they will gradually lose most of their water content. At the same time, they'll become hard, dry, black and, incidentally, both nourishing and tasty. The strips may be first soaked, if you want, either in brine or sea water. While it is still bubbling, immerse a few strips at a time for 3 minutes apiece. You can also make your own brine by dissolving all the salt possible in boiling water. After the meat has been allowed to drain, some makers sprinkle it with pepper. In many cases they also add favorite spices such as oregano, marjoram, basil and thyme for increased flavor. A common bush technique for jerking venison involves draping the strips, or hanging them, on a wooden framework about 4 to 6 feet off the ground. A small, slow, smoky fire of any non-resinous wood is built beneath this rack. The meat is allowed to dry for several days in the sun and wind. It is covered at night and during any rain. The chief use of the fire is to discourage flies and other insects. It should not be hot enough to cook the venison at all. When jerked, the venison will be hard and more or less black outside. It will keep almost indefinitely away from damp and flies.

Bradford Angier
November 1962

REAL PEMMICAN

*Equal parts venison jerky
and bacon fat*

To make real pemmican, one of the best concentrated foods, you begin by pounding up a quantity of jerky. Then take raw animal fat and cut it into walnut-sized hunks. Try these out in a pan in the oven or over a slow fire, never letting the grease boil up. Pour the resulting hot fat over the shredded jerky, mixing the two until you have about the consistency of ordinary sausage. Then pack the pemmican in commercial casings or waterproof bags. The ideal proportions of lean and fat in pemmican is, by weight, approximately equal amounts of well-dried lean meat and fat. It takes approximately 5 pounds of fresh, lean venison to make 1 pound of jerky suitable for pemmican.

—*Bradford Angier, November 1962*

FONDUE BOURGUIGNONNE

2 to 3 lbs. antelope or
    deer meat, cubed
2 cups peanut oil
2 cups butter, melted

Pour the melted butter and oil into the fondue pot over the flame. The pot is deep so that the oil won't spatter. The oil must be very hot and stay that way. Spear a cube with your fork and hold it in the hot oil for no longer than 2 minutes. It should emerge juicy and rare. Dip it into the sauce you prefer and eat it. Rice cooked in chicken broth, a green salad and cold beer are excellent accompaniments. At right are a few sauces you can use; or dream up your own.—*Jack Denton Scott, October 1967*

MAYONNAISE–CAPER SAUCE

Into a good mayonnaise (preferably homemade) squeeze the juice of 1 lemon; then stir in 1 small finely minced white onion and 2 tablespoons of capers and blend well.

GARLIC SAUCE

Mash 4 cloves of garlic with the yolks of 3 hard-boiled eggs, slowly adding a ½ cup of olive oil, until the sauce has the consistency of mayonnaise. Then add 1 teaspoon of lemon juice, season with salt and pepper, and blend well.

RED SAUCE

Use a ½ bottle of hot ketchup, adding 2 tablespoons of chili sauce and a good dash of cayenne. Blend well.

HOT MUSTARD

Blend dry English mustard with warm water into a smooth, creamy mixture. Warn guests that it is very hot. Caution: Have cold beer at hand!

Jack Denton Scott
October 1967

KABOBS

Many times, when you're really meat-hungry, you can't wait before tying into the steak portions, which is entirely okay because, despite comments to the contrary, game is at its best within minutes or hours after being killed or, depending on the temperature, after it's been hung some four or five weeks in the cooler. It's worst when a couple of days old. What I do on such occasions is thread inch-square chunks of already-salted meat onto a sharpened green stick, thrust them briefly into the blaze to form a juice-restraining glaze and then broil them a few minutes on the fringes of the heat. These I bite off one by one I punctuate alternating mouthfuls of hot, toasted sandwich. Choice cut for these kabobs? The filet mignon; that is, the small end of the tenderloin. When you get through these and the rest of the tenderloins, move to the back steaks.

Bradford Angier
November 1962

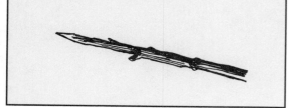

VENISON LOIN EN BROCHETTE
(SHISH KEBAB)

2 lbs. venison loin, cut
into 2-inch cubes
(for a total of 16 cubes)
4 medium tomatoes
4 medium onions
4 small green peppers
Salt and pepper to taste

Cut the tomatoes, onions and green peppers into quarters, removing the seeds from the peppers. Lightly salt and pepper the venison chunks, then spear them on skewers, alternating with the tomato, onion and pepper quarters. Broil them over an outdoor charcoal grill for several minutes per side, according to taste, turning the skewers until the meat is done evenly. (Or broil them on an oven rack with a pan underneath to catch drippings.) Do not overcook—broiled venison is best when served rare or medium and tends to dry out if cooked too long. Remove the skewers and serve the meat and vegetables on a bed of rice pilaf or a combination of ⅓ wild rice and ⅔ white rice. Serves 4.—*Dan Small, December 1981*

Venison

VENISON SAUSAGE QUICHE

1 lb. venison sausage

A pat of butter

1 lb. fresh mushrooms, sliced

¼ cup onions, chopped

4 medium eggs

½ lb. Monterey Jack cheese

1 cup heavy whipping cream

Salt and pepper to taste

2 9-inch pie shells

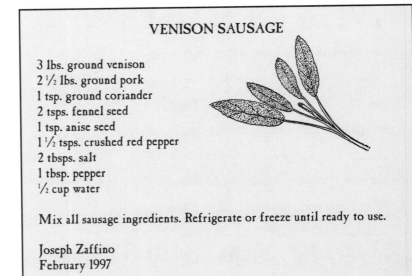

VENISON SAUSAGE

3 lbs. ground venison
2 ½ lbs. ground pork
1 tsp. ground coriander
2 tsps. fennel seed
1 tsp. anise seed
1 ½ tsps. crushed red pepper
2 tbsps. salt
1 tbsp. pepper
½ cup water

Mix all sausage ingredients. Refrigerate or freeze until ready to use.

Joseph Zaffino
February 1997

Heat the oven to 350°F so that it will be ready. Melt a little butter in a frying pan and sauté the mushrooms and onions for a few minutes. Drain and set aside. Brown the sausage and set aside. Beat the eggs slightly in a bowl and set aside. Bake the pie shells at 350°F for about 8 minutes, or until browned. (If you buy ready-to-use shells, follow the directions on the package.) Mix the sausage, mushrooms, onions, cheese, eggs and cream. Add a little salt and pepper to taste. Spread this mixture evenly into the 2 pie shells, then bake at 350°F for about 30 minutes. The two quiches will serve 5 or 6 people. The pies can be cooled, wrapped in foil, and frozen.—*A.D. Livingston (author of the* Complete Fish and Game Cookbook, *Stackpole Books), December 1991*

VENISON SMORGASBORD

As soon as the deer packed into camp, Frank skinned and quartered them. Then with John's help, Frank built a crude smoker while Jack dug a corning pit in the soft earth nearby. Some of the venison was smoked, some was corned and some was made into sausage. Two of the mule deer hind quarters were handled using a meat syringe. Frank injected them with a brine solution of curing salt, after which they were slowly, lightly smoked. Finally they were rubbed with brown sugar, placed in cheesecloth bags and hung in a cool, dry place. Venison marinated in a light brine solution makes it much better. For example, add the following to a light brine solution: crushed garlic cloves, vinegar, bay leaves, peppercorns and soy sauce. Next comes a minimum of 24 hours over smoke. First build a 5x5x5-foot frame from apple saplings lashed together with baling wire. A rack or trays to hold meat are cut from green wood. Beneath the frame build a smoke fire. Then, after placing the venison in the smoker cover the frame with odd bits of packing canvas and build the fire. The smoking is under way.

Erwin A. Bauer
December 1966

SMOKED VENISON

Electric smoker
10 lbs. lean venison meat
Salt and pepper to taste
Brown sugar
Molasses
Vinegar
Cheesecloth
Woodchips (hickory, hard maple, apple, cherry)

Cut the meat into strips. Soak them in a saltwater-and-vinegar brine overnight. Mix 1 cup of salt and a ½ cup of brown sugar in a flat pan. Dredge the meat in salt and sugar. Next, rub ½ a teaspoon of molasses onto each meat strip, then roll all of the meat in cheesecloth. Place it in a cool place for 5 hours. Rinse the excess salt off the meat, then pat the meat dry. Sprinkle black pepper onto the strips. Your meat is now ready to smoke. Place the meat on racks and smoke it from 5 to 8 hours. Check the woodchips every hour to keep the meat under a constant smoke.—*Stan Albaugh, via Dennis W. Hedberg of Logan, Utah, October 1992*

Venison

BARBECUED VENISON RIBS

3- to 4-rib section per person
3 cups barbecue sauce—
   Use your favorite brand or
   make your own with this recipe:
1 cup chili sauce or hot sauce
1 ½ cups water
½ cup Worcestershire or steak sauce
3 tbsps. lemon juice
½ tsp. salt
½ tsp. chili powder

Combine the above ingredients in a small saucepan, stir, and bring it to a boil. Let it simmer for 5 minutes. Place the ribs on a rack with a shallow pan underneath to catch drippings. Roast at 400°F for 30 minutes to remove excess tallow, then remove the ribs from the oven, transfer them to a shallow, foil-lined roasting pan and baste them liberally with sauce. Turn the oven down to 350°F and roast the ribs uncovered for 30 minutes more, basting them with sauce every 15 minutes. Cover the pan and continue roasting and basting another 30 to 45 minutes until the ribs are tender.
—*Dan Small, December 1981*

LIVING OFF THE COUNTRY

Of what we call "the red meat," we much preferred that around the ribs and loins. The best way to cook it is to roast it before the fire. Cut it in chunks about the size of a baseball. Cut a dry stick about 3 feet long and of any wood except pine or spruce, sharpen both ends and impale the chunks on it. Between each chunk of meat place a chunk of bacon if you have it to baste the meat. Stick the "totem pole" up before a highly blazing fire to roast. Turn it around occasionally, and lean it toward the blaze. Have it close to the blaze so the meat will sear on the outside and keep all the juices on the inside. Then let it roast fast enough so when the chunks are well charred on the outside they be very rare in the center.

Colonel Townsend Whelen
December 1943

DEER NECK AND SHOULDER

Treat the neck and shoulder as the haunch, but with the paste laid on thinner, from 2 to 3 hours. Serve as the haunch. The neck is best spitted by putting 3 skewers through it, and then passing the spit between the skewers and the bones. The top of the ribs should be cut out, and the flap doubled under, as in a neck of mutton for boiling. Breast of venison may be dressed as above, or baked with mutton gravy, and, when cold, cut up and made into pastry. Venison, like all wild meats, requires less cooking than tame.

Pete Byrnes
October 1964
(transcribed from
his grandmother's circa 1857
cookbook)

SPARERIBS

2 lbs. venison ribs, sawed into serving portions
Oil
1 ½ cups water
¼ cup raisins
½ tsp. salt
2 green peppers, sliced (or any other
green you have available such as
celery, peas, watercress, etc.)
1 ½ tbsps. cornstarch
1 ¼ cups sugar
1 ¼ cups vinegar
Soy sauce

For ribs that are delicious, tender and different, saw some 2 pounds into serving portions. Brown them in a frypan with oil over moderate heat about 5 minutes on each side. Add a ½-cup of water, the raisins and the salt. Cover tightly and cook over very low heat for 20 minutes. Add the sliced green peppers if you have them; a similar bulk of some other green such as celery, watercress, mustard leaves, peas and so forth, if you don't. Blend together in a small bowl the cornstarch, sugar, vinegar and 1 cup of water. Mix this with the other ingredients in the pan. Cover and continue cooking over low heat for 1½ hours. Stir occasionally and, if necessary, add more water to prevent drying. Before serving, perhaps with rice, sprinkle on some soy sauce if available.
—*Bradford Angier, November 1962*

Venison

BOILLETTES DE VIANDE
(FRENCH RISSOLES)

1 lb. venison, minced

MARINADE

½ cup carrots, finely diced

¼ cup onion, finely diced

¼ cup celery, finely diced

Pared rind of ½ lemon

Pinch thyme

2 juniper berries, crushed

2 tbsps. olive oil

1 cup port

Salt and pepper to taste

1 tbsp. currant jelly

1 tbsp. softened butter

1 ½ lbs. pie pastry

Egg yolk for glazing baked
    rissoles or cooking oil
    for fried rissoles

Marinate the venison for about 24 hours. Pour off almost all of the marinade, leaving just enough to moisten the meat. Remove the juniper berries and lemon rind. Add the currant jelly and butter and beat the mixture. Roll out the pie pastry to ¼-inch thickness and cut out into 3- to 4-inch rounds. Cover ½ the rounds with the filling; brush the edges with egg yolk. Fold the dough over the filling, form a half-moon shape and press the edges together with a fork. If you are baking the *rissoles*, brush them with egg yolk and bake them for 20 minutes in a 375°F oven. If you are frying them, use very hot fat. Cook 2 or 3 *rissoles* at a time; they take about 10 minutes. The reserved marinade can be used to make a little sauce to accompany the *rissoles*. Serves 4.—*Jane Tennant, January 1987*

MARINADES

Is marinating necessary? The answer depends largely on the age of the animal itself. The purpose of a marinade is to tenderize the meat by breaking down the tough muscle tissue and to impregnate the meat with the flavor of the marinade itself. In doing so, the marinade helps preserve the meat while masking any unappetizing gaminess that an old or improperly dressed animal might have. If the game is young and healthy at the time of killing, it probably needs no marinating at all, and the less done to it, the better. Even when a marinade is advisable, it should be kept relatively light and simple.

John Mariani
July 1994

PACK FOOD

Meat cooked in these ways over the regular wood campfire was the mainstay on all my long trips into the wilderness—venison, grouse and trout. Our transportation was always limited, so, about the only store foods we packed along were the common old-fashioned standbys—flour, baking powder, oatmeal, cornmeal, milk powder, beans, bacon and salt pork, dried prunes and apricots, peanut butter, canned butter, tea, coffee, sugar, salt, pepper and shortening. We most always had a gunnysack of potatoes and onions, and took along some oranges and apples when we could get them. All are energy and muscle-building foods that make fine, plain but wholesome, meals for hungry hunters.

Colonel Townsend Whelen
March 1958

CAMP HASH

Leftover cooked vegetables
Equal quantities of cooked:
   Venison
   Potatoes
   Onions
Bacon fat
Salt and pepper to taste

When you have cold vegetables left over and maybe not enough cooked meat to go around, here is a solution. Cut the venison up fine. If you're a bit short on meat—ideally the proportion should be about half meat and half vegetables by volume—help the flavor along with a bouillon cube. Add enough chopped vegetables, usually mostly potatoes, to go around. Season to taste. Be melting several tablespoons of fat in a frypan. If rawish onions bother anyone in the party, cook these first until thoroughly soft. Otherwise, chop up whatever amount you want and mix them with the other ingredients. Press the hash down into the pan. Cook over slow heat until a crust has formed on the bottom. Fold over and serve while hot.

—Bradford Angier, November 1962

Venison

STUFFED SLICES OF VENISON

2 lbs. venison, thinly sliced
2 tbsps. boiled ham, chopped
6 tbsps. butter
2 cups bread crumbs
1 onion, minced
2 tbsps. parsley, minced
4 egg yolks
2 tbsps. Parmesan cheese, grated
1 pinch thyme
Salt and pepper to taste

Make the stuffing by browning the bread crumbs in butter in one pan and sautéing the onion, parsley and ham in another pan. Combine these ingredients and add egg yolks, cheese, thyme, salt and pepper. Mix well. Place 1 tablespoon of stuffing on each slice, roll or turn in the edges, skewer, dip each slice in melted butter and bake at 350°F.—*John Weinrich, October 1961.*

VENISON STEAKS

Cut them from the neck and season them with salt. Heat the gridiron well over a bed of bright coals, grease the bars and lay the steaks on it. Broil them well, turning them once. Serve them with currant jelly laid on each steak.

Pete Byrnes
October 1964
(transcribed from his grandmother's circa 1857 cookbook)

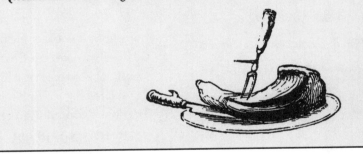

BEAR SIDES

Good dinner accompaniments with bear are baked potatoes or candied yams, or a casserole of baked corn pudding. Hot, well-seasoned applesauce (cinnamon and nutmeg) is delicious as a side dish. Green lima beans and a tossed salad of lettuce, spinach and endive with a sharp dressing complete the dinner. Fruit, cheese and crackers, and sherry make a fitting conclusion.

Grace V. Sharritt
April 1956

YEARLING BEAR ROAST

1 leg roast of bear
1 bay leaf or 1 tbsp. dried thyme
Salt and pepper to taste
2 garlic cloves, thinly sliced

Prepare the yearling leg roast (hind quarter) as you would leg of lamb. If you like bay leaf flavor, crumble one small leaf over the roast after rubbing the meat with savory salt and pepper. Cut small gashes in the meat and insert a sliver of garlic. Roast the meat uncovered in a 325°F oven until tender. If you use a meat thermometer, follow the directions given for pork. Serve with mint sauce.

—*Grace V. Sharritt, April 1956*

Bear

TENDERLOIN BEAR STEAK

1 bear steak

Flour

Salt and pepper to taste

3 ripe tomatoes (green
    tomatoes are good, too)

1 tbsp. brown sugar

Sprinkle flour, salt and pepper on the steak and fry slowly just like pork. Prepare the tomatoes, cut in halves and lightly floured. Season them with brown sugar, salt and pepper, then broil them under a slow flame and serve with the steak. A fruit salad of grapefruit segments, avocado, bits of tart apple, diced celery and orange slices is excellent. Pass French dressing at the table. Deep-dish cherry pie completes the dinner.—*Grace V. Sharritt, April 1956*

MAMA BEAR GRACE

It is worth noting that in all the 110 years of Sports Afield recipes that I looked through, the only bear recipes were these five written by Grace Sharritt in 1956. And although she extolls the wonderful taste of bear, the few times I have had it didn't get me very enthused to go shoot a bear. Bear season no longer coincides with deer season, so the incidental shooting that used to occur doesn't; and shooting a bear while over bait or with dogs has become a stunt and not too popular. The knowledge that the bear has been baited (usually over garbage) prompted me to include a bear recipe in one of my former cookbooks which called for 12 heads of garlic and cooking for 24 hours (or was that 24 heads of garlic and 12 hours of cooking?) Ms. Sharritt uses only moderate amounts of garlic and calls her article "There's More to Bear than His Skin"; but I notice she includes a soup recipe —just in case.

R.C.G.

BEAR GRAVY

Bear gravy is delicious. Brown some flour in the roaster and make a cream gravy as you would for fried chicken. Broil slices of pine-apple (they can be fried on top of the stove with a coating of brown sugar) or steam chunks of pineapple in their own liquid, and serve with the roast. Serve Floating Island, strawberry meringues, or lemon sherbet as dessert.

Grace V. Sharritt
April 1956

POT ROAST WITH PARSNIPS

5 lbs. bear rump roast
1 garlic clove
Salt and pepper to taste
Flour (optional)
2 tbsps. vinegar
2 parsnips
3 carrots
2 potatoes

Rub garlic, salt and pepper onto a 5-pound rump roast. Sprinkle with flour if you like a brown crust. Sear the meat in a Dutch oven or an iron skillet. Add 2 tablespoons of vinegar just before placing the roast in the oven; cover tightly and cook at 325°F. If water is needed, add a small amount during the cooking. During the last hour of roasting, add the peeled raw parsnips to the meat. If you like carrots and potatoes with a pork roast, these vegetables may also be added to a bear roast. [*Editor's note: No cooking time was provided for this bear pot roast, but I would cook a 5-pound roast a minimum of 2½ to 3 hours.*]—*Grace V. Sharritt, April 1956*

Bear

CHOPS AND MUSHROOM CASSEROLE

4 bear chops
Flour
1 large potato
2 onions
Salt and pepper to taste
8-oz. can cream of mushroom soup
1 cup milk
1 cup fresh button mushrooms, sliced

Grease a large baking dish. Place a layer of chops (well-seasoned and floured) on the bottom of the casserole. Slice raw potato over the chops. Cut thin slices of onion and add them to the potato. Sprinkle with flour and salt. Add another layer of chops. Then mix the can of mushroom soup with the cup of milk and pour it over the dish. Be sure there is enough liquid—yet don't make it too soupy. Add 1 small can of button mushrooms or 1 cup of fresh mushrooms. Cover the dish with cooking foil. Bake slowly for 1½ to 2 hours at 375°F. Delicious with spicy apple butter and biscuits.—*Grace V. Sharritt, April 1956*

BEAR SOAP

To make Brother B'ar's Good Laundry Soap, follow the instructions for making homemade soap given on a can of lye, which is its indispensable ingredient. After the soap is made into cakes (it will be soft) use exactly as you would any other good washday soap. Bear soap makes laundry easy on children's play clothes and men's fishing pants.

Grace V. Sharritt
April 1956

THERE'S MORE TO A BEAR THAN HIS SKIN

To render bear fat, cut it into 1 ½-inch pieces and melt them in a large kettle on top of the stove at low heat or in a roaster in a slow oven. Pour it through a cheesecloth and colander into sterilized cans, pails or jars. Store in the refrigerator, freezer or cool place. Bear lard makes unexcelled deep fat for frying doughnuts. The grease does not penetrate the dough or make it soggy as other fats may. Bear fat makes light, fluffy biscuits as well as rich, flaky pie crusts and crisp cookies. Its the best kind of lard for deep-frying potatoes, scallops, apple fritters or chicken croquettes.

Grace V. Sharritt
April 1956

BEAR SAUSAGE

3 lbs. bear meat
1 tbsp. salt
1 tbsp. ground black pepper
1 tbsp. powdered sage
1 tbsp. vinegar

Grind the meat. Season it with salt, pepper and sage. Vinegar is optional, but if you use it, use 1 tablespoon of vinegar to 3 pounds of meat. Form the meat into patties. Freeze surplus sausage meat in patties or 1-pound bricks. Bear sausage is excellent served for breakfast with broiled grapefruit. Fry the sausage patties slowly. There's nothing wrong with having buckwheat cakes at the same time. If you prefer cornmeal pancakes, hashed brown potatoes or scrambled eggs (or all three) be assured that these taste mighty good with bear sausage, too.—*Grace V. Sharritt, April 1956*

Boar

HELAINE FOPPIANO'S TENDERLOIN OF WILD BOAR

The tenderloins are the most delicate cuts from a boar, and 2 (approximately 3 to 4 pounds each) will serve 6. Marinate them up to 12 hours in the refrigerator in:

1 cup soy sauce

1 cup white wine

4 garlic cloves

1 tbsp. fresh ginger, grated

3 tbsps. frozen orange juice concentrate

3 tbsps. frozen cranberry juice concentrate

2 whole oranges

Then blend the 2 oranges, including the skins, in a food processor until no lumps remain. Do not liquefy. Place the marinated meat in a baking pan with 1 cup of marinade. Spoon the orange mixture over the meat, spreading it evenly. Bake at 325°F to 350°F until a thermometer inserted in the center of the meat reads 170°F. The key to cooking all pork, domestic or wild, is to use a meat thermometer. Current culinary thinking is that pork should reach an internal temperature of 170°F, which ensures that the meat will be done but still deliciously moist. A lighter red wine, such as Alexander Valley Vineyards Pinot Noir, or a big, oak-aged dry white, such as Foppiano Fox Mountain Chardonnay, would complement the mild, rich flavors of this dish.—*John Frederick Walker, April 1988*

APPLE PURÉE

1 lb. cooking apples, cored and peeled
Brown sugar to taste

Simmer the sliced apples in a covered pan on low heat, with little or no water. When cooked, beat them until smooth, adding sugar to taste; then continue simmering the apple and sugar mixture until the purée reaches as thick a consistency as you wish.

S.G.B. Tennant Jr.
December 1985

BROILING MEAT

Meat of any variety is never more tasty than when cooked over coals, the secret of success lying in having a mass of bright, glowing coals. We often cook beef steak over the coals in our fireplace, being sure the shades are drawn and the doors locked so that neighbors may not be surprised. In broiling out of doors, the cook usually will not wait until the fire burns down to coals, hence smoking and only partly cooking the meat. Everything else must be ready before the meat is put on to roast, so the meat can come to the table piping hot. Hickory, ironwood and maple make the best coals.

O. Warren Smith
September 1933

KATIE WETZEL MURPHY'S WILD BOAR ROAST HAM

The ham is the other prized cut from a boar, one that looks splendid on a platter. A 4- to 6-pound ham will serve 8 to 10 people. Prepare the following marinade:

3 large garlic cloves
1 large yellow onion
6 or 7 sprigs fresh parsley
½ lemon with rind
½ tangerine with rind

1 tbsp. each fresh rosemary,
    oregano, thyme, cilantro
1 cup white wine
½ cup soy sauce
½ cup olive oil

Chop the garlic, onion, parsley, citrus and herbs in a food processor or chopping bowl. Add the wine, soy sauce and oil. Place the ham flat in a large pan and pour the marinade over it. Cover and refrigerate 12 to 24 hours. Remove the pan from the refrigerator 20 minutes before cooking. Then lift out the ham and pat it dry. Grill or oven-roast it at 325°F until meat thermometer reads 170°F. This intense, rich dish calls for a big red wine, such as California Petite Sirah (1981 Foppiano Russian River Valley, if you can get it) or a cabernet sauvignon.—*John Frederick Walker, April 1988*

Boar

SADDLE OF BOAR

4 lbs. saddle or leg of young boar

2 onions, sliced

2 garlic cloves, sliced

3 carrots, sliced

6 juniper berries, crushed

9 tbsps. butter

1 bottle full-bodied red wine—
a cabernet or merlot

1 bay leaf

Salt and pepper to taste

6 strips salt pork or
bacon to cover one side

1 cup brandy

Build a marinade by softening the onions, garlic, carrots and juniper berries in 3 tablespoons of butter in a skillet. Turn the mixture into a ceramic crock and add the wine, bay leaf, and salt and pepper, adding enough water to cover the meat. Marinate it overnight, stirring occasionally. Remove the meat and drain, saving the marinade. Paint the meat liberally with the remaining butter, and cover one side with either the salt pork or strips of bacon. Braise the boar meat in a hot oven (400°F), turning once or twice to brown evenly—say 15 minutes. Lower the heat and continue cooking until tender, at least 1 hour at 325°F, depending on roast size. Baste the roast frequently with its juices and the marinade. Remove the meat and keep it warm while you prepare the gravy as follows: Pour off the fat and place the roasting pan on a burner over high heat. Add the brandy and stir vigorously, incorporating all the brown bits and adding enough marinade to form a gravy. Ignite the brandy and allow it to burn down. Lower the heat and add 1 tablespoon of arrowroot, softened in some cold marinade, if you prefer a thicker gravy. Serve the saddle with red cabbage and apple purée, the meat sauce over.—*S.G.B. Tennant Jr., December 1985*

BILL BONNETTE'S BARBECUE SAUCE

3 cups sugar

3 cups white vinegar

1 cup vegetable oil

Juice of 2 limes

$1/2$ lb. butter

2 oz. Heinz Meat Sauce

2 oz. Louisiana Red Hot
Pepper Sauce

1 oz. Worcestershire sauce

1 tsp. allspice

Salt and pepper to taste

Warm all of the ingredients until the butter melts. Blend it with a spoon. With a basting brush apply the sauce to the hog as it cooks. Heat the remaining sauce and serve with the pig.

Makes about 9 cups.

A.J. McClane
September 1980

NO WASTE HERE: USE IT ALL

All parts of the young boar (and even very young javelina and razorback) are good eating. In France he is called <u>marcassin</u> when under one year of age, and kept for special customers of the best restaurants. The only culinary application for a boar over 2 years old is the contribution the head makes to certain ceremonial occasions, and to scrap, tamales or sausage.

S.G.B. Tennant Jr.
December 1985

WILD HOG SCRAPPLE

This staple of the American frontier can be made with any porcine volunteer, but wild boar and javelina have less fat and are better than domestic pork.

1 head of boar, skinned; eyes, tongue and brain removed (supplemented by neck, shank and trimmings)
2 tsps. salt

2 bay leaves
2 cups yellow cornmeal
½ tsp. ground cloves
½ tsp. white pepper
½ tsp. red pepper, ground

Place the meat in a large pot, cover it with water, add the salt and bay leaves, and bring to a rolling boil for 2 hours. Skim the froth occasionally and add water as needed. Strain the broth and save it. Allow the head to cool, remove the meat, and mince it. Skim off any fat from the broth, then bring 1 quart of it to a boil. Stir in the cornmeal slowly, then add the spices and continue stirring vigorously as the mixture thickens. Add the meat and continue cooking and stirring for 20 minutes. Add more of the broth if necessary to accommodate all the meat. When the mix is thick, press it into greased loaf pans to a depth of 1 inch, then refrigerate it. Cut it into slices and fry them in butter. Serve with eggs and syrup for breakfast, or with a green salad for dinner. Freezes well.—*S.G.B. Tennant Jr., December 1985*

Duck

HUNGARIAN ROAST DUCK

2 wild ducks, 2 to 2 ½ lbs. each
2 apples, 2 onions, quartered
¼ cup butter, melted
6 slices bacon
Paprika, garlic salt and pepper to taste
3 cups sauerkraut

Sprinkle the ducks with the paprika, garlic salt and pepper. Place the apple and onion quarters in the cavities. Cover the breasts with bacon. Roast at 350°F, 15 minutes per pound. Serve on sauerkraut.—*Anonymous, January 1957*

DUCKS FOR DINNER

For roasting, wipe the body cavity quite dry, season with salt and pepper, add a handful of celery leaves, a bit of parsley, and some apple slices. Sew up the vent, brush the bird with oil or butter, and roast it. Some people like waterfowl roasted 20 to 30 minutes per bird, others prefer 20 to 30 minutes per pound, after the bird has been seared in a hot oven. The connoisseur's test is to prick the breast with a fork. If blood doesn't ooze out, it is done. One thing is certain: Even with the frequent basting that is necessary, cooking too long will dry out a duck or goose. It is best served rather rare.

Bill Wolf
October 1955

PRESSED DUCK À LA McCLANE

Sports *Afield* Editor A.J. McClane is a pressed-duck enthusiast. Here's the way he prepares the dish: The birds are basted with either lemon juice or cognac mixed with salt and pepper; then cooked for 20 minutes in an oven set at 450°F. Mix chopped shallot, a tablespoon of butter and a dollop of currant jelly. Sauté. Add a shot of brandy and a ½ cup of Burgundy. Stir until heated. Carve the breast meat and place it in a heated dish. Cut up and press the carcasses; add any juices released during the carving to the sauce. Serve the sliced breasts over wild rice under the sauce.

Zack and Melissa Taylor
November 1984

MARINATED WILD DUCK

2 wild ducks (about 2½ lbs. each), cleaned, rinsed, and cut into 6 pieces each
Salt and pepper to taste
MARINADE
¼ cup good brandy
2 Spanish onions, chopped
1½ cups red wine
½ tsp. ground allspice
2 sprigs fresh thyme
½ tsp. dried thyme
1 bay leaf, broken in pieces
PREPARATION
3 tbsps. unsalted butter
4 tbsps. olive oil
2 garlic cloves, minced
2 cups fresh mushrooms, thickly sliced
1 large carrot, chopped
¾ cup beef stock
2 tbsps. parsley, chopped

Sprinkle the pieces of duck with salt and pepper. Combine all of the marinade ingredients in a large, deep pan. Place the meat in the pan and turn for 2 or 3 minutes. Refrigerate the meat for 8 hours, turning it occasionally. Remove the meat from the pan; strain the marinade and reserve it. Heat the butter over a medium-high flame in a large sauté pan, preferably cast-iron. When the butter begins to sizzle, add the olive oil. Brown each piece of duck until it's golden brown (about 8 to 10 minutes). Remove the meat from the pan and set it aside. Add the garlic, mushrooms and carrots to the butter-and-oil mixture; then add ¾ cup of strained marinade and the beef stock. Cook over medium heat until the liquid starts to boil. Add the duck pieces, cover the pan, and cook slowly for 1 hour, or until the meat is tender. Sprinkle with chopped parsley and serve with the sauce from the pan. Serves 4.—*A.J. McClane, November 1981 (from Dominique's Famous Fish, Game and Meat Recipes)*

ROAST MALLARD

1 mallard
Bread sauce
Poivrade sauce
Guava jelly

Truss a mallard (Sardi's does not use dressing in the body cavity—but onion and apple dressing can be used) and roast for 25 to 35 minutes according to the size of the bird. Serve with any simple bread sauce, bread crumbs, guava jelly and *poivrade* sauce.

POIVRADE SAUCE	
2 oz. butter	*3 lbs. ground game trimmings*
2 oz. oil	*1 pt. vinegar*
1 lb. raw mirepoix	*1 pt. white wine*
1 lb. well-broken bones of	*3 qts. game stock*
mallard duck	*1 qt. Spanish sauce*
	Marinade

Melt the butter, add the oil, mirepoix, 1 pound of well-broken mallard bones and 3 pounds of ground game trimmings, sautéing until the mixture is well-browned. Drain off the grease and dilute with the vinegar and white wine. Reduce this liquid by ¾ and add the game stock and Spanish sauce. Boil it, then cover the saucepan and put it into a moderate oven for 3 hours. Then pour the contents through a fine sieve placed over a tureen. Press the remains so as to extract all the sauce they hold and pour into a tall saucepan. Add enough game stock and marinade in equal parts to produce 3 quarts of the sauce; gently reduce the latter while skimming it. As it diminishes in volume pass it through muslin into smaller saucepans. Reduction should be stopped when only 1 quart of the sauce remains.—*Vincent Sardi Jr., February 1960*

A CLASSIC
(MODERNIZED AND) UPDATED

Vincent Sardi Jr. is the well-known restaurateur (Sardi's of New York). Much about his recipes that appeared in Sports Afield in the late 1950s and early '60s reflect the food revolution that had begun; not only in a general sense but in the specific case of game. Many Americans began to take a greater interest in real cooking and looked beyond the home shores for inspiration and guidance. Julia Child helped most specifically to unravel the French techniques for us and our tastes in food began to drift toward those classics. American chefs began experimenting, using the classic techniques but creating their own signature dishes with uniquely American ingredients; except when it came to game. Up until very recently professional cooks and restaurants stuck pretty much to the standard Escoffier-type methods for cooking game. There's a problem with this. As you can see from this recipe, the process of getting the mallard cooked and sauce made would—if you made your own mirepoix, game stock and Spanish sauce—conservatively take two days or at best, a staff of four. And following the lead of professional chefs when it comes to game

has another problem. Since all restaurants in the United States cannot sell wild game and must use pen-raised critters, there can often be a difference in some of the cooking techniques, i.e., since domesticated ducks are fatter, less fat is required to keep it moist while cooking—and these elements can change the cooking time, too. In Sardi's recipe I would add olive-oil-basting to the roasting process, but would probably leave the cooking time to 25 minutes at most. And I would definitely ditch the mirepoix, game stock and Spanish sauce; these can be substituted with various purchased stocks. Better to spend your time getting the ducks than making the sauce, right?

R.C.G.

Duck

JUNIPER BERRY DUCKS

6 teal, cleaned, plucked and patted dry

6 oz. juniper berries, dried

Salt and fresh-cracked black pepper

3 tbsps. rosemary, crushed

3 onions, skinned and halved

6 celery stalks

The single most important aspect of this out-door technique is the fire; good coals, and plenty of them, capable of keeping a 375°F to 425°F heat for 30 minutes. How much fuel that takes depends on wind, temperature, elevation and your pit, but at sea level I want 8 fireplace logs the size of my arm or 10 pounds of charcoal, either one reduced to glowing coals. The whole ducks should be rinsed and drained, dry and room temperature. Rub each duck inside and out with the dried juniper berries, crushing them against the skin; throw the hulls into the cavity. Sprinkle salt, fresh pepper and rosemary over the whole birds, and stuff them with onion. Plug the birds with a stalk of celery or an apple quarter. Put the grill near the coals and place the birds breast down until singed and slightly colored, then turn them back side down until juices from the breast run clear when pierced.—*S.G.B. Tennant Jr., January 1986*

TIPS FOR PREPARING GAMEBIRDS

Make no attempt to save the giblets for any length of time in camp, but use them in camp cooking. Waterfowl should be dry-plucked; or, if scalded, they should be cooked immediately. Geese, ducks and brant should never be skinned, but coots can be. It's advisable to do so with coots, since the skin holds the taste that is objectionable. After plucking the long outer feathers, you can rub off the down with your hand. Pick out the pin feathers with a knife blade. Singe the bird over a blaze, removing the oil gland in front of the tail.

Bill Wolf
October 1955

CHINESE ROAST DUCK

The roast ducks that hang in the windows of Chinatown restaurants are as close to <u>yewei</u> as one gets in the United States. In China, cooks use domesticated ducks inflated with compressed air to separate the skin from the meat. When roasted, the skin becomes very crisp. This won't work, of course, for ducks hit with buckshot.

Glenn Smith
October 1988

CANTONESE ROAST DUCK

1 whole duck, complete with head and feet
1 tbsp. cooking oil
3 slices fresh ginger
3 garlic cloves, minced
3 whole scallions, chopped
½ cup soup stock
2 tbsps. soy sauce
1 tbsp. rice wine
1 tbsp. sugar
1 tsp. Szechuan peppercorns
8 stems Chinese parsley

Place a wok on high heat and add the cooking oil. Stir-fry the ginger, garlic and scallions for 10 seconds. Add the remaining ingredients. Lower the heat and simmer for 3 minutes. Pour the marinade into a bowl and set it aside. When cool, pour the marinade into the duck's tail vent. Skewer or sew it shut. Tie a string around the duck's neck and hang it in a cool place for 4 hours. Place the duck in the oven on a rack over a pan of water. Baste the duck with 1 cup of water and ¼ cup of honey then roast for 15 minutes at 450°F, breast up; 25 minutes at 350°F, breast up; 35 minutes at 350°F, breast down; 5 minutes at 450°F, breast down; and 10 minutes at 450°F, breast up. When the duck is done, open its tail vent and pour the marinade into a bowl. Serve the duck on a platter.—*Glenn Smith, October 1988*

D u c k

ROAST WATERFOWL WITH MADEIRA SAUCE

I duck, trussed
1 packet Knorr-Swiss Brown Gravy Mix
¼ cup Portuguese Madeira

Any roasting method can be used. I recommend 1 hour at 350°F for medium-rare meat. Before roasting, the cavity can be filled with a few skinned onions, or peeled, cored and chopped apples. Remove the roast duck from the pan, deglaze the pan with the Madeira and reduce the liquid slightly on top of the stove. Prepare the gravy as directed on the packet, add it to the pan, and stir. Add 2 additional tablespoons of Madeira; simmer 1 minute, and pour the sauce over slices of duck.—*Zack and Melissa Taylor, November 1984*

QUICK ORANGE SAUCE FOR DUCK OR GOOSE

Pour off the fat from the pan in which the bird has been roasted. Deglaze the pan with 1 cup of canned beef bouillon and reduce it slightly over medium heat. Add 1 jar of top-grade orange marmalade, simmering until dissolved. Add 1 ounce or 2 of Grand Marnier or curaçao, stir, and serve the sauce over duck slices.

Zack and Melissa Taylor
November 1984

HOME REMEDY FOR PRESSED DUCK

A substitute for pressed duck is duck cooked in its own body juices. Prepare the bird by dressing and plucking it; then roast it for about 20 minutes. Cut the breast into slices and keep them hot; collect every bit of juice from the roasting pan. Add this to the blood you saved when you prepared the duck. Crush the duck's liver in these juices, forming a paste. Add 1 teaspoon each of vinegar, pepper, salt and nutmeg or mace. Heat a chafing dish, put in the paste and add 1 glass of a dry red wine, and heat. This will form a creamy brown mixture, into which you dip the breast.

Bill Wolf
October 1955

DUCK BREASTS IN WINE SAUCE

6 duck breasts
½ cup flour
2 tsps. salt
2 tsps. paprika
½ cup butter
WINE SAUCE
½ cup butter
1 cup cooked mushrooms

1 cup cooked ham, chopped
1 cup green onions, finely chopped
1 or 2 garlic cloves, minced
3 tbsps. flour
½ tsp. salt
⅛ tsp. pepper
¾ cup canned beef bouillon
¾ cup Burgundy wine

Make the sauce by lightly sautéing the mushrooms, ham, onions and garlic in the butter. When the onion is tender, add the flour, salt and pepper. Stir, then add the bouillon and wine; cover and simmer for 45 minutes. While the sauce is simmering, prepare the breasts by dipping them into the mixture of flour, salt and paprika. Melt the butter in a shallow baking pan in an oven at 400°F. Remove the baking pan and coat the floured duck pieces in the melted butter. Arrange them in a single layer in the pan and bake at 400°F for 30 minutes. Turn. Pour the wine sauce over the breasts. Cover the pan with foil and cook the breasts until they're tender (another 45 minutes).—*Zack and Melissa Taylor, November 1984*

RAY'S PRESSED DUCK

4 mallards (or black ducks,
    canvasbacks or pintails)
Salt, freshly ground black pepper
1/8 lb. butter (1/2 stick)
2 tbsps. black currant jelly
4 tbsps. Worcestershire sauce

4 drops Tabasco
4 shallots, or 4 small white
    onions, minced
1 carrot, minced
1 tbsp. parsley, chopped
1/4 tsp. marjoram
4 oz. dry sherry

After rubbing the ducks inside and out with salt and black pepper, place them in a 425°F oven for exactly 12 minutes. Remove the skin from the breasts, then cut the meat into 1/4-inch-thick slices. Put the meat to one side. The 4 carcasses are then placed in the press and the juices extracted. Melt 1/2 the butter (2 ounces) in a large chafing dish, and stir in the black currant jelly, Worcestershire sauce, Tabasco and the essence from the duck press. Stir until merged, then add the slices of duck breast. Place a cover on the chafing dish and let the contents simmer for 5 minutes. In another chafing dish add the remaining butter and the diced duck livers. When these are slightly browned, add the shallots, carrots, parsley, marjoram, salt, pepper and sherry, and simmer for 10 minutes. Strain this and add it to the sliced breasts and sauce in the large chafing dish, merging the sauces thoroughly. Continue to simmer for 5 minutes with the cover off.—*Zack and Melissa Taylor, November 1984*

RAY CAMP, GOURMET GAME CHEF

For 20 years, Ray Camp was the outstanding outdoor editor for *The New York Times*. For years he and a group of friends held a weekly dinner meeting for devotees of gourmet game cooking. Ray wrote the finest book on cooking game ever: <u>Game Cookery in America and Europe</u>. My dog-eared copy is dotted from attempts at recreating his masterpieces. Long out of print, <u>Game Cookery</u> has just been reprinted in a 25th anniversary edition, handsomely illustrated with watercolors by Thomas Aquinas Daly. Here is Ray's pressed duck.

Zack and Melissa Taylor
November 1984

BEAT THE POOR TASTE OF GAMEBIRDS

Scaup, brant and coot usually have a slightly objectionable taste, as do other ducks and geese on occasion when their diet imparts a flavor to their flesh that the human taste doesn't find pleasing. This can be overcome very easily and should not deter anyone from eating scaup, brant and coot. Most of the flavor is in the skin and the fat. If any bird is shoved into an extremely hot oven just long enough to render out this fat, and then removed and wiped clean with a dry cloth, most of the taste will disappear. Then the bird should be cooked with vegetables. Perhaps Germans like duck with sauerkraut because sauerkraut can overrule any other flavor. Coot, as mentioned before, can be skinned and freed of any fat that is accessible to the knife. I read in an old Louisiana cookbook that the Creoles of the bayou country considered the coot, or poule d'eau (pronounced rapidly as "pool-doo"), or water chicken, as one form of meat that could be eaten on Fridays or fast days because, they declared piously, it lived its entire life in water and therefore was a fish. Last time down that way I asked whether that belief still held, and was assured that it did.

Bill Wolf
October 1955

ROAST DUCK

2 scaup
2 apples
2 onions
Celery leaves
4 bacon slices

Stuff the brace of lesser scaup with apples, onions and celery leaves. Roast the birds breast down in a covered pan for ½ an hour in a low oven. Turn the birds' breast up and lay bacon slices over them. Roast them for another ½ hour. Then baste and brown them for another 15 minutes.—*Charles Meyer, September 1961*

D u c k

SKINNED DUCKS

4 ducks

2 tbsps. salt

1 tbsp. baking soda

1 gallon water

2 apples

2 onions

2 celery stalks

2 carrots

4 bacon slices

The first step is the actual skinning. After you've severed the wings and legs at the joints, insert a knife under the skin of the breast and cut down the center. Peel the skin away, helping it separate from the flesh with a razor. As you progress, the skinning becomes easier. When all of the skin is off, remove the entrails and wash the birds well, inside and out. Clean out each shot hole individually. After the skinning and washing comes the important soaking. Lace a pan of water with about 2 tablespoons of salt and 1 of soda for each gallon of water and let the ducks soak for at least 10 hours. This will draw out the gamy taste. You can be generous with the ingredients, since washing in cold water will remove any salt or soda taste. Now the ducks are ready to be cooked or frozen.

Next comes the stuffing. Slice the apples, onions, celery and carrots 4 ways and fill each body cavity. You don't have to close the opening, as the stuffing will be discarded. Its purpose is to absorb strong flavor and add its own flavors to the meat. Bacon strips over the breasts prevent them from drying out while you bake the ducks uncovered for 1 hour at 325°F then 2 hours at 300°F. Serve with wild rice, salad and red wine.—*Wayne and Opal Judy, November 1956*

SKINNED
VS. UNSKINNED

Late-season ducks, which are completely out of the pinfeather stage, look beautiful and are excellent when prepared with the skins intact. But there are times when the appearance and flavor of wild ducks are definitely enhanced by the removal of the skins. These times are as follows: First, early season ducks should be skinned because they invariably are in the pinfeather stage, with many feathers under the skin that are absolutely impossible to remove by any plucking and waxing method yet devised. Second,

ducks badly shot should be skinned because each shot carries feathers into the meat that cannot be seen and removed unless the ducks are skinned. Third, if ducks are to be frozen for a long time, the layer of fat directly underneath the skin turns rancid and imparts a strong, "wild" flavor to the entire duck. This layer always adheres to the skin, and when the skin is removed so also is the fat. This point does not apply to ducks to be frozen for only a few weeks before cooking, but it definitely is true of ducks that are to be kept in a freezer for months. The fourth reason to skin ducks is to remove the strong taste of certain species. Even the best ducks in certain localities will have a strong flavor sometimes. Most of this strong taste is found in the fatty tissue directly under the skin, and when the skin is removed, so also is the tissue and the objectionable taste. The fifth reason given for skinning ducks is because it is much faster, easier and cleaner than plucking them. Anyone who has tried to pluck a duck in an apartment knows exactly the significance of this point. He or she is reminded of it by floating feathers from one duck season to the next. True, there will be some loose feathers and down when skinning ducks, but they by no means present the problem encountered if the plucking method is used.

Wayne and Opal Judy
November 1956

Duck

ROAST DUCK WITH PINEAPPLE

This recipe makes good use of the leftovers of Cantonese or Western-style roast duck. It is served as a cold platter.

14 oz. roast duck meat	3 tbsps. sweet-and-sour sauce
8-oz. can pineapple, in juice	1 tbsp. sesame paste
1 medium green pepper	1 tsp. mustard
3 scallions, white parts only	½ tsp. salt
10 stems Chinese parsley	2 tbsps. cooking oil
3 tbsps. warm water	3 fresh garlic cloves, minced

Cut the roast duck meat, pineapple and green pepper into equal-sized strips. Blanch the green pepper for 10 seconds and drain well. Cut the scallions into thin slices. Chop the Chinese parsley. Mix the water, sweet-and-sour sauce, sesame paste, mustard and salt in a bowl. Place the wok on high heat and add the cooking oil. Stir-fry the garlic for 10 seconds. Add the seasonings and bring to a boil. Remove from heat. When the seasonings cool, add the sliced scallions. Next, add the roast duck meat, pineapple and green pepper. Stir together. Arrange on a tray and add the Chinese parsley.—*Glenn Smith, October 1988*

CLEANING AND HANGING

It used to be that cooks would hang ducks and other gamebirds by the neck or tail feathers until the meat was so "high" that the bird pulled free and fell to the floor, whereupon the meat was considered just right for eating. Tastes have changed considerably, and such over-long aging is poor taste today. Appetites demand a bird that has been properly cared for in the field, hung a reasonable time, and then cooked well. If you must keep your bird some time, their body cavities should be cleaned out thoroughly, but don't pluck them, since the feathers help keep the meat from drying out.

Bill Wolf
October 1955

BROIL YOUR BIRD

For broiling, pick a young bird (one with a soft, pliable bill and feet) of the smaller species. Split it down the back, cut the wishbone and flatten it out. Clean the carcass with a damp cloth, then rub it well with salt and pepper to taste, and brush it thoroughly with oil or melted butter. If you're in camp, clamp the body in a wire broiler and for a short time hold it close to the red-hot coals to sear it severely on both sides. Then use reduced heat to finish the cooking. At home, use the broiler rack in the stove. The length of time depends upon your taste, but 10 minutes to a side after searing should be about right.

Bill Wolf
October 1955

SOFT TACOS WITH DUCK, AVOCADO AND FRESH SALSA

*6 duck breasts, roasted or grilled
    with chili-powder seasoning
12 blue- or yellow-corn tortillas
3 ripe avocados
8 oz. fresh salsa
2 oz. green peppercorns
1 bunch fresh cilantro
Lettuce
(If fresh salsa is unavailable, combine in a food processor 1 large ripe tomato, ¼ cup chopped onion, 2 or 3 canned Ortega chilis, 3 tablespoons vinegar, 2 tablespoons chopped fresh cilantro, a dash of light salt or salt-free vegetable seasoning.)*

Shred the duck and lettuce. Slice the avocados. Soften the tortillas by holding them over a flame; or steam or microwave them briefly. Place the tortillas on plates, and divide the duck, avocado and lettuce among them. Top off with 2 to 3 tablespoons of salsa and a sprinkle of cilantro and peppercorns. Serve with light sour cream or shredded jack cheese.—*Thomas McIntyre and Christine N. Glasser, September 1990*

Duck

PULL-DOO GUMBO

4 pull-doo (breasts, drumsticks
    and wings, all skinned)

4 tsps. salt

4 tsps. black pepper, freshly ground

½ cup flour

½ cup vegetable oil

8 tbsps. Cajun roux

1 cup onions, finely chopped

½ cup scallions, finely chopped

1 garlic clove, finely chopped

1 cup celery, finely chopped

1 cup green peppers,
    finely chopped

3 qts. water or gamebird stock,
    slightly warmed

2 tsps. ground red pepper

1 tsp. fresh oregano, finely
    chopped, or ½ tsp. ground

½ cup parsley, finely chopped

3 tsps. filé powder (sassafras)

Tabasco to taste

4 cups long-grained white rice,
    cooked

Wash the breasts; season each with salt and pepper. Dredge them in flour and brown them in vegetable oil in a skillet, turning frequently. Cool and slice them into bite-size pieces, leaving the drumsticks and wings. Blend the roux with a fork, then turn it into a 12-quart heavy casserole over medium heat. As the roux softens, stir in the onions, scallions, garlic and celery. Keep stirring over moderate heat for 5 minutes. If you need more liquid, add 1 tablespoon of butter, then add the green peppers and continue softening. Slowly add the warmed water or stock to the pan, stirring constantly. Then cover and bring the mixture to a boil over high heat. Add the pull-doo pieces and a cleaned carcass, salt to taste, then add the ground red pepper and oregano. Reduce the heat and simmer for 2 hours. Before serving, remove the carcass add the filé powder, parsley and Tabasco to taste. Serve over the rice. Serves 4.—*S.G.B. Tennant Jr., January 1984*

CAJUN ROUX

8 tbsps. flour
8 tbsps. vegetable oil

Combine the ingredients in a heavy 10-inch skillet and blend them with a spatula. Over moderate heat cook the mixture for 30 to 45 minutes, stirring constantly. At this point the mixture will begin to darken. Reduce the heat to the lowest setting and continue stirring until the mixture is a dark, nut-brown. Immediately pour the roux into a bowl and allow it to cool. At room temperature it will separate, so before using, it should be reblended. This makes enough for the pull-doo gumbo.

S.G.B. Tennant Jr.
January 1984

PORTIONING BIRDS

One of the greatest difficulties in serving ducks is estimating the number required. The smaller wild ducks such as teal are just about right for one per person, but the larger ones pose such a problem that there are a number of folk sayings to the effect that the "duck is a fool bird—for one too much, and not quite enough for two." Three ducks for two persons are about right. With geese, even the smaller ones are enough for several persons. One coot breast is a moderate serving for one. A brant will serve two diners of good appetite.

Bill Wolf
October 1955

DUCK PASTIES

This recipe makes 12 pasties you can bake on cookie sheets, then wrap in freezer-wrap aluminum foil and freeze until needed. Leftover browned pasties can be reheated in a microwave or oven. We follow Cornish tradition and splash malt vinegar on newly opened, piping-hot pasties.

CRUST
4 ½ cups sifted flour
¼ tsp. salt
½ tsp. paprika
24 tbsps. vegetable shortening
13 tbsps. ice water
FILLING
4 cups cooked duck meat,
    shredded
4 cups potatoes, in ½-inch cubes
1 cup carrots, sliced
1 onion, chopped
1 tsp. thyme
¼ tsp. salt
½ tsp. pepper
⅓ cup sherry or vermouth
EGG WASH
1 egg
1 tsp. water

For the crust, combine the flour, salt and paprika in a bowl. Cut in the shortening with a pastry blender until all is well mixed, forming pea-sized crumbs. Add ice water 1 tablespoon at a time until well mixed; or use a food processor. Form a ball, wrap it in wax paper, and chill it for 30 minutes.

FILLING: Mix all of the ingredients. Beat the egg with water. Divide the chilled dough into 24 parts. On a floured board, roll 12 parts into 6-inch circles. Place the filling in the centers of the rounds, leaving ½-inch-wide edges. Roll the other 12 parts into 7-inch circles to cover the filling. Pinch and flute the edges. Brush the crust with egg wash, place the pasties on 2 greased cookie sheets, and bake at 375°F for about 1 hour.—*Annette and Louis Bignami, November 1987*

Duck

DUCK POTSTICKERS

1 duck, skinned and boned, or
   1 ½ cups skinned and boned
    meat from backs and/or legs
1 ½ tbsps. thin soy sauce*
1 green onion, finely chopped
1 clove garlic, minced
2 tsps. fresh ginger, minced

1 cup cabbage, finely chopped
1 tbsp. cornstarch
1 tbsp. sesame oil
¼ cup water
1 package round wonton skins
PASTE
1 tsp. cornstarch
1 tbsp. water

Grind the duck meat in a blender. Remove it to a bowl and stir in the soy sauce, onion, garlic, ginger, cabbage, cornstarch and water. Place 2 teaspoons of filling in the center of each wonton skin. Mix the paste ingredients, then moisten the edge of the dough round with paste, fold the skin in half over the filling, and pinch the edges together to seal. Place the potstickers, well separated, on a cookie sheet. Keep them covered with a damp towel until needed. In a 10-inch skillet heat the sesame oil over medium heat. Set in the potstickers (do not thaw if frozen) by spoon without letting them touch. Cook uncovered until the bottoms are golden brown—about 5 minutes. Turn the heat to low, add ¼ cup water; cover and steam—6 to 8 minutes, until the water evaporates; steam an additional 5 minutes if the potstickers are frozen (you may need more water). Remove them and serve with soy sauce or a favorite dipping sauce. Makes about 3 dozen potstickers.

—*Annette and Louis Bignami, January 1988*

*Thin soy adds a more delicate flavor to this recipe than the standard type;
look for it in Oriental or gourmet markets.

SAUSAGE IN CAMP

Here is a way to prepare sausage for safe keeping for as long as a year. I take the canned sausage with me on summer camping trips. Fry or bake patties or links until they're cooked through. Put them into glass jars and pour in warm lard. Do not use hot lard, as it will further fry the meat in the jars. Let the jars chill completely and add more warm lard until the meat is covered. The meat won't absorb excess lard. Put on the jar lids. Keep in a cool place or in the refrigerator. To prepare in camp, set a jar in hot water until the lard melts. Remove the meat; wipe off excess lard. Warm in a covered skillet. Pour off melted lard.

Wilson M. Baltz
June 1976

CROQUETTES DE VOLAILLE ET DU CANARD
(CHICKEN AND DUCK CROQUETTES)

¼ lb. chicken, cooked
¼ lb. wild duck, cooked
2 tbsps. butter
3 tbsps. flour
1 cup milk, heated
Salt and pepper to taste

1 egg yolk
4 oz. mushrooms, sautéed in butter
1 tsp. tarragon
1 tsp. dry mustard
Additional flour to coat
Beaten egg and bread crumbs

Melt the butter in a small saucepan. Blend in the flour and stir over low heat for 2 minutes. Remove this "roux" from the heat and pour in the hot milk. Beat vigorously with a wire whip to blend the roux and liquid. Return the pan to moderate heat and stir continuously until the sauce comes to a boil. Boil for 1 minute until the sauce is thick and smooth. Season with salt and pepper, and when the sauce has cooled a little, whip in the egg yolk. Set aside. Chop the mushrooms and mince the meat. Add these to the sauce and mix well. Season with the tarragon and mustard and turn the mixture onto a buttered plate. Cover it with plastic wrap and leave it in the refrigerator until firm. Put the flour on a large, shallow plate. Take small handfuls of the meat mixture, dip them in the flour, and form into croquettes. Shake off excess flour, dip each into beaten egg, and coat evenly with bread crumbs. When all the croquettes are ready, deep-fry 2 or 3 at a time in hot vegetable oil until golden. Drain on paper towels. Serve these with fresh tomato sauce or a Chinese plum sauce.—*Jane Tennant, January 1987*

Duck

DIM SUM JERKY

Duck, goose or beef
MARINADE
1 cup red wine
2 tsps. oyster sauce
4 tsps. soy sauce
4 tsps. brown sugar
2 tsps. garlic powder

It is easiest to slice meat when it is lightly frozen. The cuts should be thin, long and with the grain, although they may be cut as wide as the meat allows. Remove all the fat, as it will not keep and will spoil the jerky. Marinate the strips in a glass container overnight. Pat them dry and arrange the pieces side by side, without overlap, on oven roasting racks. Cook at minimum heat, say 150°F, for 6 hours. Leave the oven door ajar to allow moisture to escape. Store the jerky in a cool, airtight container. Alternate drying techniques include a "hard cure" in an electric smoker for 12 hours. Crisp jerky means the heat was too high. For sweeter jerky, baste with molasses or honey and water just before drying. You can vary the marinade given above by adding more sugar, salt or some juniper berries to taste. If the cut and type of meat used produce extremely tough jerky, slice against the grain next time.—*S.G.B. Tennant Jr., September 1983*

SAVE THOSE HEARTS AND LIVERS

I would no sooner think about tossing away the heart and liver of a gamebird than I would those of a deer. In the field, I store the tiny treats in a plastic bag. At home, I transfer them to a small plastic container. When serving gamebirds, I use the hearts and livers as a side dish. Defrost them, dredge them in seasoned flour, then fry them quickly in butter with browned onions. Hearts can be cooked whole, whereas the larger livers should be cut into 1-inch pieces. They require no more than 1 minute or 2 to cook.

Fred Everson
November 1991

CITRUS GOOSE

In waterfowl cooking, there's an affinity between waterfowl and oranges that makes for the most agreeable eating. I prefer roasted duck (or goose, or brant) cooked this way: Clean 2 ducks, or 1 goose or 1 brant, and rub thoroughly inside and out with lemon juice and mixed salt and pepper. Peel an orange (1 for each bird), removing the pith, put it in the body cavity, and sew up and truss the bird. Rub the skin with melted butter and then sear the fowl at high heat in the oven (500°F) for 15 minutes. Then cover it with a napkin or other cloth soaked in butter, and continue roasting it in a moderate oven (350°F) for almost 1 hour until it is tender. Now for the gravy or sauce, which you can be preparing while the fowl is roasting: Peel 1 large orange, scrape the white from the peel, cover the peel with a bit of water in a pot, and cook it for about 10 minutes. Discard the water and mince the peel very fine, adding it to 8 ounces of dry white wine. Into the sauce, put the giblets, and cook 30 minutes or more until tender. Make a roux by browning 2 tablespoons of flour in 2 tablespoons of melted butter, and add it to the mixture of giblets and orange peel. Chop up the orange from the body cavity and add it to the sauce. Carve the duck or goose and serve the sauce (which has been seasoned afresh with salt and pepper to taste) over the meat. Decorate with the sections of 2 fresh oranges.

Bill Wolf
October 1955

GRILLED GOOSE BREAST

2 goose breasts
Ground black pepper
½ cup vegetable oil
Dash of soy sauce
¼ cup red wine

Take goose breast fillets and slice off the outer membranes. Rub both sides of the breasts with ground pepper and beat them flat with a mallet. Marinate them in vegetable oil with a shot of soy sauce. Depending on his mood, John adds a ½-glass of red wine or a shot of gin to give character. Marinate the breasts from a ½-hour to 2 hours. Get your charcoal or gas grill as hot as possible and cook the fillets 5 minutes maximum on each side. Cut them into thin slices with a sharp knife and serve. The marinade stays dryness and adds a wonderful flavor.—
Zack and Melissa Taylor, November 1984 (from John Easton)

ROAST PHEASANT
(VIENNA)

1 large cock pheasant
    (should be aged at least
    3 days in refrigerator)
1 stick (8 tbsps.) butter
Salt and pepper to taste

6 shallots, minced
8 large chicken livers
    (and pheasant liver)
3 tbsps. Madeira
2 cups chicken broth

Truss the pheasant, then rub it with ½ the butter and sprinkle it with salt and pepper. In a frypan melt the rest of the butter and sauté the minced shallots; dice the livers and add them to the shallots, sautéing until the meat is pink. Stir in the Madeira and lightly season with salt and pepper. Spoon the liver mixture into the pheasant cavity; sew or skewer the skin over the cavity so it is securely closed. Place the pheasant on its side in a roasting pan and pour in the chicken broth. Cover and cook in a 350°F oven for 1 ½ hours (at the halfway mark, turn the bird onto the other side), basting every 15 minutes. Cook another 15 minutes, breast up, with the top of the pan removed, basting every few minutes. Now turn the bird breast down for 10 minutes, so the juices flow into the breast. Serve the bird whole on a warm platter, surrounded by wild rice or mashed potatoes. Pass lingonberries instead of cranberries and pour a crisply cold Chablis. Give each guest a spoon of the liver dressing.
Serves 4.—*Jack Denton Scott, September 1967*

A WORD ABOUT WINE

In the countries I visit I always prefer what they call their "local" wines. For example, in Rome it is intelligent to drink Frascati, which comes from the nearby seven hills rather than an Orvieto, which comes from many miles away. This also applies in the United States. Why drink French wine when we produce superb wines here? Some of the California and New York State wines can hold their own with any of the European. So drink local when you can. Instead of mentioning wines by name and brand I'll just mention types that I think go with the various meals outlined here.

Jack Denton Scott
September 1967

PRESSURE-COOKED PHEASANT

I think you'll enjoy pheasant the way we serve them in Bowling Green, Kentucky—where, likely as not, the dinner conversation will turn to horses and hounds, shooting, or how the bream are biting. Here's our recipe: Disjoint the pheasant, discarding the back and wings. Season it with salt and pepper. Brown it in a saucepan with butter. Then place the bird in a pressure cooker with an ⅛ cup of water. Cook at 15 pounds pressure for 15 minutes. Return the bird to the saucepan, cover it with 1 pint of heavy cream, add 3 tablespoons of sherry, and let it all simmer until the cream is thick. Serve with wild rice.

Duncan Hines,
with Bradford Angier
March 1959

PHEASANT KIEV (HUNGARY)

2 pheasant breasts (boned)
1 stick (8 tbsps.) butter
Salt and pepper to taste
¾ cup flour
2 eggs, beaten
1 ½ cups fine bread crumbs
Small can cooking fat

Place 4 half breasts under wax paper and flatten them with a wooden mallet to ½-inch thickness. Place the thin fillets in the refrigerator for 2 hours. Shape the butter into 4 pieces the size of a medium walnut; roll them in flour and place them in the freezer. Remove the fillets from the refrigerator and sprinkle them with salt and pepper; place a "nut" of frozen butter in the center of each and carefully roll it, folding the edges over so the butter is completely encapsulated. Dip each rolled fillet into flour, then into beaten egg, then roll it in the bread crumbs so it is completely coated. Fasten the ends with toothpicks and fry the fillets in hot cooking fat. Pheasant rolls should be completely immersed and cooked until deep gold. Remove the fillets, drain them on paper towel and serve them on warm plates immediately. A crisp green salad and asparagus make good accompaniments. Pour a cold white Burgundy. Pheasant Kiev is perfect if, when the breast rolls are cut, the captured butter escapes in a jetting golden stream, dramatically providing the sauce the breast meat needs. Serves 4.—*Jack Denton Scott, September 1967*

Pheasant

STIR-FRIED SWEET-AND-SOUR PHEASANT

1 pheasant, boned and sliced
2 tbsps. cooking oil
$2/3$ cup celery, sliced
$1/2$ cup green onions, sliced
1 can water chestnuts, sliced
1 package frozen snow peas
1 can pineapple chunks
$1/2$ cup chicken broth
$1/4$ cup sugar
1 tbsp. cornstarch
$1/2$ tsp. powdered ginger
2 tbsps. vinegar
2 tbsps. soy sauce

LEMON PHEASANT (CANTON)

1 pheasant, approximately
    $2 1/2$ lbs.

5 tbsps. cooking oil

3 slices fresh ginger

3 garlic cloves

$1/2$ lemon

5 large mushrooms

Cornstarch

MARINADE

2 tbsps. soy sauce

2 tbsps. rice wine

1 tsp. water

3 garlic cloves, minced

1 tsp. salt

SEASONINGS

8 tbsps. soup stock

2 tbsps. lemon juice

1 tbsp. sesame oil

2 slices fresh ginger

$1/4$ tsp. sugar

$1/4$ tsp. salt

Clean the pheasant and wipe it dry. Mix the marinade ingredients in a bowl. Rub the marinade into the pheasant's body cavity. Set the bird in the marinade, turning it from time to time, for 2 hours. Place the wok on high heat and add the cooking oil. Stir-fry the ginger and garlic for 10 seconds. Brown the pheasant. Reduce the heat and remove 4 tablespoons of oil. Next, add the seasonings ingredients and bring them to a boil. Cover the wok and simmer for 10 minutes. Turn the pheasant over, cover the wok, and simmer for another 10 minutes. When the pheasant is done, take it out of the wok. Remove the bones and cut the meat into pieces. Strain the ginger and garlic from the seasonings mix and set aside. Skin the lemon and cut it into pieces. Slice the mushrooms. Reheat the wok and add 1 tablespoon of oil. Stir-fry the mushrooms for 30 seconds. Add the lemon and the strained seasonings. Bring to a boil and thicken with cornstarch. Pour it over the pheasant meat and serve with rice.

—*Glenn Smith, October 1988*

In a wok, heat the oil, add the pheasant, and stir-fry for 5 minutes. Add the celery, onions and water chestnuts and stir-fry for 2 minutes. Add the pea pods, pineapple chunks, with syrup; stir-fry for 2 minutes. Mix the broth, sugar, cornstarch, ginger, vinegar and soy sauce; pour it over the pheasant and vegetables. Lower the heat, stir, and simmer. Serve over rice.

A. J. McClane
November 1981

COLD PHEASANT CURRY

Once, when there were only three of us in camp, we performed a major miracle with 2 cups of cold pheasant meat in a curry sauce. Here's how: We removed bones, fat and skin from the leftover meat, and chopped the meat finely. Boiled and buttered noodles were placed in a ring in a shallow baking dish and the cold pheasant heaped in the middle. Here is the curry sauce:

1 tbsp. melted butter
1 tbsp. flour
½ cup undiluted evaporated milk
1 ½ tsps. curry powder
½ cup consommé
1 tsp. onion juice
Salt and a trace of black pepper

Stir the butter and flour together in a double boiler until smooth, then add the remaining ingredients. The sauce is blended and cooked until it's smooth and thick, then it's poured over the pheasant and noodles, dusted with a freckle of paprika, and baked at 300°F for 25 to 30 minutes. Glorious in taste and flavor, especially when served with a salad of drained canned tomatoes, finely diced onion, a pinch of thyme and a dash of wine vinegar.

Harry Botsford
February 1953

PEKING PHEASANT SALAD WITH RICE NOODLES

4 pheasant breasts, cooked, skinned, and shredded
2 cups Chinese napa cabbage, chopped
1 small yellow onion, chopped
½ cup bean sprouts
½ red bell pepper, cut into matchsticks
1 small can water chestnuts, sliced
SESAME DRESSING
2 tbsps. low-sodium soy sauce
3 tbsps. dark sesame oil
⅓ cup seasoned rice vinegar
¼ tsp. powdered, or 1 tbsp. fresh or
*   pickled, ginger, minced*
1 garlic clove, minced
3 tbsps. fresh cilantro
Sesame seeds for garnish
Rice noodles (crispy variety)

In a large bowl combine the poultry and vegetables. Mix the dressing and toss it with the salad. Serve over rice noodles. Serves 4.—*Thomas McIntyre and Christine N. Glasser, September 1990*

ETRUSCAN PHEASANT

2 whole pheasants, thawed

1 lemon

Salt and pepper to taste

1 large purple onion, quartered

2 tbsps. butter

2 cups small vegetables
    (onions, carrots, etc.)

½ cup white wine

½ tsp. thyme

3 tbsps. parsley, chopped

The clay or terra-cotta pot, both top and bottom, should be immersed in clean, cold water for at least 30 minutes. Wipe the birds thoroughly with the cut lemon, squeezing juice directly onto the flesh, rubbing it in with the pulp. Rub the birds with salt and pepper, inside and out, and place it in the drained pot. Sprinkle the birds with bits of the butter, then add the purple onion, vegetables and wine to the pot. Sprinkle the thyme and parsley over all. Cover the pot with its lid and place in a cold oven. Bake at 450°F for 90 minutes. With a bottle of *chenin blanc*, say Bargetto, you may toast the ancient Etruscans and ask them to forgive modern man his culinary short-cuts.—*S.G.B. Tennant Jr., December 1984*

CLAY-POT COOKING

The form of this recipe is generic, ubiquitous and legendary. The most authoritative announcement came from the doyenne of modern gastronomes, M.F.K. Fisher. Clay-pot cooking is accommodating, forgiving and flexible. Avoid the partially glazed sets; they are like a kiss blown from across the room, compared to the completely unfinished and authentic version.

S.G.B. Tennant Jr.
December 1984

PHEASANT PIE

1 pheasant, 3 to 4 lbs.
1 bay leaf
1 celery stalk
6 peppercorns
½ cup butter, melted
Flour
1 cup cream
Chicken broth
1 pkg. frozen peas
2 onions, sliced
1 cup mushrooms, sliced
1 tbsp. pimentos, diced
Salt and pepper to taste
1 lb. pastry dough
   (see the next recipe or purchase a pie crust)

Cook the pheasant in a kettle with the bay leaf, celery, peppercorns and enough water to cover for 2 to 3 hours. Remove the pheasant, discard the bay leaf and reserve the remaining broth. Take the meat off the bones. Make a roux from the melted butter and flour, then slowly add the cream and broth (using water/broth from the cooked pheasant and enough chicken stock to make 2 cups.) Combine the sauce, pheasant meat and vegetables and place them in a casserole dish lined with pastry. Top with dough and bake in a 375°F oven for about 35 minutes.

Anonymous
March 1957

PHEASANT SOUVAROFF

1 pheasant
6 fair-size truffles
½ lb. foie gras
1 glass Madeira
1 glass light meat glaze
   (meat stock, preferably veal or game)
Bacon slices

Cook the truffles for 5 minutes in a glass of Madeira wine and an equal amount of light meat glaze. Remove the truffles and put them in a tureen in which the pheasant will complete its cooking. Cut a ½-pound of foie gras into large slices. Stiffen these in the truffles' cooking-liquor and stuff the pheasant. Truss the bird, wrap it in slices of bacon, and cook it until it is ⅔ done. Remove the pheasant, put it into the tureen containing the truffles, add the truffles' cooking-liquor and the same quantity of game drippings. Tightly close the tureen and continue to cook for about 15 minutes.

—*Vincent Sardi Jr., January 1960*

Pheasant

VENISON AND PHEASANT PIE

Use tougher cuts of venison and older pheasant for this classic dish that's good hot or cold. Make it ahead if you like. As with most game and gamebird pies, it improves with reheating.

¾ lb. venison	3 tbsps. melted butter
¾ pheasant, boned	1 cup sliced onions
1 cup water	¼ lb. fresh mushrooms,
¼ lb. bacon, diced	quartered
½ cup seasoned bread crumbs	2 hard-cooked eggs, quartered
¼ tsp. thyme	1 cup game or beef stock
¼ tsp. oregano	1 egg
¼ tsp. parsley	1 tsp. water

Make the butter crust and chill it for 45 minutes. In a small saucepan bring the water to a boil, add the bacon, and cook it for 5 minutes. Drain. Slice the venison and pheasant into ½-inch-wide strips, 1 inch long. In a small bowl mix the seasoned bread crumbs with thyme, oregano, parsley and melted butter. Layer the venison, pheasant, bacon, onions, mushrooms and eggs in a 9-inch pie plate. Sprinkle the bread crumb mix over the filling and pour on the stock. On a lightly floured board roll the butter crust into a 10-inch circle. Cut a 1-inch hole in the middle. Beat the egg with water and brush the pie plate rim with the wash. Place the dough over the filling and press the edge onto the rim, crimping it. Brush the crust with egg wash. Bake at 400°F for 20 minutes (to brown the crust). Lower the heat to 350°F and bake for 1 hour.—*Annette and Louis Bignami, November 1987*

BUTTER CRUST

1 ½ cups flour
¼ tsp. salt
1 cube (1 lb.) butter
1 tbsp. lemon juice
4 tbsps. ice-cold water

In a bowl combine the flour and salt. Cut in the butter with a pastry blender or fork until pea-sized crumbs form. Add the lemon juice and water, 1 tablespoon at a time, and stir until well mixed. Form a ball; then wrap it in waxed paper and refrigerate.

Annette and Louis Bignami
November 1987

ROAST PHEASANT

1 young pheasant
1 bay leaf
1 lemon
1 garlic clove
2 cans button mushrooms
1 cup chicken broth
Butter, bacon, onion

Sprinkle the pheasant with salt and pepper. Put the bay leaf, garlic and lemon in the cavity. Cover the breast with bacon. Place the bird in a roasting pan with the onion and mushrooms. Pour on the broth and roast for 30 minutes per pound at 350°F.

Anonymous
February 1957

TOUGH-PHEASANT STEW

A tender young pheasant isn't difficult to cook, or to chew. Older birds, however, present problems. I can recommend the following stew, which I usually make in a slow-cooker. If you don't have one, use any pot with a lid that fits tightly, put it on very low heat, and check the water level from time to time. Here's what you'll need:

1 tough pheasant, either skinned
   or plucked
2 bay leaves
16-oz. pkg. frozen gumbo
   vegetable mix
6-oz. can tomato paste

1 medium onion, chopped
1 tsp. salt
½ tsp. pepper
½ tsp. thyme
16-oz. can tomatoes

Dress the pheasant, cut it into pieces, and cover it with water in a pan. Add the bay leaves and bring it to a boil. Cover, lower the heat, and simmer for 1 to 2 hours, or until the meat is tender enough to come off the bone easily. While the bird is cooking in the pan, put the frozen vegetables, tomato paste, salt, pepper and thyme into a pot. Add the canned tomatoes, chopping as you go, and pour in the juice from the can. Cover the pot and turn the heat to low. When the pheasant is tender, remove the pieces and put them aside to drain. Add to the pot 2 cups of the stock from the pan. If you don't quite have 2 cups, add water. (Discard the rest of the broth and the bay leaves.) Pull the meat from the pheasant pieces and add it to the pot. Cover and cook on low heat for 6 or 7 hours. Serve the stew in bowls with lots of hot bread, or serve it over rice.—*A.D. Livingston, August 1991*

Quail

QUAIL IN CREAM
(SPAIN)

8 quail

1 lb. butter

Salt and pepper to taste

1 cup heavy cream

4 cups fine bread crumbs,
    warmed and buttered

Red currant jelly

Melt the butter in a frypan and, over a medium flame, sauté (perhaps poach or baste are better words, or maybe "bathe in butter") the quail for 30 minutes, spooning the butter over and into the cavities of the birds; sprinkle with salt and black pepper; reserve on a warm platter. Pour the heavy cream into the same frypan in which the quail were cooked (there will be browned particles and some butter left); stir well and bring it to a simmer for just under 5 minutes. Two quail on a bed of warm, buttered bread-crumbs—with a dollop of currant jelly on the side—should be given to each person. The hot cream is served separately. In Spain we had cold white Rioja and a green salad. I certainly can't suggest any improvement on that. Serves 4.—*Jack Denton Scott, September 1967*

THE BOUNTY OF SPAIN

I remember the castles and the rivers and the mountains wreathed in blue haze and the constant golden sunshine and the wind in the lacy leaves of the olive trees and the proud, handsome people, but I also remember the quail of Spain. They are small, fast quail. But they can be bagged if you are quick enough and know where to go for them. A friend told me where to go, and I either was quick enough or I managed to run into idiot birds. As a result, the quail I bagged made a fine dish. The memory of it returns to me often, as does some poetry, some music and some recollections of a beautiful place.

Jack Denton Scott
September 1967

A CHALLENGING SHOOT

The Greek island of Lesbos doesn't have the ordinary kind of tourists. Most fly in under their own power. Most are quail. They are tough to shoot because they keep to the mountainous parts of the island, but when you do manage to bag a dozen, after several days of trying and many miles of climbing, you are anxious to see how they go between knife and fork—a blessed relief from the ubiquitous lamb.

Jack Denton Scott
September 1967

QUAIL ALLA GRECA (GREECE)

8 quail
1 ½ cups flour
Salt and pepper to taste
Paper bag

4 tbsps. olive oil
2 cups white onions, minced
2 garlic cloves, minced
3 cups of chicken broth

Place the flour, salt and pepper in the paper bag. Put the quail in and shake well until the birds are thoroughly coated. Sauté them in the olive oil until they are browned, then remove them. Place the onions and garlic in the frypan and sauté them until the onions are golden. Stir in the chicken broth; using a wooden spoon, blend the ingredients well to make an onion gravy. Arrange the quail in a roasting pan and pour the onion gravy over them. Cover the pan and roast the birds in a 300°F oven for 1 hour, or until they are tender but not falling apart. Broiled tomato halves, sprinkled with butter and seasoned bread crumbs, are good with this. So is a glass of cold white wine. The Greeks served Retsina. I would have preferred a California mountain white Burgundy.—*Jack Denton Scott, September 1967*

Quail

SPORTS AFIELD RECIPE —BRUNCH QUAIL

4 quail
Salt and pepper to taste
Flour
¼ cup butter
6 small mushrooms
Water
2 tbsps. parsley, chopped
4 slices of toast, buttered

 Sprinkle the quail with salt and pepper, and dust them with flour. Sauté the quail quickly in the butter until they're brown, then add the mushrooms and enough water so there is approximately 1 inch in the pan. Cover and cook slowly for 10 minutes. Add the parsley and cook an additional 10 minutes, or until the birds are tender. Serve on buttered toast.—*Editors, March 1957*

GAME COOKING I'VE LIKED

The matter of quail takes me back to when I was 22 and visiting a friend of mine, Bob Geary, at his father's Wyoming ranch. The Gearys were big cattlemen and politicians. Old Bob and then Bob himself both served as U.S. senators and governors of Wyoming. At the time, however, Bob Jr. was more interested in pranks than in either ranching or statesmanship. Once he and I followed an Indian burial party across the range, gathering up the cigarettes that the Indians had put along the funeral trail to pacify evil spirits. The Indians caught us red-handed and chased us all the way back to the ranch where it took all the old Senator's eloquence to pacify them. Another time we opened up a locked gate, and 400 prize bulls joyously romped off to mingle with the scrubbier range cattle. It took the cowboys several days to separate them and to get them back into their private corral. But it was not until we blasted at the old Senator's imported Austrian quail, by some always-regretted freak of chance, killing almost all of them with one salvo from the shotgun, that his patience reached an end. He called me aside and came to the point with admirable directness: "Look," he said, "just when in hell are you going home?"

Duncan Hines, with Bradford Angier
March 1959

RASPBERRY WALNUT VINAIGRETTE

¹/₃ cup walnut oil
2 to 3 tbsps. raspberry vinegar
1 tbsp. hot sweet mustard
1 garlic clove, pressed
¹/₂ tsp. sugar or fruit
    sweetener

Thomas McIntyre and
Christine N. Glasser
September 1990

SALAD OF GRILLED QUAIL WITH PAPAYA AND MANGO

3 quail, skinned and marinated
    overnight
1 large ripe Hawaiian papaya
    (select one with fragrant
    yellow or orange skin with
    slight yield to the touch)
2 ripe mangoes (soft to the touch,
    no bruises)

2 heads limestone or
    butterhead lettuce
1 red onion
MARINADE
2 tbsps. olive oil
1 garlic clove, crushed
Dash of red or white wine
Dash of low-sodium soy sauce

Marinate the quail overnight. Grill it (barbecue or indoors) until it's slightly pink. Baste it with the marinade while grilling. Let it sit while you prepare the rest of the salad as follows: Wash and dry the lettuce leaves; do not tear or cut them. Arrange several leaves to form a cup. Peel the papaya, cut it in half lengthwise, and seed it. Cut each half lengthwise into about 10 thin slices. On each plate, fan 3 slices across the lettuce. Peel the mangoes. Cut the meat away from the bone, as thickly as possible, into about 12 chunks each. Place 4 chunks on one side of the papaya fan. Add a few slivers of onion. Cut thin medallions from the quail breast—1 breast for each plate. Arrange it in a fan opposite the papaya. Dress the salad with commercial vinaigrette or use the recipe for raspberry walnut vinaigrette given at left. Garnish if desired. Serves 6.—*Thomas McIntyre and Christine N. Glasser, September 1990*

Quail

BRITTANY QUAIL

8 quail, picked and cleaned
2 cups seedless green grapes, peeled
⅓ cup brandy marinade
½ tsp. salt
½ tsp. white pepper,
    freshly ground

4 tbsps. butter, melted
2 cups chicken stock, warmed
    and mixed with:
    2 tbsps. arrowroot
    2 tbsps. chilled butter bits

Before making the pastry or cooking the quail, peel the green grapes and set them aside to marinate in the brandy for at least 1 hour; stir occasionally. A frozen pie crust can be substituted for the pastry shell. Once it is done, you can delay cooking the birds until ½ an hour before dinner time. When the birds are cooked, remove them to the pastry shell or serving dish and keep them warm. The sauce should then be prepared and the dish served immediately.

The quail should be seasoned with salt and pepper and browned in a skillet with butter at fairly high heat. When the birds are browned, put the skillet into a 500°F oven for 10 minutes. After the quail are completely cooked, remove them to the pastry shell or serving dish. Separate the grapes from the marinade and scatter them over the quail. Drain most of the butter from the used skillet, then add the brandy marinade and cook it over moderate heat. Scrape up the browned bits with a spatula, incorporating them into the sauce. Slowly add the warmed stock and arrowroot mixture, stirring until the sauce thickens. Add the chilled butter bits. Strain the sauce through cheesecloth, pour it over quail, and serve immediately. Serves 4.—*S.G.B. Tennant Jr., October 1983*

PASTRY SHELL

3 cups flour
¼ tsp. salt
12 tbsps. butter bits, chilled
2 egg yolks, beaten
½ cup (or less) ice water
1 tbsp. butter, melted

Mix the first 3 ingredients in a large chilled bowl. Add the egg yolks and enough water to make a dough ball that will not crumble. Preheat the oven to 400°F and roll out the dough on a floured board to 15 inches square, ¼-inch thick. Brush the melted butter inside a 10x10x2-inch baking pan and press the dough into this pan. Trim off the dough at the rim. Bake, covered with foil, for 20 minutes; remove the foil and continue baking until brown, about 20 minutes more.

S.G.B. Tennant Jr.
October 1983

SOUR CREAM QUAIL

Here is my favorite recipe for sour cream quail, for which I thank the Huntington Hotel in Pasadena. Fasten a piece of salt pork around each quail with a toothpick. Fry the birds in 3 tablespoons of butter, turning them until brown. Then mix 12 crushed juniper berries with 1 cup of boiling water and put in with the quail. Simmer for 1 ½ to 2 hours, adding water from time to time if necessary. Afterward, salt and pepper to taste. Pour 1 pint of sour cream, 5 or 6 days old, over the quail and boil it well for 30 minutes. If the cream curdles, add 1 teaspoon of hot water slowly until the cream becomes smooth.

Duncan Hines
(with Bradford Angier)
March 1959

GIBLETS WITH PASTA

1 lb. gizzards and hearts from
*   quail (duck, pheasant and*
*   chukar can also be used)*
4 tbsps. olive oil
1 medium onion, chopped
1 small celery stalk,
*   cut into ¼-inch pieces*
1 small carrot, cut into
*   ¼-inch pieces*

1-lb. 2-oz. can whole
*   tomatoes, chopped*
1 tsp. Italian seasoning
1 tsp. garlic powder
¼ tsp. each salt and pepper
2 tbsps. butter
2 cups fresh mushrooms, sliced
¼ cup grated Romano cheese
1 lb. pasta

In a skillet heat 3 tablespoons of oil over medium heat. Add the onion, celery and carrot. Cook until tender, about 10 minutes. Add the tomatoes and seasonings. Cook over low heat, stirring frequently, until thickened—about 30 minutes. Simmer until ready to serve. Trim the gizzards and hearts into ½-inch slices. In a saucepan boil 3 cups of water and cook the meat for 15 minutes over medium-high heat. Drain. Cook the pasta according to the package directions. Meanwhile in a skillet, melt the butter and the remaining oil over medium heat. Add the hearts, gizzards and mushrooms and cook for 8 minutes. Mix the pasta with the sauce, giblet mixture and Romano cheese. Serve with additional cheese if desired. Serves 4 to 6.

—Annette and Louis Bignami, January 1988

Q u a i l

QUAIL IN WINE

4 quail

3 tbsps. butter

2 large onions, chopped

1 can cream of mushroom soup

1 cup white wine

Lightly sauté the chopped onions in a Dutch oven. Take out the onions and sear the split birds quickly. Lower the heat, add the cream of mushroom soup, thinned with white wine. Put the onions back in and cook slowly, covered, until the meat begins to fall from the bones. Serve with peas and rice.—*Charles R. Meyer, September 1961*

WHICH WINE?

For gamebirds, I like to go lighter still, but stay red. Some Burgundy whites like Puligny-Montrachet are terrific with pheasant or quail, but I prefer luscious, well-priced French country wines like Chinon Bourgeuil and Beaujolais-Villages; a California Pinot Noir from the Beaulieu Vineyard; or an Italian Dolcetto.

John Mariani
November 1994

SCALOPPINE OF PARTRIDGE (ITALY)

2 partridges
2 eggs, beaten
Salt and pepper to taste
1 ½ cups fine bread crumbs
¼ lb. butter
1 lemon

Remove the breasts from each partridge (saving the rest of the carcass). Skin them, then slice into scaloppine—4 1-inch-thick slices from each ½-breast; 16 from the 2 partridges. Place each scaloppine between double folds of wax paper and gently flatten it with a wooden mallet or the side of a meat cleaver. Season the beaten eggs liberally with salt and pepper. Dip each flattened scaloppine in egg and then lightly in bread crumbs. Don't use too much batter or you will overwhelm the flavor of the partridge. Separate each dipped scaloppine with wax paper and place them in the refrigerator for 2 hours. Melt the butter in a frypan. Cook the scaloppine 1 minute (no more) on each side. They will be golden and juicy. Try one for taste; the key here is not to overcook. Serve 4 per person with a wedge of lemon, which should be lightly squeezed over the scaloppine before it is eaten.

—*Jack Denton Scott, September 1967*

Partridge

PARTRIDGE VOL-AU-VENT (ITALY)

2 partridge carcasses
    (breasts removed)
Salt and pepper to taste
3 carrots
4 celery stalks, with tops
4 small white onions
1 bay leaf
6 sprigs Italian parsley
Sprinkle of thyme

3 tbsps. butter
2 tbsps. flour
1 jigger brandy
1 cup heavy cream
2 tbsps. baby peas
    (lightly cooked)
1 jumbo pimento-stuffed
    green olive, sliced
8 patty or pastry shells

Place the partridge carcasses in a large pot. Sprinkle liberally with salt and pepper and cover with cold water. Add the carrots, celery, onions, bay leaf, parsley and thyme. Cover and simmer for 2 hours, or until the meat is tender. Take the meat from the bones and cut it into small pieces. Reduce the stock in the pot by 50 percent by cooking uncovered over high heat. Then put the liquid and vegetables through a fine sieve. Keep them hot. Melt the butter in a large saucepan. Stir in the flour until it is a smooth golden paste. Now add 1 ½ cups of the reduced, hot stock—a spoonful at a time—stirring constantly so that the sauce is smooth. (Meanwhile you have baked the pastry shells in the oven.) Now add the brandy and the cream, the peas, the sliced olive and the pieces of meat; blend well and simmer for 5 minutes. Taste and correct the seasoning. If the mixture is too thick, add more stock; it should be smooth and not runny, but it shouldn't be gummy, either. Fill the pastry shells with the partridge mixture and serve immediately.—*Jack Denton Scott, September 1967*

MARINADES CAN MAKE THE DIFFERENCE

For most wild birds, deer, antelope, bears, moose and other game on the hoof, red wine is the best of all simple marinades, and the gamier the animal, the heartier the red wine should be. For light birds such as quail and pheasant, you might want to use a medium-bodied red like an Italian Chianti or Spanish Rioja Tinto, while a bold, big zinfandel or cabernet sauvignon is better with rich meats like venison, squab or grouse. One last thing: Pouring expensive Burgundies or Bordeaux over a piece of meat is unnecessary. Rather, save it for the meal itself.

John Mariani
July 1994

COOKING WITH CURRY

Particular Parsons was a masterly cook. He didn't use curry powder often. He used it frugally; his dishes were never offensively hot, but just delicately sauced. After a day in the woods and fields, nothing hit the spot, that vast empty space in the hunter's stomach, like a well-prepared curry dish. Curry powder comes from India. There is no mystery about the ingredients in a commercial curry powder. The principal ingredients include turmeric, garlic, onion, chili, ginger, aniseed, coriander, black cumin, fenugreek, black and cayenne peppers, mustard seed, cardamom, citrus and a few other items that balance and bind in the assorted ingredients. Like garlic, it should be used with discretion.

Harry Botsford
February 1953

CURRIED GROUSE BREAST

3 lbs. grouse breast
4 tbsps. seasoned flour
2 tsps. curry powder
1 cup sour cream
4 tbsps. butter
1 tsp. salt
3 ¼ cup consommé

Skin the breasts, removing the bone. Roll the breasts in seasoned flour and brown them in the butter in a deep skillet. Add the consommé and the curry powder, which you've mixed to a paste with a little of the consommé. Cover the skillet and simmer the breasts for 25 to 30 minutes, or until meltingly tender. Add the sour cream (or use undiluted evaporated milk), pouring it in just a little at a time while stirring. Correct the seasonings with the addition of a little salt. Decant the contents of the skillet onto a hot platter; surround with broken hot biscuits.—*Harry Botsford, February 1953*

GROUSE STEW

2 grouse
2 cups veal or chicken stock
1 onion, sliced
1 tbsp. parsley, chopped
1 tsp. basil
1 tsp. tarragon
4 tbsps. butter
Flour
3 egg yolks
1 tbsp. lemon juice

Cut the fowl flesh into small pieces and put them in a stew pan with good broth, sliced onion, parsley and sweet herbs. When the broth has boiled enough, strain it off; then put in a bit of butter rolled in flour and let it stew another moment. Then put in the hash of fowls; cook; thicken it with 3 egg yolks; put in the lemon juice; and serve up hot.—*James Brakken, October 1995*

COLONIAL GROUSE

It's hard to believe that grouse were once so abundant that New England farmers requested a bounty to cope with the birds' taste for apple tree buds. And that early Americans took fantail ruffed grouse by trapping them with horsehair nooses, or simply knocking them out of the trees with sticks. Judging from this 1753 recipe, ruffed grouse must have been a tasty dish in colonial times.

James Brakken
October 1995

BREADED GROUSE FILLETS

Grouse are soft-skinned and difficult to pick, so many hunters simply skin them. This does not ruin the bird, but cooking grouse does require special measures. One approach is to bread the bird to help keep moisture in it while cooking.

4 grouse breast fillets
¼ cup milk
2 tbsps. seasoned flour
1 egg, beaten
Dash of hot sauce
½ cup Italian bread crumbs
4 tbsps. Chinese duck sauce

Dip the fillets into milk, then into flour, then egg, then bread crumbs. Place them on a baking sheet and cook them in a 375°F oven for about 15 minutes. Do not overcook. Spoon the duck sauce onto the fillets and serve them with a dash of hot sauce, with rice pilaf and/or a vegetable of choice. Serves 2.—*Almanac, July 1990*

Grouse

ELEGANT BRIMBLE JERKY

4 grouse breasts
2 cups apple cider
¼ cup brown sugar
¼ cup salt
1 tsp. grated orange peel

1 tsp. ground clove
1 tsp. ground ginger
Grated rind of ½ a grapefruit
Juice of ½ a grapefruit
Dash of Cointreau

Slice the grouse breasts in horizontal sheets. Combine all of the ingredients in a glass container and marinate the strips overnight. Pat them dry and arrange the pieces side by side, without overlap, on oven roasting racks. Cook at minimum heat, say 150°F, for 6 hours. Leave the oven door ajar to allow moisture to escape. Store the jerky in a cool, airtight container. Alternate drying techniques include a "hard cure" in an electric smoker for 12 hours. Crisp jerky means the heat was too high. For sweeter jerky, baste with molasses or honey and water just before drying. When drying outdoors, the meat—whether laid on rocks and turned every few hours or hung from a rack on the porch—must be protected from moisture and creatures at all times. A cool fire keeps the flies at bay, sometimes. An original Pacific Indian procedure included a marinade of seawater reduced to enhance its saltiness. You can vary the marinade given here by adding more salt, sugar or juniper berries to taste.—*S.G.B Tennant Jr., September 1985*

PIT COOKING

Frank dug a pit larger than the Dutch oven. He piled split wood in over the pit, fired the wood, and let the coals drop into the pit. As the fire burned, he lined the Dutch oven with strips of ham, onions, chunks of the hind legs of rabbit, the breasts of 3 grouse, potatoes, 4 diced carrots and 1 cup of shredded cabbage. Over this went evaporated milk, salt and pepper. The cover went on the pot and Frank set the Dutch oven on a bed of coals, surrounding the kettle, side and top. Dirt covered the pit tightly. All day long the pot simmered and when it was served the meat, potatoes and onions were meltingly tender.

Harry Botsford
December 1955

INDIAN INSPIRATION

While hunting tigers in the jungles of India, I discovered that I preferred shooting the plentiful ring-necked doves to hunting the elusive cat—it not only had more action, but made much more sense. You could eat the doves. Our cook, Joakium Cleamanto Rodriguis, was from Goa and a master. He also didn't mind my watching and cribbing his recipes. His curried doves with rice pilaf has become my favorite method of serving those superb gamebirds. This is truly Indian and a real taste treat. It is not campfire cookery as we know it, even though it was prepared in a jungle camp.

Jack Denton Scott
September 1967

CURRIED DOVES
(INDIA)

8 doves
1 tsp. dry English mustard
Salt and pepper to taste
1 cup olive oil
1 tbsp. wine vinegar
1 cup canned tomatoes
2 cups water
1 tbsp. butter
½ cup white onions, chopped
2 garlic cloves, chopped
1 small piece fresh ginger, chopped
1 ½ tbsps. Madras curry powder

Marinate the doves for 3 hours in a mixture of the mustard, salt, pepper and ½ of the olive oil and vinegar. Turn the birds often so they are well coated. Sauté them in a frypan in the remaining olive oil until they are browned. Remove the doves and place them in a large pot, to which you add the cup of tomatoes. Pour the 2 cups of water into the frypan that the doves were browned in. Stir well so as to mix the cooked particles in the bottom of pan with the water. Pour this over the doves in the pot and stir with a wooden spoon, blending well. Now melt the butter in the frypan and sauté the onions, garlic and ginger until they're brown but not burned. Stir in the Madras curry, blending well. Add this curry mixture to the doves in the pot. Cover the pot and simmer slowly until the birds are tender, about 1 ½ hours.—*Jack Denton Scott, September 1967*

Dove

TERRINE OF PIGEON

4 cups dove or squab, skinned,
    boned and diced
4 bacon slices
Salt and black pepper to taste
1 tbsp. tarragon, dried
1 cup gelatinous game
    (or beef) stock

2 slices hard bread,
    crust removed
1 garlic clove, crushed
1 tbsp. quatre-épices
4 eggs
½ cup heavy cream
⅓ cup Madeira (Malmsey)
1 cup pistachio nuts, shelled

Brown the bacon in a skillet, lower the heat, and add the meat, salt and black pepper. Cook until the meat is firm but not cooked through. Drain off excess grease and sprinkle tarragon over the meat, allowing the seasoning to soften. Remove the meat to a mixing bowl. Over reduced heat add the stock to the skillet, stirring to incorporate any brown bits, then add the bread, stirring until it forms a paste. Add the garlic and the quatre-épices, stir, then add them to the meat. Purée this mixture in a food processor. Remove it to a mixing bowl and whisk in the eggs, cream and Madeira (Malmsey has enough body, but port will do, too). Adjust the seasonings, add the nuts, and pour the mixture into a 6-cup terrine previously buttered and underlaid by a strip of buttered wax paper or parchment paper. Set the terrine in a pan of water, cover it, and cook at 350°F for 1 hour. Refrigerate it overnight and unmold before serving.—*S.G.B. Tennant Jr., March 1986*

MOURNING DOVES IN HISTORY

In Old Carolina, the dove has been a gamebird for nearly 300 years. Grainfields brimming with what they used to call Egyptian millet, bennet and even rice were cultivated to lure the long-tail pigeons. In the old days the hunt took on the trappings of a ceremonial English pheasant drive. The birds were chased out into nearby woods by the field hands. When the guests had finished a stately luncheon in the great house, they were positioned in blinds around the field. The hands would drive the birds out of the trees and toward the fields, and the great outdoor spectacle was under way.

S.G.B. Tennant Jr.
September 1983

RICE PILAU (INDIA)

2 tbsps. olive oil
½ cup white onions,
    chopped
1½ tbsps. almonds, slivered
2 tbsps. white raisins
2 tbsps. butter
2 cups long grain rice
4 cloves
1 piece fresh cinnamon
4 cups chicken broth
Salt to taste

Sauté the onions, almonds and raisins in olive oil until brown. Drain and reserve. Melt the butter in a frypan, sauté the rice with the cloves and cinnamon until the rice absorbs the butter. Brown the rice and transfer it to a pot; add the broth and salt. Cover and cook until boiling. Place the pot in a low oven and cook the rice until it's dry, then sprinkle it with the drained onion, nuts and raisins. Serve with curried doves.

Jack Denton Scott
September 1967

GULLAH COUNTRY CHARLESTON DOVE PILAU

12 doves, picked and cleaned
1 cup dried raisins
2 cups boiling water
6 bacon slices
1 cup celery, finely chopped
1½ cups white rice
2 cups chicken or duck stock
1 tbsp. each salt and freshly
    ground black pepper
4 eggs, beaten
1 cup vinegar, mixed with
    3 tbsp. powdered mustard
1 tbsp. olive oil

To plump the raisins, drop them in the boiling water for 2 minutes, then set the pot aside and allow the raisins to steep until needed. Fry the bacon in a skillet until medium- to well-done, then set aside. Add the celery to the skillet, browning it lightly in the grease. With a slotted spoon, remove the celery to a large mixing bowl. Simmer the rice in the stock, stirring until the liquid is completely absorbed. Add the rice, drained raisins and chopped bacon to the mixing bowl. Stir in the salt, pepper and beaten eggs, blending it all together well. Stuff the birds with this mixture. Brush the outside of each bird with the vinegar-and-mustard mixture and place them in a shallow baking dish. Sprinkle a few drops of olive oil on each bird and place the dish, uncovered, in a 375°F oven for 30 minutes. Baste the birds frequently with the remaining vinegar-and-mustard mixture. Serve them on a platter inside a ring of freshly cooked white or wild rice, mixed with more plumped raisins if you like, and pour the basting juices over everything. Serves 4.—*S.G.B. Tennant Jr., September 1983*

Gamebirds

MIXED-BAG PURLOO

Breasts and giblets from
    6 small birds
2 bay leaves
¼ lb. venison sausage,
    cut into bite-size pieces

1 medium onion, chopped
Salt and red pepper flakes
    to taste
1 cup rice
1 tbsp. fresh parsley, chopped
2 ripe tomatoes, chopped

Put the breasts and giblets into a pot, cover them with water, add the bay leaves, and simmer (do not boil) for 1 hour. Add the sausage, onion, salt and red pepper, plus a little hot water, if needed. Simmer for 30 minutes. Discard the bay leaves. Bring the ingredients to a boil and add the rice, parsley and chopped tomato. Cook for 25 minutes, watching the pot closely and adding water as needed. (As it cooks and expands, the rice will quickly absorb lots of water.) Serve in bowls as a soup, or cook it down like a pilaf and serve on plates. I prefer it in bowls, served with hot French bread.

—A.D. Livingston, May 1996

AN ASIDE ON THE BAY LEAF

In cooking school I was taught that all bay leaves should be removed from a stew, or a purloo—as in this recipe, because they are dangerous. My instructor believed the edges of a bay leaf were so sharp as to cause the stomach lining to be perforated by one. My cooking teacher was very dramatic and was concerned about proper presentation of food. This may have been her way of reinforcing the idea that bay leaves should be removed if for no other reason than floating leaves in food doesn't look very appetizing, except perhaps to an outdoorsman.

R.C.G.

WOODCOCK APPETIZER

I have the greatest respect for A.J. McClane. Not only because of the expertise and knowledge he possesses in order to have written the fishing encyclopedia, but because he is a master of the culinary art as well. His experience and creativity have produced some of the very best there is in wild fish and game cookery. But when it comes to recipes for woodcock, if the stew at right is any example, I'm squinting my eyes. I suggest instead of stewing, sautéing slices of woodcock breast in olive oil for a minute or two and combining it with a little reduced cream seasoned with thyme. Serve on toast points as an appetizer.

R.C.G.

WOODCOCK STEW

4 woodcock, plucked and dressed
½ cup of vegetable oil
1 cup lean uncooked bacon, diced
2 medium onions, thinly sliced
2 medium carrots, diced
2 medium turnips, diced
1 veal knuckle or shank bone,
   cracked
Hot water
1 bay leaf

½ tsp. thyme
5 peppercorns
1 tsp. salt
2 stalks celery, diced, tops included
2 tbsps. fresh parsley, minced
½ tsp. Worcestershire sauce
1 tbsp. tomato paste
½ cup wild rice, cooked
Sherry
4 slices French bread,
   toasted and buttered

In a large stew kettle, heat the oil over high flame and brown the birds on all sides. Add the bacon, onions, carrots and turnips and cook them over medium heat until all are browned. Add the veal knuckle and hot water to cover. Add the herbs and seasonings. Cover and simmer for about 1 ½ hours, or until the birds are tender. Remove the birds and set them aside. Simmer the liquid 30 minutes more. Remove the veal bone. Add the celery, parsley, Worcestershire sauce and tomato paste. Simmer until the celery is tender. Return the birds to the pot. Correct the seasoning to taste with salt and pepper. Stir in the wild rice and heat it through. Serve the stew in bowls with a dash of sherry and the toasted French bread floating on top. Serves 4. Note: Partridges, doves, quail or a mixture of birds may be used.—*A.J. McClane, October 1979*

BROILED WOODCOCK

2 whole woodcock, plucked
Salt and pepper to taste
2 bacon strips
White wine for basting

Season the woodcock inside and out with salt and pepper and wrap the brace in bacon strips. Broil the birds under moderate heat for 15 minutes. Serve with peas and mushroom slices, broiled apple slices and cornbread. For basting and drinking, a tangy white wine is ideal. The sweet flesh needs little seasoning.

—*Charles R. Meyer, September 1961*

TASTY MEAT SAUCE

1 $1/2$ cups meat or chicken broth
2 tbsps. cornstarch
2 tbsps. water
$1/2$ cup spiced rum
2 tbsps. lime juice

Bring the broth to a boil. Dissolve the cornstarch in the 2 tablespoons of water and add it to the broth. Simmer the broth until it thickens. In a separate saucepan, warm the rum, then ignite it with a match. Quickly remove it from the heat and when the flames are extinguished, pour it into the broth. Add the lime juice and serve the sauce atop woodcock breasts.

Almanac
December 1991

MULLED WINE

Mulled wine is the traditional specific against long mornings in drenching cold. This is Harry Bourne's recipe, and he was always smiling, no matter the weather.

½ tsp. black peppercorns
½ tsp. whole cloves
2 cinnamon sticks
¼ cup sugar
2 bottles red wine
1 cup cognac

Simmer the spices, sugar and wine for 5 minutes. Add the cognac and pour the wine into heated mugs or a vacuum bottle. Makes about 12 servings.

S.G.B. Tennant Jr.
February 1986

STEELHEAD QUICHE

2 cups steelhead fillets, cooked and flaked (any fish may be used)
2 cups heavy cream
6 eggs, beaten

Salt and pepper to taste
½ tsp. ground nutmeg
Grated cheese
2 lemons

Whisk the cream, eggs and seasonings together and fold into the flaked fish. Spoon this carefully into the pastry shells (see below), sprinkle with cheese, and bake at 375°F for 30 minutes, or until they are set and puffy. Sprinkle with lemon juice. Serves 4.

PUFF PASTRY
2 cups flour
½ tsp. salt

4 tsps. powdered sugar
2 sticks butter, cool and soft
2 egg yolks

Use quiche molds that have false bottoms to facilitate removal. Mix the flour, salt and sugar on a pastry board, forming a circle to mix the butter and egg in the middle, and incorporate the flour with quick turnings of a palette knife. When all of the moisture is absorbed, scrape the dough into a plastic bag and refrigerate it for 1 hour. Roll the dough out into 2 circles, drape each over a quiche ring, settling the dough in the corner and trimming the edges with a roller. With aluminum foil, build a cast to fit inside each pastry shell. Chill the dough before baking it at 400°F for 8 minutes until set, then remove the foil, baste the inside of the shells with butter, and bake them for 3 minutes longer. Cool the shells before uncasing them.—*S.G.B. Tennant Jr., February 1986*

Winter

UNLESS YOU'RE A CRAZY ICE fisherman or really into the last part of rabbit or quail season, there isn't a whole lot to hunt and fish for in winter—but it's a great time to dream. A few people are lucky enough to be able to go to the Bahamas for bonefish; but I'm not really certain that deters the dream season. In fact, I think it may promote it.

"The best thing about hunting and fishing," the old man said, "is that you don't have to actually do it to enjoy it. You can go to bed every night thinking of how much fun you had twenty years ago, and it all comes back clear as moonlight."—Robert Ruark, The Old Man's Boy Grows Older, *1961*

I was in the Bahamas one winter several years ago, and we'd spent the day fishing on the flats; a long, sultry and lazy day when even the ocean water seemed to steam. We were trying to organize ourselves to go cook supper but some of us had become dizzy, so dizzy we almost couldn't stand up. There were a variety of explanations offered for our vertiginous behavior: The incessant sun made us dizzy (I'm sure it wasn't the dark rum and tonics we'd had the previous evening).

No—I knew what it was. We were in a beautiful place and having magnificent fishing. It was the release; we'd taken a mental vacation and our minds had just drifted off. Our brains simply flitted away out to sea so that we couldn't even be bothered to stand up straight.

When these symptoms appear there is only one possible

method for cooking your fish: grilling. You need some technique that's simple while your brain has gone on holiday, some method that requires little attention in order to let your mind continue to travel. Don't let it be brought back to the harsh reality of elaborate meal-making and order. Let your mind stay on the Bahama flats, or on a Florida bass pond, while your eyes meander, without seeing, around the backyard. The smoke from the grill will be drifting off into the neighborhood. I think most happy fishermen know what I'm talking about.

One of the very best reasons for eating what you've caught or shot is that it conjures up an event, a nice memory, the time and place of when you caught the fish or shot the critter. And if you're not in the Bahamas or at your grill, wintertime cooking can also help summon the moment. The partridge is pulled from the freezer and unwrapped. The memory of this particular bird, shot in the wild grapes in an old nearby covert, comes back. Stuff the bird with thyme and roast it hot and fast, then make a sauce using wild grape jelly for the base. Tie all the ingredients together—a good adage in cooking as well as in memory-making.

RABBIT PIE

Potpie has long been a favorite on Yankee tables and it's still fine fortification for autumn days in the field. Here's how it's done with rabbit. Place 2 jointed rabbits in a stew pan with ½ a cup of water. Add salt, pepper, a generous amount of minced parsley, 1 large onion, chopped, 3 cloves, 4 stuffed olives, chopped, and ½ a pound of diced salt pork. Boil the mixture until the rabbit is tender. Thicken with browned flour and, if necessary, add a little water. Let it boil again and add ½ a cup of butter. Remove from the fire and bone the pieces of rabbit. Mix in 3 or 4 sliced, boiled potatoes and 2 or 3 sliced, boiled carrots. Put the whole works in a baking dish lined with pie crust and cover with another crust. Cut several slits in the top crust to allow steam to escape. Bake until the crusts crisp.

Erwin A. Bauer
December 1955

BREADED RABBIT

1 small rabbit, cut
⅛ tsp. oregano
Salt and pepper to taste
2 tbsps. milk
1 egg
¼ cup flour
¼ cup bread crumbs

Sprinkle the rabbit with oregano, salt and pepper. Combine the milk and egg; beat. Dip the meat pieces in the milk and egg mixture, then dredge them in flour and bread crumbs. Brown them in ½-inch of fat at 375°F. Lower the heat and cook for 25 minutes, until tender.—*Editors, February 1957*

R a b b i t

RABBIT STEW

2 fat rabbits (about 3 pounds each),
 dressed and disjointed into
 serving pieces
4 cups chicken broth or stock
3 cups water
1 cup dry white wine
2 tsps. salt
1 bay leaf
¼ tsp. thyme
3 whole cloves

3 peppercorns
4 large parsley sprigs,
 stems removed
2 cups fresh or frozen green peas
3 celery stalks, sliced thick, tops
 removed
12 fresh or frozen baby carrots
12 fresh or frozen baby onions
4 large scallions cut in
 ½-inch pieces

Frozen options are included in the recipe because these ingredients are often hard to find in fall hunting country. Place the rabbit pieces in your stew pot and add the broth, water, wine, salt, herbs and spices. Bring to a boil, then lower the heat. Skim the surface as needed and simmer covered for 1¼ hours or until the meat is almost tender. Add the peas, carrots, celery, scallions and onions if fresh (reserve if frozen), simmering until the vegetables are cooked. Frozen baby onions won't stand much heat, so these and other frozen vegetables should be added during the last few minutes. Remove the bay leaf and correct the seasonings with additional salt, if desired. Serve in large soup bowls with vegetables and broth and crusty sourdough bread for dunking. Serves 6.—A.J. McClane, October 1979

LIVING OFF RABBITS

To people doing the hard muscular work that life and hunting in the wild entails, there is inordinate craving for fats, particularly in cold country and where sugar is scarce. Indeed, under such conditions fat and a lot of it is absolutely necessary for health, energy and ultimately for life itself. Indians who are reduced to a diet of rabbits exhibit every symptom of starvation, for as a rule rabbits have no fat. There is a saying in the North: "Starving on rabbits!"

Colonel
Townsend
Whelen
December
1943

SOUTHWESTERN RABBIT WITH A MEXICAN INFLUENCE

Mexicans in the Southwest have devised splendid methods to cook rabbit. Joint one or two rabbits and dust them generously with chili powder. Brown the pieces in hot olive oil. Now place the pieces in a well-greased casserole, salt and pepper them, sprinkle with chopped onions and parsley and cover with white wine. Bake the rabbit until it's tender and most of the wine is absorbed. The liquor remaining can be made into a gravy by thickening with flour and cream. Use on the rabbit or on a baked potato, which fits into the meal perfectly.

Erwin A. Bauer
December 1955

HASENPFEFFER WITH GRAVY AND DUMPLINGS

1 rabbit, cut into pieces
2 cups vinegar
1 cup claret
1 ½ cups water
1 onion, sliced
½ tsp. salt
⅛ tsp. pepper

1 tsp. mustard seed
1 tsp. juniper berries, crushed
8 whole cloves
6 bay leaves
Flour
⅓ cup butter or salt pork
Salt and pepper to taste

Place the meat in a marinade of vinegar, claret, 1 cup of water, onion, salt, pepper, mustard seed, crushed juniper berries, whole cloves and bay leaves. Marinate for 1 or 2 days, turning at least every 12 hours. Then dry the meat carefully and sprinkle it with flour. Sauté it in either butter or salt pork until it's well-browned on all sides. Drain it, then place it in a pot. Strain the marinade through a sieve, add ½ cup of water and pour it over the pieces of rabbit. Bring to a boil, cover and simmer over low heat for about 45 minutes. Add salt and pepper if desired. Serve on a platter with the gravy—thickened somewhat with flour if you want—poured over it. Traditionally, hasenpfeffer is served with dumplings.—*Duncan Hines (with Bradford Angier), March 1959*

 *Rabbit*

HASENPFEFFER—1981

3 lbs. rabbit, skinned and cut into chunks
1 ½ cups cider vinegar
1 ½ cups cold water
½ cup sugar
3 bay leaves
2 tsps. salt
1 tsp. whole cloves
¼ tsp. black pepper
⅛ tsp. allspice
1 medium onion, sliced
½ cup flour
Butter or shortening
Cornstarch or arrowroot

Combine the vinegar, water, sugar, spices, seasoning and onion in a bowl. Add the chunks of rabbit. Cover and refrigerate for at least 12 hours, preferably longer. Remove the rabbit and drain it. Save the marinade. Dredge the rabbit in flour and fry until brown in ¼ inch of hot butter in a skillet. After browning, place the rabbit in a clean frypan. Add the marinade. Simmer covered until the rabbit is tender; about 1 hour. When the rabbit is tender, remove it from the pan and thicken the liquid with a paste made of a small amount of cornstarch and water. Serve the sauce over the rabbit.—*A.J. McClane, November 1981*

MIDWESTERN HASENPFEFFER

For a robust dish, try hasenpfeffer as it's served in German farm kitchens of the Midwest. It's solid nourishment for cold winter nights. Combine 2 cups of vinegar, 1 cup of red wine, 2 cups of water, 1 unpeeled and thinly sliced lemon, 3 sliced onions, 12 whole cloves, 3 bay leaves, 2 teaspoons of mustard seed, 12 whole black peppercorns, 2 tablespoons of sugar and 2 tablespoons of salt in a bowl. Cut a pair of rabbits into chunks and place them in the mixture. Keep the meat in the refrigerator, turning occasionally, for 1 or 2 days. Remove the meat and dry it. Roll the pieces in a mixture of ¼ cup of flour to 2 teaspoons of salt. Melt ¼ cup of shortening in a Dutch oven and add the meat, browning it. Pour ½ of the marinating liquor into the Dutch oven. Add an extra onion, several whole cloves and black peppercorns. Simmer until tender, about 2 hours for young cottontails. When blended with flour, the liquor remaining makes a gravy. Serve over egg noodles, dumplings or spätzle.

Erwin A. Bauer
December 1955

BUTTER CRUST

1 ½ cups flour
¼ tsp. salt
1 cube (8 tbsps.) butter
1 tbsp. lemon juice
4 tbsps. ice cold water

In a bowl I combine the flour and salt. Cut in the butter with a pastry blender or fork until pea-sized. Add lemon juice and water, 1 tablespoon at a time, and stir until well mixed. Form into a ball; then wrap in waxed paper and refrigerate.

Annette and Louis Bignami
November 1987

BRITISH RABBIT PIE

Before disease decimated wild rabbits in England, every ditch and hedge held them. Today the British use domesticated rabbits and wild hares for pies. In America, tender cottontails or young hares suit this recipe best.

MARINADE
3 tbsps. red-wine vinegar
3 tbsps. olive oil
2-inch sprig fresh rosemary
½ tsp. thyme leaves
1 garlic clove, minced
½ tsp. black peppercorns, crushed
1 small bay leaf
FILLING
1 rabbit, jointed

¼ cup plus 1 tbsp. flour
¼ tsp. salt
¼ tsp. pepper
3 tbsps. olive oil
3 tbsps. butter
1 medium onion, sliced
¾ cup red wine
½ cup game or chicken stock
2 stalks celery, sliced
1 tbsp. fresh parsley, chopped

Combine the marinade ingredients. Place it with the rabbit in a plastic bag; seal and refrigerate overnight. Drain and reserve the marinade. Pat the rabbit dry with a paper towel. Season the flour with salt and pepper and dust the meat with it. Make the butter crust and chill it for 45 minutes. In a Dutch oven, heat the oil and butter and brown the rabbit. Add the onion and cook till tender. Stir in the tablespoon of flour. Add the wine, stock, celery and parsley and bring to a boil. Lower the heat, cover and cook for 30 minutes. Transfer to an 8x10-inch casserole. Roll the dough for the crust. Place the dough on top to cover, crimp the edges and brush the crust and edges with an egg wash. Bake at 400°F for 20 minutes; reduce to 350°F and bake 40 minutes.—*Annette and Louis Bignami, November 1987*

 *Rabbit*

SHISH KABUNNY

4 rabbits, skinned, boned, and
   cubed for skewers
½ cup cooking oil
½ cup onion, chopped
¼ cup parsley, chopped
¼ cup lemon juice
2 tsps. salt
1 tsp. dried marjoram (or oregano),
   crushed
1 tsp. dried thyme, crushed
1 garlic clove, sliced

½ tsp. fresh-ground
   black pepper
3 tbsps. olive oil
3 medium onions, cut into
   quarters for skewering
2 green peppers,
   cut into 8 squares each
1 cup medium mushrooms,
   stems removed
1 cup sweet red peppers,
   cut into pieces

Combine the cooking oil, onion, parsley, lemon juice, salt, marjoram, thyme, garlic, pepper and rabbit cubes in a bowl. Cover and refrigerate overnight, or at least 6 hours, stirring occasionally. Remove the meat and reserve the marinade. Pat the cubes dry. In a hot skillet brown the meat cubes in the olive oil, turning frequently until they are evenly colored. Thread four skewers, alternating meat with chunks of onion, green and red peppers and mushrooms. Grill over hot coals (or rotisserie), turning often and brushing with the marinade, until the rabbit is well done and the vegetables have softened (about 12 minutes).—*S.G.B. Tennant Jr., September 1984*

A TREAT FOR WHEN YOU SCORE YOUNG RABBITS

Stews are delicious, quite an appropriate fate for a senior bunny. If, on the other hand, you are so fortunate as to put a few young and tender cottontails in your bag, allow me to suggest a departure from the soup-and-gravy routine—rabbit shish kebob. It is important to marinate the meat, particularly if your rabbits are long in the tooth; the marinade also serves nicely as a baste for the skewered vegetables during cooking. This recipe serves 4.

S.G.B. Tennant Jr.
September 1984

TRY SOMETHING NEW IN THE WOK

Stir-frying preserves the fresh flavor of meat. When preparing this dish, Cantonese chefs use an intense flame and the rabbit meat is in and out of the wok in minutes, tender and juicy. Brevity also applies to the other ingredients: the bamboo shoots and mushrooms retain their own flavors.

Glenn Smith
October 1988

STIR-FRIED RABBIT WITH BAMBOO SHOOTS

12 oz. rabbit meat
8-oz. can sliced bamboo shoots, drained
8-oz. can Chinese mushrooms, drained
3 slices fresh ginger, minced
2 whole scallions, minced
2 tsps. rice wine
4 tbsps. cooking oil
SEASONING A
1 egg white
2 tsps. cornstarch

1 tsp. baking soda
¼ tsp. salt
4 tbsps. soy sauce
½ tsp. sesame oil
SEASONING B
4 tbsps. broth
    (stock from rabbit bones)
1 tbsp. oyster sauce
1 tsp. sesame oil
1 tsp. sugar
¼ tsp. cornstarch
¼ tsp. salt
¼ tsp. black pepper

Clean the rabbit and slice the meat. Place it in a bowl and add Seasoning A. Mix until the meat is evenly coated. Set aside for 20 minutes. Blanch the bamboo shoots and Chinese mushrooms in boiling water for 30 seconds. Drain well and set both aside. Mix Seasoning B ingredients in a bowl and set aside. Mince the ginger and scallions. Place the wok on high heat and add the cooking oil. Stir-fry the rabbit meat until lightly browned. Remove and keep warm. Reheat the wok and stir-fry the ginger and scallions in the remaining oil for 30 seconds. Next add the bamboo shoots and mushrooms and stir-fry for 30 seconds. Add the rabbit meat. Pour the rice wine onto the side of the wok. Add Seasoning B and stir the ingredients until the broth thickens. Serve with rice.—*Glenn Smith, October 1988*

R a b b i t

DEEP-FRIED RABBIT IN GINGER SAUCE

In this recipe the rabbit is deep-fried to make it crisp, and then it is stir-fried with ginger. It sounds like extra work, but the dish takes only 10 minutes to prepare. All ingredients must be ready before cooking begins because hesitation while stir-frying can ruin the texture.

6 oz. rabbit meat

1 whole scallion

2 slices fresh ginger, chopped

2 garlic cloves, chopped

Cooking oil

½ tsp. rice wine

SEASONING A

1 egg white

1 tbsp. cornstarch

½ tsp. sugar

½ tsp. salt

½ tsp. peanut oil

SEASONING B

6 tbsps. broth (stock from
     rabbit bones)

1 tsp. sesame oil

1 tsp. cornstarch

1 tsp. sugar

¼ tsp. salt

¼ tsp. black pepper

Cut the rabbit into cubes. Place the meat in a bowl and coat with Seasoning A. Mix the Seasoning B ingredients in a bowl. Place the wok on high heat and add 1 inch of cooking oil. When the oil is hot, begin deep-frying the meat piece by piece. Move the cooked pieces to the upper portion of the wok. When all of the meat is cooked, remove it from the wok and set aside. Reheat the wok. Stir-fry the chopped scallion, ginger and garlic in the leftover oil (about 2 tablespoons) for 10 seconds. Add the rabbit meat and stir-fry until warm. Pour the rice wine onto the side of the wok. Add Seasoning B and stir-fry for 1 minute. Serve with rice.—*Glenn Smith, October 1988*

FRIED RABBIT

Years ago we stayed at a backcountry inn where fried rabbit appeared on the menu three times a day. It required cajolery and bonded sour mash to pry the formula from the chef. But it was a sound investment indeed. Parboil a pair of quartered rabbits in water containing 2 tablespoons of salt, ¼ cup of white vinegar, several whole black peppercorns and 1 large onion, chopped. Right there is the secret: parboiling is the difference between this and ordinary fried rabbit. Now dry the pieces, dip them in flour, sprinkle with pepper and fry in hot fat until tender. It's as quick and easy as that.

Erwin A. Bauer
December 1955

RABBIT SHOOTING IN IOWA

W hen you go after Bunny, don't take the ferret; don't take the dog—it isn't his place to hunt rabbits. Take the little hammerless, fill your pockets with shells and jump the rabbits yourself. Hunt them where you will—in the cornfields, in the woods, in the swamp—and you will enjoy yourself more than you can imagine. When you have bagged four or five, bring them home and make one of those old-fashioned rabbit pies. If you do not think that it is about the sweetest morsel you have ever tasted, then your Uncle Reuben misses his guess.

Ralph E. McCord
March 1905

SNOWSHOE TERIYAKI

MARINADE
1 cup soy sauce
½ cup beer
¼ cup brown sugar
4 whole cloves
½ tsp. black pepper

2 cloves, coarsely ground
CASSEROLE INGREDIENTS
2 snowshoe rabbits
2 onions, chopped
2 green peppers, chopped
4 celery stalks, chopped
2 10-oz. packages frozen broccoli
2 cups rice, uncooked

P lace 2 quartered rabbits in a shallow baking dish. Mix the marinade ingredients and pour it over the rabbit. Cover with plastic wrap and refrigerate, turning the meat every 6 hours or so, for at least 24 hours. Remove the meat from the marinade, reserving the liquid. In a large skillet, brown the quarters over medium-high heat, about 3 minutes per side. Add ¼ cup of the marinade, cover and reduce heat to simmer. After 1 hour, add the chopped onions, peppers and celery, and more marinade if necessary. Cover and simmer for another hour. Remove the skillet from the heat. Separate the rabbit pieces from the veggies and refrigerate the meat until it's cool. Debone and cut the meat into bite-sized chunks. Add it to the vegetable mixture in the skillet, but do not reheat. In a large pot (4-quart or better) with a tight-fitting lid boil enough water, mixed with the remaining marinade, to cook 2 cups of rice. Add the rice. Reduce to a simmer, then add the skillet contents and frozen broccoli. Simmer with the cover on for at least 30 minutes. Test the rice. All should be done. Serve with additional soy sauce, Chinese mustard or duck sauce. Serves 4 to 6.—*Fred Everson, June 1991*

 *Rabbit*

NEW ENGLAND RABBIT

1 rabbit
Butter
Salt and pepper
Flour
1 large onion, sliced
Sour cream
Mushrooms

Preheat the oven to 350°F. Melt the butter in a skillet. Salt and pepper the rabbit pieces, dust them with flour, then brown them. Place the meat in a well-greased casserole, then cover them with onion slices and sour cream to taste. Cover tightly and bake in the oven for about 45 minutes until the rabbit is done, basting several times. Serve the rabbit with its gravy, with green beans and mashed potatoes or peas and rice. Note: This is also a very good dish to cook in a Crock-Pot. It's even easier than using an oven and virtually foolproof. Brown the rabbit as directed above, then put the pieces in the pot and cover with onion slices, mushrooms and sour cream. Cook on the high heat setting for 4 or 5 hours, or until the rabbit is tender.

—A.D. Livingston, October 1995

BROILED RABBIT

Charcoal grill fans can have a holiday broiling rabbits. The most uncomplicated method is to salt and pepper pieces of rabbit, then douse them with melted butter. After a bed of charcoal subsides to glowing coals, place the pieces right on top. Turn them frequently, basting each time with butter. Cooking time is about 15 minutes. For something really choice, make a sauce (for 1 rabbit) of ⅓ cup of vinegar, the juice of ½ a lemon, ⅔ cup of salad oil, 1 teaspoon of salt, ½ teaspoon of pepper, ½ teaspoon of paprika, several basil leaves and a finely chopped onion or kernel of garlic. Marinate the rabbit in this sauce for about 15 minutes, then sear it quickly on both sides on the broiling rack. Turn the rabbit often and baste it each time. Try to keep a steady heat—you can do this by maneuvering it around over the charcoal—until the meat is tender and evenly browned all over. The result is something to remember.

Erwin A. Bauer
December 1955

MORNAY SAUCE

2 cups light cream
½ lb. Gruyère cheese, grated (2 cups)
Salt to taste
¼ tsp. cayenne pepper
1 tsp. white pepper
2 oz. butter
4 tbsps. flour

Combine the cream, grated cheese, salt, cayenne and white pepper in the top part of a double boiler over a low flame. In a separate pan make a roux with the butter and flour (melt the butter until it foams, stir in the flour and cook for 2 minutes). Scald the cream mixture in the double boiler over steaming water, but do not let it boil. Whip in the roux. Cook for 8 to 10 minutes. Adjust the consistency with leftover fish broth from poaching. Makes about 3 cups.

A.J. McClane
February 1980

FISH FILLETS MARGUERY

6 thin fillets, 4 oz. each
6 large shrimp, butterflied
24 mussels
Water and wine in equal parts to cover fish
1 bay leaf
2 parsley sprigs
Salt
Mornay sauce
Chopped parsley

Starting with the tail end, roll up each fillet and fasten with a toothpick. If in the 4-ounce size (perch fillets are often smaller), cut each roll into halves to make 12 small paupiettes. Combine water, wine, bay leaf, parsley stems and salt to taste in a deep pan. Poach the rolled fillets for 6 to 8 minutes or until they are translucent but still firm. Remove the fish to a platter and keep warm. Poach the shrimp and mussels in the same broth until the shrimp are tender and the mussel shells open. Arrange the fish fillets on a heatproof serving platter and top with Mornay sauce. Brown under the broiler. Garnish with the mussels and shrimp. Sprinkle with parsley.

—A.J. McClane, February 1980

POMPANO EN PAPILLOTE

3 whole pompanos

3 cups water

1 shallot, chopped

5 tbsps. butter

2 ¼ cups white wine

1 cup crabmeat, chopped

1 cup shrimp, chopped and cooked

1 garlic clove, slivered

2 large onions, chopped
  (1 ½ cups)

Pinch of thyme

1 bay leaf

2 tbsps. flour

2 egg yolks

Salt and pepper

Oil

Parchment paper or foil

POMPANO BAKED IN A PAPER ENVELOPE

Having started with simplicity, you might as well try something on the fancy side, but don't let its name discourage you. It simply means pompano baked in a paper envelope. And it does not have to be pompano, although this was the fish used when the dish was created in New Orleans more than half a century ago. If fortunate to catch pompano anywhere from Florida west to Texas, use them by all means; but if you live in the North as I do, employ substitutes. I like flounder fillets, but fillets from striped bass, fresh salmon or weakfish can be used. Recipes for this vary widely from the original conceived by Jules Alciatore, son of the founder of Antoine's in New Orleans, which was, in turn, a modification of a still older recipe for baking fish fillets in a sauce in an envelope. The one which follows is a bit complicated, but well worth the trouble if you want something out of the ordinary.

Bill Wolf
April 1956

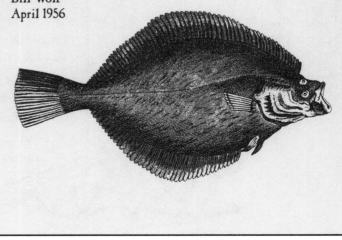

154

There are several steps. Fillet the fish and save the heads and backbones to make a stock. Three pompanos will yield 6 fillets—as will 3 weakfish, flounders or whatever you use. Simmer the heads and backbones in 3 cups of water until the water is reduced to 2 cups of stock. Save this, discarding the bones. Sauté 1 chopped shallot (or 2 tablespoons of minced onion) and the fish fillets in 2 tablespoons of the butter, then add 2 cups of the white wine; cover and simmer gently for about 8 minutes. Lift out the fillets. Save the wine stock. In another pan, sauté the crabmeat, shrimp and garlic in 1 tablespoon of butter. Add the chopped onion and cook gently for 10 more minutes. Then add a pinch of thyme, a bay leaf and all but ¼ cup of the 2 cups of fish stock. Simmer an additional 10 minutes.

Meanwhile, heat 2 tablespoons of butter in a separate saucepan, blend in the flour, then add the remaining ¼ cup of fish stock. Add the flour mixture to the crabmeat and shrimp mixture, plus the wine in which the fillets were poached, and stir constantly while cooking until it thickens somewhat. Stir in the egg yolks, which have been beaten, the remaining ¼ cup of white wine, and salt and pepper. Remove from heat. Cut 6 large paper hearts about 1 foot deep and 8 inches wide from clean butcher's paper or parchment paper, and oil or butter these 6 hearts well on both sides. I have also used aluminum foil for these envelopes and found it perfectly satisfactory. Only the inside of the foil is buttered. Divide the crabmeat and shrimp sauce among the 6 paper cut-outs, using ½ the heart only. On each sauce bed, lay 1 fillet. Fold over the other ½ of the heart and crimp the edges of the paper or foil to seal in the contents, then lay them on an oiled baking sheet and bake at 450°F for 15 minutes, or until the paper begins to brown. They must be served immediately but should not be opened until placed in front of the diner. Then the paper is snipped open with scissors, and the heavenly aroma that emerges justifies all the effort. Make no mistake about it—this is one of the world's great fish dishes. Serve with a good dry white wine.—*Bill Wolf, April 1956*

Perch

FISH PUDDING

1 ½ lbs. fresh perch,
*   skinned and boned*
1 tbsp. butter, softened
2 tbsps. dry bread crumbs
½ cup light cream
1 cup heavy cream
2 tsps. salt
4 tsps. cornflour

Coat the inside of a 4-cup mold with the butter and sprinkle with bread crumbs. Mix light and heavy cream together. In a blender, purée the fish with a small amount of cream; continue adding cream until you have a smooth blend. Place the puréed mixture in a large bowl and add the salt and cornflour. Beat vigorously until fluffy. Pour the purée into the mold. Gently shake the mold sharply to remove any air pockets. Cover the mold with a sheet of buttered aluminum foil and set in a baking dish deep enough to hold water ¾ the height of the mold. Place in a 350°F oven and bake for 1 to 1¼ hours. Make certain that the water is simmering (if it boils, the molded fish will become perforated). Serve pudding hot or cold, with a suitable sauce such as lobster, dill, caper or egg.

—A.J. McClane, November 1981

POWDERED MILK

To make milk, stir 1 heaping tablespoon of powdered milk in cold water, or 2 for cream. It's a little tedious to mix, but an egg beater will do it; or better, have a can with a tight top to use like a cocktail shaker, and afterward as your cream pitcher. You also use the powder dry in mixes for breads and puddings. In its dry state it keeps indefinitely without ice so long as you keep bugs away. I never cared for powdered eggs cooked as eggs straight, but it's fine in breads, cakes and puddings, and also scrambled with chopped up liver, kidneys or dried beef.

Colonel Townsend Whelen
July 1953

YELLOW PERCH BAKED IN APPLES AND MUSTARD

3 tart green or red apples, sliced
6 tbsps. butter
4 yellow perch fillets
⅔ cup Dijon mustard
1 cup clam juice
2 cups white wine
1 green onion, chopped

Preheat the oven to 350°F. Core and slice the apples ¼-inch thick. Sauté them in a skillet in 3 tablespoons of butter over medium heat until lightly browned. In a buttered baking pan, layer the fillets and spread the mustard evenly over them. Place the apples over and around the fish. Cover with clam juice and 1 cup of wine. Bake 8 to 10 minutes or until the fish flakes with a fork. While the fish cooks, put the remaining cup of wine with the onion into the skillet and reduce to 1 tablespoon. Add the liquid from the baking pan to the skillet, putting the fish back into the oven to keep warm. Reduce the liquid by ½; add the remaining butter and cook until the sauce becomes glossy. Pour the sauce over the fish. Buttered green noodles complete this meal.—*Annette and Louis Bignami, May 1989*

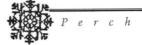

Perch

SMOKED PERCH

Perch
Brown sugar
Saltwater
Wood chips

Seventy degrees Fahrenheit is the point that determines whether a fish is cold smoked or hot smoked. The only difficulty in cold smoking is in making the smoke circulate around and penetrate the fish. You can generate the smoke several feet away from the smokehouse so it cools as it travels to the fish. This is most easily accomplished by "cooking" wood chips (usually hardwood such as alder or maple) in a cast-iron skillet over a hot plate inside a closed container— an air-tight barbecue will do—and then piping it to the smokehouse. Once the issue of how to make the smoke is settled, the next step is to freeze the fish for 8 days or so. Freezing breaks down the cell structure in the tissue, enabling the meat to absorb the sugar-and-salt cure at a uniform rate. To make lox, remove the fins from the thawed salmon (perch). Split the fish along the backbone and carefully remove the rib bones. If the fillets are thick—more than ¾ inch—turn them flesh side down and score the skin with a razor blade to a depth of ½ an inch. Make a line of cuts 1 inch long, ½ inch apart, with ¾ inch separating the rows of cuts. You need only make the scores at the thickest part of the back. If you do not want to smoke whole sides simply cut the fillets into 4-inch strips and proceed to the curing

RAW PLEASURES

Smoked fish is an ambiguous term. There is hot smoked fish, commonly called kippered fish, which is partially cooked as it is smoked. And there is cold smoked fish—what many people call lox. Many types of fish respond well to smoking, particularly the salmon species and steelhead from the coastal areas and the freshwater fish—trout, crappies and perch—from the inland sections of the country. White fish from the ocean, such as cod, haddock, tuna and sturgeon, as well as fish that are not usually eaten fresh, such as whiting, shad, buffalo fish, butterfish and eel, are delicious when smoked.

Stuart E. Mork
June 1987

stage. Make the cure by mixing equal parts brown sugar and salt. Rub it gently on the surface of the meat and into the scores on the skin. Spread some of the sugar-salt cure over the bottom of a deep glass dish and lay the fish in it, skin side down. You can layer fish 4 pieces deep if you sprinkle ¼ inch thickness of the cure between each layer. Spread some over the top of the last layer and keep the dish in the refrigerator for 3 days. On the 4th day rinse the fish, which will be a little stiff and shrunken because the salt has removed some of the fluids from the flesh, then put it back in the dish. Make a strong brine solution by dissolving 3 pounds of salt in 1 gallon of water, then dilute it 4 parts brine to 6 parts water. Pour this over the fish and put the dish back into the refrigerator for 2 more days. Agitate the fish once a day to make the brining uniform. If the fish try to float, weight them with a plate on top. On the morning of the 6th day, remove the fish from the brine and soak it in a tub of cold, fresh water for 6 hours. Change the water periodically to leach out the salt from the fish tissue. After the fish has soaked, it will be pale and soft. Handle the meat gently to avoid breaking it. Put the fish on the smoker racks. Place the racks in a cool, shady place to let the fish dry for a few hours. A fan blowing air across the fish will help to form the glaze that indicates it is time to begin smoking. Smoke the fish for 3 days at 70°F. Don't let the temperature go any higher, or you will have cooked fish or spoiled fish. You can cut off small slices to check the depth of the smoke penetration. At the end of 3 days you will have the most exquisite smoked fish you ever tasted. Store the smoked fish in the refrigerator.—*Stuart E. Mork, June 1987*

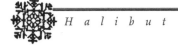 *Halibut*

CALIFORNIA CIOPPINO

2 medium Dungeness crabs
2 dozen clams in shells
1 ½ pounds halibut or rockfish fillets
1 lb. large shrimps in shells,
    split and deveined
1 medium onion
2 large garlic cloves (or more)
6 parsley sprigs
¼ cup olive oil
3 ½ cups canned Italian
    plum tomatoes

1 ¼ cups canned tomato purée
1 cup Burgundy or
    other dry red wine
1 cup water
2 tbsps. wine vinegar
1 tbsp. mixed herbs (basil,
    rosemary, marjoram
    and oregano)
Salt and pepper to taste
12 to 16 potatoes,
    boiled and peeled

Use a Dutch oven or a large pot with a lid. Finely chop the onion, garlic and parsley. Cook in the olive oil over moderate heat until soft but not browned. Add the tomatoes, tomato purée, wine, water, vinegar, herbs, salt and pepper. Bring to a boil and reduce the heat to simmer for 40 minutes. (This sauce may be made ahead of time, if desired, but heat it before adding to fish.) When the sauce is completed, reserve it in a separate container. Dress the crabs, crack the claws, and break into serving pieces. Layer the crabs, clams, halibut and shrimp in the pot. Pour the sauce over all. Cover tightly and cook over low heat for 20 to 25 minutes. Serve in heated bowls. Serves 6.

—A.J. McClane, June 1980

IN A STEW

Cioppino is legendary in California. However, Cioppino is from the Genoese dialect and defined in the venerable Gaetano Frisoni dictionary as "a tasty stew of various qualities of fish." What isn't in contention is the meaty Dungeness crab, without which no modern day cioppino could be labeled "California." I've substituted blue crab with excellent results, and if you make the substitution, remember: The Dungeness is a big crab of 2 ½ to 4 pounds, so you'll have to figure on at least 4 blue crabs for each Dungeness in this recipe.

A.J. McClane
June 1980

CLAMS IS CLAMS

There aredozens of clams worldwide. The hardshell clam is the smallest little neck and usually eaten on the half shell. Next in size is the cherrystone, eaten in any way that suits. Hardshell clams larger than cherrystone are called quahaugs and are used in chowders or stuffed clam recipes. Softshell clams are also known as longneck clams or steamers. The hen clam is a softshell more than 5 inches long. A squeeze of lemon is appreciated when they are eaten raw. Littleneck clams, razor and geoduc are usually fried, steamed or chopped into a chowder. The tiny butt clam is a rare, raw treasure.

S.G.B. Tennant Jr.
June 1985

YANKEE CHOWDER

2 cups cooked clams
2 cups codfish, in chunks
2 cups fish stock (or chicken stock)
¼ cup salt pork, finely diced
½ cup sweet onion (or one bunch
    scallions and greens), chopped

1 cup clam juice
4 tbsps. flour
1 cup raw potatoes, sliced
1 cup cream, heated
¼ tsp. cayenne pepper
3 tbsps. fresh parsley, chopped

One-half peck of clams in the shell will produce 2 cups shucked clams. In a heavy stew pot, barely cover the scrubbed clams with water; cover and steam for 10 minutes. When done, the shells will open. Remove the clams from the shells and save the broth. If you use canned clams (whole clams, not bits), separate the liquid from the clams; rinse the clams and strain the liquid through a linen napkin. Place the fish and stock in the empty stew pot and simmer until the flesh barely flakes. Separate the stock and fish, and reserve. In the same, again-empty stew pot, heat the salt pork to soften it. Add the chopped onions, allowing them to soften thoroughly but not brown. Add the clam juice and stock (if necessary, add water to the latter to reach a total of 3 cups) and bring to a simmer. Mix the flour in ½ cup of stock, then stir into broth. Simmer and stir. If the potatoes are raw, add them immediately and allow them to reach the al dente stage. Ten minutes before serving, stir in the fish, cream, clams and cayenne pepper. Two minutes before serving, chop the parsley with great furious whacks, stir into the chowder and serve in great clay bowls. Serves 4 —*S.G.B. Tennant Jr., June 1985*

LOUISIANA OYSTER SOUP

24 oysters
6 shallots, minced
2 tbsps. butter
2 garlic cloves, minced
2 cups boiling milk
1 cup hot water

Finely mince the shallots (or use young green onions), including some of the tender green part. Melt a chunk of butter the size of a walnut (about 2 tablespoons) in a pan. Add the shallots and cook slowly. Add the 2 toes (cloves) of minced garlic, then the 2 dozen raw oysters, including the oyster water. When the oysters begin to curl, add the 2 cups of boiling milk and 1 cup of hot water. Season to taste with salt and pepper. Simmer 2 minutes and serve.—*Roy L. Alciatore, September 1955*

BUTTER CRACKERS

2 cups flour
2 tbsps. butter
¼ tsp. soda, dissolved in hot water
1 tsp. salt
1 cup sweet milk

Blend the butter and flour, cutting the two together on a pastry board. Add the salt, milk and soda, mixing the very wet dough rapidly to keep it together. Work until the dough forms a ball, then beat it, turning it regularly, with a rolling pin for at least 20 minutes or until your arm gives out. Roll out the dough in the thinnest sheet possible, not more than ¼-inch; thinner is better. A pasta roller will do the job. Cut out the crackers with a small-diameter cookie cutter (you can also use half a clamshell) and bake them hard in a 350°F oven for 1 hour. Finish the crackers by letting them dry overnight in the oven at the lowest heat with the door ajar. Serves 4.

S.G.B. Tennant Jr.
June 1985

CANNING THE CATCH

Pack the smoked clam or oyster meat tightly in pint jars, leaving a ½-inch of space at the top. Brush the top of the meat with vegetable oil and close the jars. Process the jars for 2 hours at 10 pounds of pressure (240°F).

Erling Stuart
April 1983

OYSTERS ON THE HALF SHELL, FRENCH-STYLE

6 oysters
Rock salt
2 shallots finely chopped
  (or substitute young green onions)
3 toes (cloves) garlic, finely minced
1 tbsp. parsley, chopped
8 tbsps. (1stick) butter
2 bacon slices, partially cooked

Open your oysters, leaving them on the deep shell. Fill a pie pan with rock salt and place the oysters, each in its shell, on the rock salt. In a bowl, mix the shallots, garlic, parsley and butter into a thick paste. Place 1 teaspoon of the green paste onto each raw oyster, and on top of the paste, place a 1-inch-square slice of partly cooked and drained bacon. Place the pan with the prepared oysters under the oven broiler just long enough to curl the bacon and melt the butter paste. Serve immediately.—*Roy L. Alciatore, September 1955*

S h r i m p

SHRIMP IN SHELLS IZAAK WALTON

Raw shrimp
Olive oil
8 tbsps. butter (1 stick)
3 tbsps. English powdered mustard
2 tbsps. Lea & Perrins Worcestershire sauce
A pinch each salt and cayenne pepper

Take the raw, unpeeled shrimp and split each down the center of the back through the shell to the center, all the way to the tail. Dip each shrimp in olive oil or cooking oil and lay flat in a single layer in a shallow pan. Prepare a butter paste by taking 1 stick of butter and mashing it with a fork in a bowl until smooth. Add the English powdered mustard and Lea & Perrins sauce. Add a pinch of salt and a pinch of red pepper. Mix well until thoroughly blended. Now dot each shrimp with the paste and place the shallow pan under the oven broiler only long enough to cook the shrimp and melt the butter. When the shrimp are done on one side, turn each in pan to cook the other side. You will find that shrimp cooked in this manner are the most tender you have ever tasted. Serve piping hot. Guests will remove the shells with their fingers.—*Roy L. Alciatore, September 1955*

CATCH A CRAB

All you need is a long wooden wharf and a collapsible basket, usually made of cord and iron rings. A few scraps of fish or meat laid in the basket is all the bait that's required. Highly pungent bait is the best, for crabs have an excellent sense of smell. Let the basket down to the ocean floor by rope, lean back against a piling and relax. After a few minutes pull up the basket—full of crabs if your location is good. If your efforts have been unrewarded, move to another spot. You've nothing to do but enjoy the ocean air, and one good basket is all you'll need for a meal. Crabs are plunged live into boiling salt water. Purists may insist on genuine sea water with perhaps a bay leaf added, while others just add salt to tap water. I can't notice a difference, so I'm not going to get caught in that argument. After a few minutes of seething in any event, the crabs are bright red and ready to be eaten. Brought to the table steaming hot, and served with melted butter, they are unforgettable.

Duncan Hines, with Bradford Angier
March 1959

CANNED CLAMS

Scrub the clam shells and place those that are tightly closed in a steamer. Discard any clams whose shells have opened; these clams are dead and may be spoiled. Steam clams until the shells open. Next, open the steamed clams and keep the liquor. Heat the liquor in a saucepan and reduce until it is ⅔ the original volume. Snip off the siphons of the clams and throw away the dark portions of the intestinal system. Wash the clam meats in a weak brine made by mixing ¼ cup of salt per gallon of water. Mix a solution of either 2 tablespoons vinegar per gallon of water or 3 teaspoons of lemon juice per gallon of water and bring it to a boil. Blanch the clam meats in the boiling solution for 1 or 2 minutes. Pack 1¾ cups of clams into each pint jar and fill each to within half an inch of the top with the boiling clam nectar. Put the lids on the jars and process them at 10 pounds of pressure (240° F) for 1 hour and 10 minutes.

Erling Stuart
April 1983

GRILLED SHRIMP SMOKEHOUSE

36 raw shrimp
Salt and pepper
8 tbsps. butter
6 shallots, minced
3 garlic cloves
1 tbsp. parsley
Juice of 1 lemon
1 tbsp. liquid smoke
Dash of Lea & Perrins Worcestershire sauce

Shell the raw shrimp. Remove the black line with a knife and flatten each shrimp into a butterfly shape. Salt and pepper to taste. Melt the butter, add the minced shallots (or young green onions). Cook 2 minutes and add the cloves of minced garlic and the chopped parsley. Cook 1 minute and add the shrimp. Cook 2 or 3 minutes until the shrimp curl and are done. Squeeze over the top the juice of 1 small lemon and add 1 tablespoon of liquid smoke and a dash of Lea & Perrins sauce. Serve immediately with squares of toasted bread.

—Roy L. Alciatore, September 1955

FRIED SHRIMP
À LA BRINY DEEP

5 dozen raw shrimp
Salt
Red pepper
2 eggs, beaten
2 cups all-purpose flour
4 tbsps. oil

Remove the shells from the raw shrimp and with a sharp knife split each shrimp down the back and remove the black line. Season the shrimp with salt and red pepper and moisten with the beaten eggs. Place the all-purpose flour in an ordinary paper bag and set aside. Heat the cooking oil until it just begins to smoke. Drop the dozen shrimp, one at a time, into the flour and shake the bag. Remove them one at a time and drop them into hot oil. Cook in the oil for 2 minutes and remove to a piece of absorbent paper to drain. Repeat the procedure until all the shrimp are fried. (Do not cook more than a dozen at a time.) These shrimp are really tender and delicious.—*Roy L. Alciatore, September 1955*

NEW ENGLAND CHOWDER ON THE BEACH

While on the subject of soups and stew, let me recall the clam chowders compounded by Uncle Lou Higgins on the sandy shores of Cape Cod. Uncle Lou's chowders were the full-bodied, New England brand and they were made not with soft clams but with quahaugs. He prepared them many years ago as the crowning feature of our trips together after striped bass. While I cast my squid over the bar, guzzle holes covered by an incoming tide, Uncle Lou waded knee deep in the shallows, catching his quahaugs with his short-handled rake. When he had a quart or so, we shucked them on the beach beside a driftwood fire. To assemble his chowder, he diced 2 cups of potatoes and put them on to boil. Then he chopped the quahaugs in a mixing bowl and simmered them in their juice. He browned 3 strips of salt pork and 1 large, sliced onion. When they were done, Uncle Lou added onion, pork and clams to the potatoes in the kettle. Last of all, in went 1 quart of milk. Bring to a boil. Then, just at that precise instant, the kettle was lifted from the fire. The recipe was alleged to serve 4 persons, but there was very little chowder left when Uncle Lou and I laid down our spoons.

Ted Janes
April 1957

CORN OYSTERS

One of the top cooks of all was old Pete Lufkin, a stalwart State-of-Mainer, who contrived his culinary miracles in a pail. "Give me a bucket," he once declared, "and I'll get along. I can fry, bake, boil and roast all in one pot." One of Pete's specialties was corn oysters, which he made from 1 can of corn, 1 beaten egg, 4 crumbled crackers and a pinch of salt and pepper. These ingredients he mixed with enough condensed milk to make them stick together, coated the oysters and fried them in deep fat in his pail.

Ted Janes
April 1957

FISHERMAN'S OYSTER CANAPÉ

24 raw oysters
3 tbsps. butter
3 shallots, minced
2 garlic cloves, minced
1 tbsp. parsley
Salt and pepper to taste
1 tbsp. flour
½ cup hot milk
Toast

On chopping board, chop the raw oysters. In a pan, melt a piece of butter the size of a walnut (about 2 tablespoons) and add the minced shallots (or substitute young green onions) and minced garlic. Add the minced parsley and make a thick cream sauce with the flour, butter and hot milk. Stir and cook until smooth, and set aside. Toast a slice of bread for each person. Assemble the dish as follows: Cook the shallots, butter, garlic and parsley for 2 minutes, then add the minced oysters. Add salt and pepper to taste. Then add the cream sauce to make a thick paste. Cook, stirring all the while, until the proper consistency. Remove from the fire and spread paste on slices of toast. Devour while still warm.—*Roy L. Alciatore, September 1955*

Flounder

FISH MOUSSE

3 cups flounder fillets
    (other fish may be substituted)
1 ½ cups heavy cream
2 anchovy fillets, drained
5 eggs

1 cup small shrimp, boiled
    and peeled
Salt and pepper
¼ cup capers
1 tsp. paprika
1 tsp. cayenne

Warm the cream slightly, taking care not to boil it, and add the anchovy fillets, stirring until they disappear. Purée the flounder and cream together. Pour into a mixing bowl, add the eggs, shrimp, capers and seasonings. Pour into a 6-cup terrine previously buttered and underlaid by a strip of buttered, waxed, or parchment paper. Set the terrine in a pan of water, covered, and cook at 350°F for 1 hour. Refrigerate overnight and unmold before serving.

—*S.G.B. Tennant Jr., March 1986*

CILANTRO MAYONNAISE

2 egg yolks
Salt and pepper
2 tsps. lemon juice, strained
1 ½ cups olive oil
¼ lb. fresh cilantro (coriander) leaves

Have all ingredients at room temperature. Whisk the yolks, salt and pepper in a warm bowl for 1 minute, add the lemon juice, and continue whisking until blended. Then add the oil, a drop at a time, until the mixture thickens. Continue whisking, and pour in the remaining oil until the desired consistency is reached. Parboil the cilantro for 1 minute, then rinse in cold water and drain well. Chop the cilantro, then stir into the mayonnaise, blending well.

S.G.B. Tennant Jr.
March 1986

SAUTÉED FISH FILLETS WITH SAUCE

Milk
6 flounder fillets
Flour
Salt, pepper and paprika
4 tbsps. butter
Parsley sprigs
Juice of 1 lemon wedge

Dip the fillets in milk. Dust with flour. Sprinkle with salt, pepper and paprika. Gently sauté in a skillet with ½ stick butter. Turn once and remove. Add a finely chopped parsley sprig and the juice of 1 lemon wedge to the butter; stir and pour over the fish.

Charles R. Meyer
June 1959

SAUTÉED FISH FILLETS WITH WINE

6 flounder fillets
4 tbsps. butter
1 onion, finely chopped
Salt and pepper
½ cup dry white wine

Melt the butter in a skillet and lightly sauté the onion. Add the fillets (baby flounder is preferred) and gently sauté. Add salt, pepper and the ½ cup of dry white wine. Bake in a 325°F oven for about 15 minutes, basting every so often.—*Charles R. Meyer, June 1959*

 *Cougar*

COUGAR CASSEROLE

6 cougar chops
8 tbsps. sweet butter (1 stick)
Salt, pepper, powdered thyme
1 cup bread crumbs, sifted
1 cup beef broth
1 cup dry white wine
1 onion

2 cloves
1 garlic clove
1 bay leaf
2 celery stalks
2 tbsps. parsley, minced
2 tbsps. chives, minced
2 tbsps. shallots, minced
Splash of lemon juice

Melt the sweet butter in an earthenware casserole, then brown six cougar chops that have already been seasoned with salt, pepper and powdered thyme. When the chops are brown, remove and keep hot. Next stir a cup of sifted bread crumbs into the butter in the casserole, cooking them over a low heat until golden. Put the cougar back into the casserole and pour the beef broth and white wine over the chops. Correct your seasoning and add the onion, whole with 2 cloves stuck into it, 1 whole clove of garlic, 1 bay leaf and 2 celery stalks. In a 350°F oven, bake the covered casserole for 45 minutes. Now sprinkle the cougar with a mixture of minced parsley, chives and shallots combined with a little lemon juice, and cook uncovered for 15 minutes more. Take the casserole from the oven, remove the bay leaf, celery, onion and garlic, skim away the fat and serve the cougar. Have a bite and see if the old free trappers of backcountry fame were not on the right track—a round, four-toed one with the claws retracted—all along.

—*Thomas McIntyre, June 1984*

LIVING OFF THE LAND

The Western writer Louis L'Amour reports on the mountain men, that "they lived off the country, eating nothing but the meat they shot themselves. They had it all—deer, elk, moose, mountain sheep, bear, beaver tail, buffalo hump and tongue. Oddly, they preferred panther meat." To describe cougar meat, it is like the palest of pale milk-fed veal. It is rather fat-free, and when prepared needs to have moisture returned to it.

Thomas McIntyre
June 1984

MOUSE STEW

One morning I rigged a neat little configuration of sticks and stones known as a Paiute deadfall, and with the kind of dubious luck I've almost grown accustomed to having, rather promptly caught a mouse...a standard-variety *Peromyscus*, squished a little under the trap's fallen rock. I debated casting the little beast into the brush and rebuilding the trap for another try, perhaps this time for a rabbit or squirrel, but the survivalist's law and a low-guilt threshold won out. I carried my bounty back to camp. My companion was delighted. He placed the mouse on a large, flat rock. Without skinning or gutting it, he then used another heavy rock to mash and grind the little mammal into pulp. This material was then scraped off the rock and put into a cooking vessel, where it was covered with river water, sprinkled with campfire ash for sodium, and simmered for an hour over the fire. Mouse stew. I could barely keep it down, and I won't venture to describe the taste, but the survival expert wolfed his share. "In a survival situation," he said, "you've got to eat anything that's edible." He also pointed out that we didn't skin and gut the mouse because too many vital nutrients would be lost. Since then I've made every possible effort to stay out of survival situations. I'll take a Hirschpfeffer Jädgerart (stag simmered in blood) over mouse stew anytime.

Anthony Acerrano
June 1984

CHICKEN-FRIED IGUANA

1 iguana
Flour
1 egg
2 cups finely crushed cracker crumbs
Salt and pepper
Oil

Don thick leather gloves and catch one big, ugly lizard. Dispatch quickly, skin out and cut into thumb-sized pieces. Dredge in flour. Dip in whipped egg and roll in crushed cracker crumbs, then skillet fry until golden brown. Then, as you munch, keep thinking, "Chicken wings, chicken wings..."—*Homer Circle, June 1984*

B a t

FRUIT BAT

1 fruit bat (1 to 1 ¼ lbs.)
Coconut milk (lots of it)

Shampoo the fruit bat and rinse thoroughly. Do not eviscerate; do not skin; leave intact, including head, tail, wings and feet. Fill a large iron pot (8 or 10-gallon) ⅔ full of coconut milk. Add the fruit bat and simmer several hours until tender. Turn bat halfway through cooking time. Serve with lots of rice and other side dishes for the faint-hearted. One fruit bat will serve about two *Chamorros* or 15 *haoles.—Kit Harrison, June 1984*

ROAST BEAVER

Working on a furbearer management story for <u>Sports Afield</u> in January 1983, I had flown by ski plane to an Indian family's tent camp 100 miles north of the last road in Ontario's taiga forest. Mrs. Josephine Diamond, matriarch of this traditional trapping family, was expecting us and had planned a sumptuous repast for her guests: roast beaver, burnt caribou foot and boiled lynx. Mrs. Diamond and her daughter-in-law, Gerthe, were skinning marten and beaver carcasses on the teepee floor while the dinner cooked. With deft strokes of sharp knives and handmade bone scrapers, they removed and prepared the pelts and stretched them to dry. On top of the wood stove, portion-sized pieces of hindquarter meat from a young lynx simmered in a pot to which salt and pepper had been added. Close to the stove, transfixed by a birch skewer pushed through its hind legs, hung a beaver carcass that had been rubbed with salt and pepper. The skewer was attached to a long thong tied to a crossbar high in the teepee's cone. Every so often Mrs. Diamond or Gerthe would reach out and give the carcass a spin. The ladies had removed the entrails from the beaver, then cut off its tail and stitched that up inside the carcass, where it roasted in the internal juices. Both the lynx and beaver cooked in this manner for three or four hours as we talked....It was a fine dinner, and when it ended we licked our fingers clean, spilled boiling water over the platters and put them back into the box to dry.

Jerome Robinson
June 1984

CHAMPAGNE ASPIC

3 cups chicken stock
2 egg whites
3 packages gelatin
2 cups chilled dry champagne

If you use store-bought gelatin, soften it in half a cup of the cold stock. Beat the egg whites and mix with the stock and gelatin. Bring the mixture to a light boil, stirring to prevent scorching. Let stand 5 minutes while the eggs clarify in the aspic, then pour through a sieve. Set a bowl containing the aspic inside a larger bowl filled with ice and refrigerate. When cooled, stir in the champagne. Pour half the aspic into the bottom of a garnished serving dish, arrange the nymphes à l'aurore around and sprinkle the remaining aspic over it.

S.G.B. Tennant Jr.
April 1985

NYMPHES À L' AURORE
(FROGS' LEGS)

10 pairs of frogs' legs, skinned and separated	Salt and peppercorns
Fresh chervil	CHAUD-FROID SAUCE
Tarragon leaves	6 tbsps. melted butter
COURT BOUILLON	8 tsps. flour
1 qt. white wine	1 qt. stock, chicken or fish
1 qt. water	Salt, white pepper and nutmeg
1 cup onions, minced	1 package gelatin
1 cup chopped herbs, parsley, tarragon, etc.	1 cup stock
	1 cup heavy cream
	Paprika

The legs should be poached 15 minutes in a simmering court bouillon. Cool, dry and trim the legs. Make the *chaud-froid* sauce by blending the butter and flour over low heat and stirring for 15 minutes to create a white roux. Slowly stir in the stock and seasonings and bring to a boil. Cook over medium heat for 30 minutes to reduce it by ¼, skimming the foam. Soften the gelatin in 3 tablespoons of liquid from the 1 cup of stock. Add this gelatin mixture to the sauce and continue simmering and stirring. Slowly stir in the cream and continue cooking until the sauce has a thick consistency. Remove from the fire and stir in paprika. Refrigerate. The frogs' legs are dipped in the *chaud-froid* sauce to coat with a thin, uniform glaze. Arrange them on a bed of aspic and garnish with the chervil and tarragon, or you can cover them with diced champagne aspic jelly.—*S.G.B. Tennant Jr., April 1985*

Crow

CROW STEW

1 large onion, chopped
2 tbsps. bacon fat
1 crow
Salt and pepper
1 tsp. flour
½ cup sour cream

Brown the onions in the bacon fat—one onion for each bird. Add the meat; salt and pepper to taste. Cook for a few moments, then add water to cover. Simmer over low heat until tender, then stir in the sour cream mixed with the flour. The usual other ingredients can then be added. If you have never eaten crow (literally), give it a try.—*Bill Palmroth, June 1992*

CROWS

In England, young crows are considered a great delicacy. In France and Germany, crow meat is added to vegetable stew, as well as to beef soups. Most of us think of the crow as a pest, but when properly prepared, crows are good to eat. Here are a few hints: Older birds should always be skinned instead of plucked. Young birds may be roasted like squab. Butter or slabs of bacon are absolutely necessary because the meat tends to be quite dry.—*Bill Palmroth, June 1992*

CROW BROTH

1 crow, breasts and legs
3 tbsps. butter
2 celery stalks, sliced and
    with leaves
6 cups water
Salt and pepper to taste

The breast and legs should be browned a little in butter and boiled with small quantities of chopped celery until tender. The amount of water depends on the quantity of broth desired and the amount of meat you have.

Bill Palmroth
June 1992

CROW SANDWICH SPREAD

1 crow, breast and legs boiled
1 tsp. mustard
1 small onion, minced
Salt and pepper to taste
1 tbsp. mayonnaise
Dash of paprika (optional)

Carefully inspect the boiled meat and remove all bones. Run through a meat chopper. Add the mustard, finely chopped onion, salt, pepper, mayonnaise and perhaps 1 dash or 2 of paprika. May be kept for a reasonable length of time in the refrigerator.—*Bill Palmroth, June 1992*

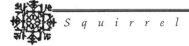

Squirrel

BRUNSWICK STEW

*2 large squirrels or 3 small ones,
    dressed and cut into serving pieces*
2 qts. fresh or canned chicken broth
¼ cup raw bacon, diced
1 cup onion, chopped
2 cups raw potatoes, diced
2 cups baby lima or butter beans

2 cups corn, cut from fresh cobs
*2 cups canned plum tomatoes,
    drained*
*½ tsp. fresh-ground
    black pepper*
2 tsps. Worcestershire sauce
2 tsps. granulated sugar
2 tbsps. butter or margarine

Put squirrel pieces and chicken broth in a large kettle and simmer until the meat is tender—about 1½ hours. Skim the broth to remove fat and foam. Remove the squirrel from the broth and when cool, remove the meat from the bones and return it to the kettle with the bacon, onion, potatoes and beans. Continue to simmer until the vegetables are just tender—about 30 minutes. Add the corn and all the remaining ingredients, except the butter. Cook 10 minutes longer, stirring to prevent sticking. Serve in bowls, with a lump of butter whisked through. Serves 6. Note: rabbit or pheasant may be substituted for squirrel.—*A.J. McClane, October 1979*

A COLONIAL FAVORITE

There are a few stews that follow a strict ingredient formula. Brunswick stew is the most famous squirrel presentation, a papillary favorite of Thomas Jefferson and John Adams, and while its original is claimed by several geographic Brunswicks, the recipe's authorship was probably in Brunswick County, Virginia. It was a favorite in the colonial capital of Williamsburg, where the first American cookbook (with the pre-lib title The Compleat Housewife, or Accomplish'd Gentlewoman's Companion) was published in 1742.

A.J. McClane
October 1979

PIT COOKING

One of the best things that ever came out of the pit was a happy combination of squirrel, tomato soup, leeks and mushrooms. The squirrels were parboiled for 25 minutes, quartered, dropped into a Dutch oven on a bed of fat bacon. There were 6 squirrels and on them went 6 diced leeks, 2 cans of sliced mushrooms, 2 cans of diluted tomato soup, salt and pepper. Ten hours after being placed in the pit, the Dutch oven's seal was broken and the stew removed. The squirrels were so tender that the meat literally fell off the bones. The liquid had become a thick, delicious gravy.

Harry Botsford
December 1955

SQUIRREL POT PIE

6 squirrels, cut in half
1 onion, quartered
A few celery tops
1 bay leaf
4 tbsps. butter or margarine
4 tbsps. flour

1 cup squirrel stock
1 cup milk
3 tbsps. Madeira or cream sherry
Salt to taste
1 can (1 lb.) whole carrots
1 can (1 lb.) whole potatoes
1 pie crust

Place the onion, celery tops and bay leaf in the bottom of a pressure cooker. Place the squirrel pieces on top of the vegetables and add 1 cup of water. Cook under 15 pounds of pressure for 20 minutes. Cool the cooker immediately. Strain the resulting stock and reserve for use in the sauce. Remove the meat from the bones and cut it into bite-size pieces. For the sauce, melt the butter in a medium saucepan and blend in the flour. Slowly stir in the stock and milk. Add the wine and salt to taste. Place the meat, carrots and potatoes in a casserole and pour the sauce over them. Make a pie crust or use a frozen shell to cover; be sure it is securely fastened to the rim of the casserole. Make slits in the crust and bake at 425°F for 25 to 30 minutes, or until the crust is brown and the sauce bubbles. Serves 4 to 6.—*A.J. McClane, November 1981*

Squirrel

BACKCOUNTRY SQUIRREL STEW

2 squirrels
2 qts. boilng water
2 potatoes
1 onion
1 cup corn
1 cup lima beans
1½ tsps. salt
½ tsp. pepper
2 cups tomatoes
1½ tsps. sugar
¼ cup (4 tbsps.) butter

Put the 2 squirrels, each cut into 6 pieces, into boiling water in a Dutch oven, along with the potatoes, onion, corn, lima beans, salt and pepper; cover and simmer for 2 hours. Add the tomatoes and sugar, and simmer for an additional hour. Add the butter and simmer again for 30 minutes. Then bring the stew to a boil, move the pot to the edge of the fire to keep it warm, and sneak out of camp for an hour of hunting or fishing before dinner. (One large chicken cut into 6 pieces can be substituted for the squirrels.)—*J. Wayne Fears, October 1985*

DUTCH OVEN APPLES

Wash and core 1 large apple per person. Fill the holes with sugar, raisins and butter, plus cinnamon if desired. Put the apples on a greased pie tin with a small amount of water. Place the tin in the Dutch oven on a cake rack to prevent scorching. Cover and bake for about 30 minutes.

J. Wayne Fears
October 1985

PAN-SEARED MUSKRAT

For years the muskrat has been sold under the name of marsh rabbit and is served in some high-class eating places under its Indian name of musquash. In preparing the muskrat, you should cut away the abdomen flesh because that's where most of the strong taste comes from. Wash and cut the remainder in pieces. Don't forget to remove all the little kernels of fat you can. Then sear and brown the meat in a deep iron skillet. When it's browned, season, add a little water, put the cover on and let it simmer until the meat falls from the bones. Cook it as dry and brown as possible without burning.

R.N. Hamilton
August 1961

BUTTERFLIED SQUIRREL

4 squirrels, skinned, cleaned, and split up the middle
MARINADE
½ cup soy sauce
½ cup white wine or vinegar

2 garlic cloves, chopped
3 tbsps. sugar
1 tbsp. lemon juice
¼ lb. butter
Salt and pepper to taste

Skin the squirrels by running a sharp blade around the midsection, being careful not to puncture the stomach. Pull the skin off toward the tail, chopping off legs at the first joint, and the tail the same. Reverse the process toward the head, cutting off the neck as close as possible and the forelegs at the first joint. Split open the chest by running a knife up the middle, being sure to clean out all lung tissue. Combine the soy sauce, wine, garlic, sugar and lemon juice in a crock, or some other pot, and add the squirrels. Add enough cold water to the marinade to cover the squirrels, and allow them to stand overnight, or least 3 hours. If you have very young squirrels you may be able to get by without the marinade, but it adds an interesting quality, and certainly helps to soften those rear leg muscles. Remove the squirrels and pat dry. Salt and pepper all over, then spit them. A simple skewer running over the backbone and piercing the front legs, and another, for the back legs, will keep them spread eagle during grilling. Allow 5 minutes a side over hot coals, basting with butter. Serves 4.
—S.G.B. Tennant Jr., December 1983

O p o s s u m

OPOSSUM

1 possum
1 lb. stuffing mix
¼ cup vinegar
3 heaping tsps. grated horseradish
4 tsps. sugar
Pinch of salt
1 can (6 oz.) of evaporated milk

Remember, as with all other animals discussed in this book, to remove the fat kernels. Hang the carcass in a cold, airy place for a day or two but don't freeze it. Parboil the possum whole. While it's parboiling get ready a stuffing. By the time you have the stuffing prepared, the possum will be sufficiently parboiled. Stuff with the filling, pin or sew shut, put into a roaster with a little water and roast in a medium-hot oven until done. Roast the last 15 minutes with the cover off to brown well. Make a horseradish sauce to serve with the dinner. Here's how: Take a large glass, ¼ full of vinegar, add water to make it ½ full, then add the grated horseradish, sugar and salt. Add canned milk to fill the glass.—*R.N. Hamilton, August 1961*

SOMETHING DIFFERENT FOR DINNER

Cut a possum into serving-size pieces and parboil in salted water. While it's parboiling, boil some sweet potatoes. When the taters are cooked, peel and cut into chunks. Put the possum in a roaster. Place the chunks of taters around the meat. Season with salt and plenty of pepper. If you can get some real Southern cane syrup, pour about a cupful over the taters. If not, the same amount of brown sugar will do. Roast slowly without a cover until the meat is crusty brown. Pour off the excess grease and you have that delicious Southern dish known in Dixie as possum pie. I know a Florida cracker who scalds the possum and scrapes off the hair, cuts off the head, tail and feet, dusts the inside rather liberally with salt and pepper and stuffs the animal with white potatoes and parboiled swamp cabbage. Then he roasts his possum beside a bed of hot coals, turning often, until the skin becomes real brown and cracks open.

R.N. Hamilton
August 1961

CLEAN, CORN-FED CRITTERS

The raccoon, or coon as it is more commonly known, inhabits a good portion of North America, and has taken its rightful place as a game animal in many sections. Like its big brother, the coon hibernates during the extreme cold of winter. But given a few warm nights, it's on the prowl, looking for something to fill its belly. At this time it's not too choosy. But usually a coon is a fairly clean feeder. It eats frogs, crabs and fish. When it finds a farmer's sweet corn patch it really lives high because it must put on great layers of fat to see it through the winter. Should you catch one in a cornfield, you would be reasonably sure of getting a clean-feeding animal.

R.N. Hamilton
August 1961

RACCOON

1 raccoon
2 small onions
2 carrots
1 celery stalk
6 whole cloves
2 bay leaves
8 to 10 apples
8 to 10 tbsps. butter
8 to 10 tbsps. brown sugar

Skin and cut the raccoon into pieces. Remove the kernels and all the fat you can. Wash the meat well in cold water. Put in salt water and set in a cold place or freeze until wanted. Put a kettle of water on the stove, add the onions, carrots, celery, whole cloves and bay leaves. When the water is boiling, put in the meat and parboil until tender. While the meat is parboiling, wash and core the cooking apples and fill them with butter and brown sugar. When the meat is done, remove it from the kettle and scrape off any fat you can. Place your coon in a large roasting pan with ½ inch of water and stand the apples throughout the meat. Bake in a slow heat without a cover until the apples are done and the meat is crusty and brown on top.—*R.N. Hamilton, August 1961*

Spring

S PRINGTIME IS USUALLY WHEN YOU catch the first trout of the year, or maybe it's the first time you manage to call a turkey within range. It's the time when everything seems new once more. (How do I cast this big surf rod again?)

Spring requires you to come out of the winter fog, to re-focus, to concentrate, and to try again. It can be a bit jolting. Trout simply will not tolerate my tying on some tiny beige fuzzy thing bearing no resemblance to any insect within 200 miles. I need to know precisely which size elk-hair caddis fly imitates the real one, and what stage of that caddis hatch to expect where and when. Then there's turkey hunting. What exact sound is it that makes a turkey call sound turkey-seductive? Can putting those strange contraptions in your mouth accomplish anything but a gagging reaction or, as I have seen so artfully done, the clever calling in of a large brown-eyed Vermont Guernsey?

The saving-grace is that spring is when we stop freezing. We're done with ice and cold and will eat everything, maybe anything, as long as it is fresh. And, of course, it is the season when it's all fresh, it's all just begun. The fiddleheads are brilliant green, tightly curled and still without chaff; the morels are tender and moist and springing up seemingly every day.

"Cooking is like love. It should be entered into with abandon or not at all."

—Harriet Van Horne, Vogue,

October 15, 1956

Spring

The brook trout are caught at noon and by half-past the streamside lunch is being devoured. We crave what hasn't been in the freezer, the new bounty, the taste of a beginning. It is no wonder that Truite au Bleu (Blue Trout), a recipe which requires as its basic ingredient a live trout, was developed specifically for one of spring's favorite fish.

There's a truth here: All food seems better tasting if it's eaten the instant we take it from nature. My farmer father walks between the rows of his vegetable garden at lunchtime with a jar of Hellman's mayonnaise tucked under his arm. His garden inspection includes a pause at the cherry tomato vine where he plucks the just-ripe and sun-hot fruit off one by one, dipping each in cool mayonnaise until he's finished lunch. He maintains it's the best way, the only way, to eat them.

We are reminded that one of our great rewards as hunters and fishermen is instant gourmet chef-hood because everything we procure to eat is by definition the freshest. And as Master Chef Pierre Franey says, "Remember in any of these [recipes], simply choose a fresh fish and take care not to overcook it....Some of the simplest dishes can be food for the gods."

FAMOUS TROUT RECIPES

Do not overcook. This injunction applies to all fish, but especially to trout. A few minutes to each side is all that's needed in broiling or frying the average trout. As for eating them, hold the head in the left hand, free the top fillet by running a knife along the backbone, turn the trout and free the other fillet, then lift out head, backbone, small bones and tail in one movement. The meat alone remains on the plate. Back home, more elaboration in cooking is possible. Dredge the trout in seasoned flour before frying in butter. The flour gives a slight crustiness to the fish.

Bill Wolf
March 1956

PAPA'S TROUT

3- to 4-pound
   trout or steelhead
1 cube butter
1 medium onion, chopped
3 celery stalks, chopped
1 tsp. ground sage
1 tsp. thyme leaves
1 tsp. parsley flakes
2 cups cooked rice
6-oz. can green olives
   with pimentos
Salt and pepper to taste

Clean the whole fish, pat it dry, and place it on a greased baking dish or sheet. Spread the fins and tail. Fold aluminum foil over them to protect against burning. If you leave the head on, replace the eye with an olive just before serving. Melt the butter in a skillet over medium heat and sauté the onion and celery until tender. Add the sage, thyme, parsley, cooked rice and drained green olives with pimentos, and mix well. Stuff the trout with the mixture just before you bake it. (Place the extra rice in a buttered casserole and bake it with the trout for 30 minutes; baste occasionally with any juice from the trout.) Salt and pepper the trout and bake at 150°F for 45 minutes, or until the fish flakes with a fork. The rice stuffing may be made a day early and refrigerated. If you like crisp, brown trout skin, baste the fish with melted butter as it bakes. If you dislike skin, neatly remove it from the upper side of the trout before serving; then decorate the trout with scales made from a second can of sliced green olives and a gill formed with diced red pimentos; brush with melted butter. Serves 6 to 8. This dish can be served cold.—*Annette and Louis Bignami, April 1986*

Trout

TROUT FILLETS WITH MACADAMIA NUT SAUCE

2 lbs. skinless trout fillets
1 cup buttermilk
1 cup buttermilk biscuit mix
2 tsps. salt
Clarified butter or peanut oil
MACADAMIA NUT SAUCE
1 cup macadamia nuts, coarsely chopped
¼ lb. sweet butter or margarine, melted
2 tbsps. finely chopped parsley

If necessary, cut the fillets into serving-size portions. Place the trout in a single layer in a shallow pan. Pour the buttermilk over the fish and let it stand for 30 minutes, turning once. Combine the biscuit mix and salt. Remove the trout from the buttermilk and roll each fillet in the biscuit mix. Pan fry the fish in ½ an inch of hot oil for 3 to 4 minutes, turning once. The fillets should be yellow rather than brown. Drain on absorbent paper. Serve with the macadamia nut sauce. Make the sauce by browning the nuts in butter; then adding parsley. Makes 1 cup. Serves 4.—*A.J. McClane, February 1981*

A WEEK'S OUTING IN MAINE

About 4 o'clock Chick and I started out to try for some trout for dinner. Acting upon the advice of the guide, we did not try the pond, as he said it was too warm for the trout to bite well there. Instead we tried our luck on the little brook which flowed by our camp. We decided to use worms this time, as we were out to stock the larder and not for sport. We smeared our hands and faces with tar and oil, for the black flies hereabouts have very "hot feet." I was having great luck catching trout, though they ran rather small, when, glancing back, I saw Chick trying to land a big fellow. This monster put up a good fight but Chick at last succeeded in landing him. And what a beauty he was! He must have weighed at least 3 ½ pounds. On counting up we found we had caught 50, and though the trout were biting so well we concluded to return to camp. My! but didn't those fish disappear that night at the supper table.

J.A. Linscott
July 1898

I kill each trout with a blow to the back of the head, or break its back by hand, and clean it as soon as I can. Slit it up the belly from vent to gills, the gills from the head and pull everything free at one time. Use your thumbnail to clear the dark line along the spine, and wrap the trout. Try cooking trout over coals right beside the stream from which they came a short while before. They can be spitted on a sweet green wood stick and broiled briefly over the heat with only some salt and pepper in the body cavity, or they can be fried in butter or bacon drippings.

Bill Wolf
March 1956

TROUT STUFFED WITH CRABMEAT

4 trout, 12 to 14 oz. each, boned	1 tbsp. minced parsley
3 stale rolls	1 tsp. dried oregano
1 cup milk	Juice of ½ lemon
1 egg	½ tsp. Worcestershire sauce
1 egg yolk	Dash of Tabasco
⅓ cup raw bacon, chopped	Salt and pepper
⅓ cup onion, chopped	Melted butter
8 oz. crabmeat	Paprika

Make the stuffing first by soaking the rolls in milk, then squeeze them dry and drop them in a bowl with the eggs. Sauté the bacon and onion until the onion is limp and amber, not brown. Add the crabmeat and sauté for 5 minutes. Combine this with the bread mixture in the bowl and add all the other ingredients except the melted butter and paprika. Add salt and pepper to taste. The rolls should be broken into pieces, of course. Spread equal amounts of stuffing in each trout and fold closed. Brush the top half of each trout with melted butter, and sprinkle generously with paprika only during the last few minutes of cooking (paprika crystallizes under prolonged heat and turns bitter). Bake in a 400°F oven for 20 minutes or until the skin is brown and crisp.—A.J. McClane, February 1981

Trout

SHERIFF HOUSE TROUT

4 trout, 12 to 14 oz. each, boned

1 lb. sole fillets

3 egg whites

⅔ cup fresh heavy cream

Salt and white pepper to taste

Butter

SHERIFF HOUSE SAUCE

2 shallots, finely chopped

2 tbsps. butter

½ cup white Burgundy wine

1 oz. cognac

1 tbsp. fresh parsley, minced

Cut the sole fillets into small pieces and place in a food processor or blender. Beat, adding a little cold water until the sole has a smooth texture. Break the egg whites with a fork and beat these into the sole, a little at a time. Gradually beat the heavy cream into the mixture and season with salt and pepper. Spread some of this stuffing onto the inside of each trout. Reshape the fish and arrange in a fireproof casserole dish that has been well buttered. Wipe the exposed parts of the trout with more butter. Bake at 350°F for about 20 minutes. Cover with the sheriff house sauce; it can be made while the trout are baking: Sauté the shallots in butter just to soften them, then add the wine and boil for a few seconds. Reduce heat, add the cognac and parsley. Bring to a boil again while stirring, then pour the sauce over the trout. Serves 4.—*A.J. McClane, February 1981*

TROUT À LA CHARLES COTTON

Charles Cotton, the more or less forgotten man who wrote the second half of Izaak Walton's famed book on angling, apparently preferred his trout cooked in a court bouillon, or short broth. Nearly three centuries ago, he advised in his portion of <u>The Compleat Angler</u> to: "Give him (the trout) three scrotches with a knife to the bone, on one side only. After which take a clean kettle, and put in as much hard stale beer (but it must not be dead), vinegar, and a little white wine, and water, as will cover the fish you intend to boil; then throw into the liquor a good quantity of salt, the rind of a lemon, a handful of sliced horse-radish root, with a handsome little faggot of rosemary, thyme, and winter savory. Then set your kettle upon a quick fire of wood, and let your liquor boil up to the height before you put in your fish; and then, if there be many, put them in one by one, that they may not so cool the liquor as to make it fall. And whilst your fish is boiling, beat up the butter for your sauce with a ladleful or two of the liquor it is boiling in. And, being boiled enough, immediately pour the liquor from the fish; and, being laid in a dish, pour your butter upon it; and, strewing it plentifully over with shaved horse-radish, and a little pounded ginger, garnish your sides of your fish, and the fish itself with a sliced lemon or two, and serve it up."

The "handsome little faggot" he mentions is a bouquet garni, of course, of the several fresh herbs tied together with a string. Unless you grow your own in an herb garden, fresh rosemary, thyme and winter savory are hard to find, but the dried leaves (available in almost any large store in packets) can be substituted if you wish to try Charles Cotton's recipe.

Bill Wolf
March 1956

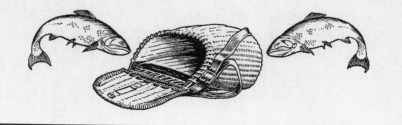

WALNUT STUFFED TROUT

This recipe best suits small, firm wild trout but even the softer hatchery trout can delight the most discerning palates when crusted with crisp walnuts and stuffed with spinach and mushrooms. Trout vary in size, so begin sautéing the larger ones first.

STUFFING

1 bunch fresh spinach or
     10-oz. package of frozen

1 tsp. fresh parsley, chopped

1 tsp. dried tarragon

Salt and pepper to taste

3 tbsps. butter or margarine

4 green onions, chopped

2 cups fresh mushrooms, sliced

4 10- to 12-inch trout

1 cup flour

¼ cup walnuts, finely chopped

⅛ tsp. salt

⅛ tsp. pepper

2 eggs, beaten

¼ cup butter or cooking oil

Cook the spinach and squeeze it dry. Mince it and season with parsley, tarragon, salt and pepper. Melt the butter in a skillet, add the onions and mushrooms and cook until soft. Add the spinach mixture, cook 5 minutes more, then cool. Clean the trout and pat it dry. Mix the flour, walnuts, salt and pepper in a shallow dish. Dip the trout into the beaten eggs, then into the flour/walnut mixture. Set the trout aside on wax paper for 10 minutes, then stuff the trout with the cooled spinach mixture. Heat butter or oil over medium heat, and brown the trout slowly for about 5 to 7 minutes on each side, or until it flakes and the stuffing is warmed through. Garnish with sautéed orange slices sprinkled with sugar.—*Annette and Louis Bignami, April 1986*

BAKED TROUT

Butter a baking dish, and put the cleaned trout, seasoned with salt and pepper on the inside of the body, in the dish. Place a thin film of water, not more than a few tablespoons, in the pan, plenty of chopped chives and chopped parsley, plus the juice of a whole lemon, and some extra salt and pepper. Bake in a moderate oven for 10 minutes, and make a cream sauce (melt the butter in a saucepan, add the flour, cook slightly but do not brown, gradually adding cream while stirring constantly) of the quantity desired. Pour the sauce over the fish, sprinkle liberally with bread crumbs and brown in the oven.

Bill Wolf
March 1956

POACHING: THE ART OF THE "BLUE TROUT"

Among the classic poached-fish dishes popular throughout Europe is "blue trout." The fish must be alive until the last instant, just before poaching, in order to change color. You can do it by using freshly killed trout a few hours out of the water. The blue color comes from the slime that keeps it waterproof. A trout that has dried out, been handled too much or frozen won't turn blue. Trout flavor is subtle and poaching enhances that delicate flavor. Small trout of about 10 inches in length are ideal for bluing.

A.J. McClane
February 1980

TRUITE AU BLEU (BLUE TROUT)

1 trout	1 tsp. coriander
1 qt. water	½ tsp. dill
1 small onion	½ tsp. rosemary
2 carrots, chopped	1 cup vinegar
2 cloves	Parsley, chopped

This is perfect for that speckled trout netted from the Fox River in Michigan, the river that inspired Hemingway to pen his short story "The Big Two-Hearted River." Okay, Hemingway may have been a jerk, but he knew his cooking. (This dish the Paris Ritz will still cook up on command, but bring a jacket, please.) Put the spices together in a sandwich bag with a twist-tie beforehand. Bring to a boil the quart of water, onion, carrots, cloves, coriander, dill and vinegar. Keep the fish alive as close to cooking time as possible. A Ziploc bag works wonders. Leave the head on the fish and lightly rinse him but do not, repeat, do not wipe off the slime. Put the fish in boiling water after slitting and cleaning. Let the water come to boil again and remove the pan from the heat and cover it, allowing it to stand at least 5 minutes. The eyeballs bug out white when done, but not to worry. Serve with a sprinkle of parsley and a Hemingway quote. Something about the earth moving will work. The trout's skin will be blue like clean water and summer sky.—*John Eckberg and David Lowery, May 1993*

Trout

TROUT MEUNIÈRE

In making trout meunière you may use cottonseed or some oil other than peanut, but the latter is preferred by most professionals.

6 whole 8- to 10-oz. trout, dressed
¼ lb. sweet butter
1 tsp. salt
½ tsp. pepper
½ cup flour
Peanut oil
2 lemons, quartered
12 parsley or watercress sprigs

Clarify the butter and set aside. Mix the salt and pepper with the flour and coat the fish inside and out with the seasoned flour. Pour the oil into a heavy skillet, using enough to keep the trout from sticking, and bring to a high heat. Add the trout, 2 or 3 at a time, cooking at a moderate temperature for 4 to 5 minutes on each side until brown. The tails, a gourmet bonus, should be crisp. Remove the trout to absorbent paper. Reheat the clarified butter until it's pale brown. Arrange the trout on a warm serving platter and pour the hot butter over each fish. Garnish with lemon wedges and parsley or watercress.—*A.J. McClane, February 1981*

TROUT MEUNIÈRE

Roll the required number of trout in flour seasoned with salt and pepper, then fry them briefly in plenty of hot sweet butter in a pan. Transfer them to a previously heated platter and keep warm while you: 1) Add enough butter to the pan to make ½ a cup for each 6 moderate-sized trout and bring up the heat until the butter foams. 2) Remove the pan from the fire and quickly stir in 1 tablespoon of lemon juice, then 3) Pour the sauce over the trout on the platter and serve at once, or pour it over the fish and thrust the fish under a broiler flame for a few moments of intense heat. Don't try to stir the lemon juice into the butter, but sprinkle it on the warm fish—which have been garnished with chopped, scalded parsley—and pour the foaming hot butter over this. On contact with the parsley, the butter will come to a froth. The main thing in fish cooked à la meunière is to have the butter sizzling hot when it is poured on. Also, the fish should be done just right, an art in itself. They should not be crisped in butter too hot, nor made soggy from lukewarm butter.

Bill Wolf
March 1956

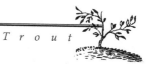

HOW TO FRY TROUT

Clean the fish and let them lie a few minutes wrapped singly in a clean, dry towel; season with pepper and salt; roll in cornmeal, fry in $1/3$ butter and $2/3$ lard; drain on a sieve and serve hot.

Henry Wurzbach
July 1898

TROUT MEUNIÈRE (AND WE AREN'T KIDDING)

6 brook trout
½ cup flour
Salt and pepper
Oil
3 tbsps. butter or margarine
Lemon wedges
1 tbsp. parsley, chopped

An excellent recipe for those times along New Hampshire's Pemigewasset River, when, like Henry David Thoreau so many years before, you're hunting for the falls and can't remember if you brought matches. Salvation is three pairs of brookies. Cut the trout, pat them dry, dip them inside and out with ½ a cup or so of seasoned flour. Cook the trout in oil about ¼-inch deep— enough to keep the fish from sticking. Fry for about 5 minutes, flipping halfway until golden brown and tender. Set the trout aside, melt the butter or margarine and pour it over the trout, which you've placed on a plate, surrounded by lemon wedges and sprinkled with parsley. Eat with your fingers and listen for the sounds of owl and wind.—*John Eckberg and David Lowery, May 1993*

Trout

LEMON TROUT

4 medium trout, chilled
6 tbsps. butter
Juice of 1 lemon
½ cup heavy cream
½ tsp. tarragon leaves

Clean the trout (head and tail removal is optional) and pat dry with paper towel. In a skillet over medium heat, melt 5 tablespoons of butter and fry the trout until brown—about 7 minutes per side, or until the flesh flakes with a fork. (The basic rule for cooking fish is 10 minutes per inch of thickness. The other rule is, If you can smell the fish cooking, the skillet is too hot.) Remove the trout to a warm platter and keep it warm. Melt the remaining tablespoon of butter and deglaze (scrape) the bottom of the pan; then add the lemon juice, cream and tarragon. Cook over low heat until the sauce thickens. Serve the sauce over the trout.—*Annette and Louis Bignami, May 1989*

FAMOUS TROUT RECIPES— THE SERVING OF TROUT

Trout should be garnished in keeping with their status in the fish world. Don't just throw them on a plate and put them on the table. On the other hand, don't overload the platter with fanciful decorations. All the garnishing needed are quarters of lemon and sprigs of bright green parsley; and keep the side dishes simple. The trout is the dinner. You can have potatoes and meat any old day.

Bill Wolf
March 1956

COURT BOUILLON

Fish are boiled or, preferably, poached in court bouillon as a means of cooking them before the application of a sauce. There are various court bouillons and an infinite variety of fish sauces—too many to give in detail here. A typical court bouillon will contain these ingredients: 3 quarts of water; 1 cup of vinegar; 12 peppercorns, roughly crushed; 2 teaspoons of salt; 2 carrots, scraped and sliced thin; 2 sliced onions; a bouquet garni of 2 bay leaves, 1 ounce or more of fresh parsley, and a little thyme tied together. Bring to a boil and simmer for nearly 1 hour, then strain. Some chefs advise putting the pepper in only during the last 10 minutes, else it will impart a slight bitterness. A court bouillon with white wine is made the same way, except the vinegar is substituted with equal parts white wine and water to make 3 quarts. Red wine court bouillon is made like the white wine product except red wine is substituted for the white, and in the proportion of 2 parts wine to 1 part water. Vinegar, wine and lemon juice have the virtue of "firming" the flesh of poached fish. If, however, you have trouble poaching fish without having them fall all apart when you lift them from the court bouillon, lower them into the liquid and lift them out with a wire basket.

Bill Wolf
March 1956

CORNMEAL TROUT

1 trout
Salt and pepper to taste
Cornmeal
3 tbsps. butter
2 tbsps. white wine

Clean, wash and drain the trout. Season it with salt and pepper and roll it in cornmeal or flour. Place 2 sheets of broiler foil on a rack over coals. Turn up the edges to keep the fat in. Melt the butter; when sizzling, place the fish on the foil. Cook 5 minutes on each side, or until brown. Pour the white wine over the fish during the last 5 minutes.—*Anonymous, April 1958*

Trout

TROUT AMANDINE

2 lbs. trout fillets
½ cup butter or margarine
½ cup unblanched almonds
⅓ cup sauterne
2 tsps. lemon juice
2 tbsps. parsley, chopped

Melt the butter, add the almonds, and cook slowly. Stir often until browned. Remove. Add the wine, lemon and parsley. Pour the sauce while hot over broiled or pan-fried fillets.—*Anonymous, April 1958*

TROUT AMANDINE—1956

This is just the same as trout meunière, with the addition of chopped or shredded blanched almonds, which you can buy at almost any nut roasting store. These are almonds that have been boiled or steamed enough to loosen the skin. You will have to shred them yourself. There are two ways to add almonds for trout amandine (and by the way, almonds work in some mysterious way to impart a new flavor to things). 1) Stir 2 large tablespoons of shredded almonds into the butter before the final heating and cook for 1 minute or 2 while rocking the pan; then pour them over the fish, or 2) Place the almonds on the trout on a platter, pour the sizzling butter over the fish, and place under a broiler flame until the almonds are lightly roasted.

Bill Wolf
March 1956

SHORE LUNCH—TROUT

Trout, especially lake trout, can be an exceptional delight either for a shore lunch or at home if baked with a little ingenuity. Their flesh contains oil, which makes it difficult to fry suitably in deep fat—a favorite cooking method for walleyes, pike and many other fish. Here are three ways our guide, Garry Powers, cooked our lake trout on the shore of Great Bear Lake, Northwest Territories, Canada. Each method is simple, and the result is a great deal more delicious than fried lake trout. Garry followed one basic procedure, but varied his recipe with either ketchup, beer or hot sauce as flavoring. Each gave the fish a wonderfully unique, piquant flavor. Here is how Garry prepared it: First, he filleted the trout. Then he spread butter in the center of sizable pieces of aluminum foil. A generous portion of lake trout was placed on each. Next he buttered the top and side of each fillet and sprinkled it with salt and pepper. Then he placed sliced potatoes and onions atop the fish. When ketchup or hot sauce was the desired flavoring he spread the fish with it before placing the potatoes and onions on, then added more sauce. The fish was then sealed tightly in the foil. When the beer was used, Garry made sacks of the foil holding the fish-potato-onion concoction and poured the liquid on it from the open end, filling each sack about halfway. Then he carefully sealed the open ends. Each foil sack was placed on the hot coals of our campfire and baked on each side for 10 minutes.

Hank Bradshaw
March 1967

BROILED TROUT

2 6- to 8-inch trout
Salt and pepper
Olive oil
4 tbsps. butter, softened
1 tbsp. parsley, chopped
Splash of lemon juice

Select 2 pan-sized trout, draw them and wipe dry. Season with salt and pepper, inside and out. Brush with oil. Broil 8 minutes to the side or until golden brown. Cream the butter until soft and add the salt, pepper, chopped parsley and lemon juice. Place a dollop of the butter combination on cooked trout.—*Charles R. Meyer, April 1959*

Trout

SIMPLE BAKED TROUT

2 trout
Salt and pepper to taste
4 tbsps. butter
Parsley
Lemon

Simplicity should be the rule with such a delicacy. Season your selected trout lightly with salt and pepper; spread butter over the entire surface. Place the fish on a baking pan and bake until golden brown—about 15 minutes. Serve with nothing more than parsley and lemon.—*Charles R. Meyer, April 1959*

HOLLANDAISE SAUCE

4 egg yolks
1 tbsp. light cream
1 tbsp. tarragon vinegar
$\frac{1}{4}$ lb. butter
1 tsp. lemon juice
Salt
Cayenne pepper

In a double boiler over low heat, beat the egg yolks with the cream and vinegar using a wire whisk. Continue beating the yolks until they begin to thicken. Add $\frac{1}{3}$ of the butter; when that's melted, add the remainder bit by bit. Beat until the sauce is thick. Should the mixture curdle, immediately beat in 1 or 2 tablespoons of boiling water to rebind the emulsion. Add the lemon juice, salt and cayenne to taste. Set the pan in lukewarm water until serving time. Makes about $1\frac{1}{2}$ cups.

A.J. McClane
February 1980

TROUT BOURGUIGNONNE

This is for 6 trout weighing about ¾ of a pound each. Salt and pepper well. Place them in a baking pan and spread 2 tablespoons of finely chopped mild onion or shallots over. Use a string and tie together 1 large bay leaf, 1 stalk of parsley leaves, 1 sprig of thyme. Put this bouquet garni in the pan and bring 2 cups of Burgundy wine to a boil. Pour the wine over the fish and cover them with foil, then bake in a moderate oven for 15 to 20 minutes. Lift the trout from the pan when cooked, draining them as much as possible, and strain the wine in the pan into a smaller pan. Put the trout aside on a heated platter, and boil the strained wine until it is reduced to about 1½ cups. Remove from the heat and immediately stir in 3 beaten egg yolks, a bit at a time, stirring constantly. Return the sauce to the heat, still stirring vigorously, until it comes to a boil, whereupon you remove it from the heat and reseason if necessary. Squeeze lemon juice over the fish, pour the sauce over them and serve.

Bill Wolf
March 1956

POACHED FISH (NOT AS IN "A BIG DADDY BASS POACHED FROM A COUNTRY CLUB POND AT MIDNIGHT")

If you find yourself along the Little Divide Lake and stream in Wyoming's Wind River Range, half-frozen in July since you dropped your sleeping bag in a creek, all is well if there's a nice cutthroat or Dolly Varden belly-up in a bed of fern.

1 lemon, sliced ¼-inch thick
2 bay leaves
1 tbsp. parsley, chopped
Several small trout

Slice the lemon. Place a bed of the slices at the bottom of a pan. Add 2 bay leaves and sprinkle with parsley—lots of it. Pour water over the slices, just enough to cover the lemon. Bring to a near-boil. Place the fish onto the lemon bed. Do not allow the mixture to boil. Cover the pan with foil, a big pot or even your hat, and cook 6 to 8 minutes until the fish is tender. Serve with a flourish and don't drop any in the dirt. If dropped, brush off the twigs and eat it anyway.—*John Eckberg and David Lowery, May 1993*

Trout

MALABAR CURRIED TROUT SOUP

2 lbs. trout fillets, cut into
    1-inch cubes
4 tbsps. butter
2 cups onions, chopped
2 celery stalks, sliced
2 carrots, chopped

1 tbsp. curry powder
4 cups fish or chicken stock
1 tbsp. parsley flakes
1/3 cup uncooked rice
1 cup heavy cream
    or half-and-half
Salt and pepper to taste

Melt the butter in a saucepan and add the onions, celery, carrots and curry powder. Cover and cook for 10 minutes over low heat or until the vegetables are tender. Add the stock, parsley, trout and rice. Cover and cook for 20 minutes or until the fish flakes when tested with a fork and the rice is tender. Add the cream or half-and-half and simmer for 10 minutes more. Season with salt and pepper. Cooled and blended, this soup slides smoothly down the throat on hot, humid summer days. And ½-inch cubes of old homemade or French bread, toasted in butter over low heat until golden brown, add textural contrast. Serves 4 to 6.—*Annette and Louis Bignami, April 1986*

TROUT SALAD

Boil a medium-sized lake trout in slightly salted water, take up, remove the bone and skin, break the fish into flakes and put into spiced vinegar for 2 hours. Drain, put in a salad bowl on a bed of lettuce leaves, pour over 1/2 a cup of mayonnaise, and garnish with hard-boiled eggs.

Henry Wurzbach
July 1898

TROUT
À LA CHAMBORD

Make a forcemeat with 1 pound of boneless fish by pounding it well in a mortar, adding the whites of 3 eggs. When well-pounded, add ½ a pint of cream, ½ a teaspoon of salt, and a little white pepper and nutmeg. Mix well and use it to stuff three ½-pound trout. Well butter a deep baking dish and lay in the trout, add ½ a glass of white wine, a bouquet of herbs, and salt and pepper. Bake for 15 minutes, basting often. Put the fish on a dish to keep hot. Remove the gravy to a saucepan, add 1 truffle and 4 mushrooms, sliced; also a glass of wine. Heat and pour over the fish.

Henry Wurzbach
July 1898

SMOKING RAINBOWS

4 rainbow trout, whole, cleaned and without gills
1 qt. fresh water
¼ cup salt
½ cup honey
1 tsp. white pepper, freshly cracked
½ cup lemon juice
3 tsps. fresh dill
Additional water to cover

The little electric smokers generate just enough heat to actually smoke-cure fish, but the first step is the brine cure. Simmer the water and ingredients until the salt is dissolved and the honey blended. Pour the mixture into a crock tall enough for the fish to stand on end. (Do not use wooden or aluminum crocks.) Soak 4-inch fish for 4 hours, a few hours more for larger fish. Stir the liquid occasionally. Remove the fish and rinse with cold water. Expose them to air for 1 hour. A glaze called a pellicle will form over the fish, which indicates they are ready for smoking. Plug in the electric gizmo and allow a dense smoke to build up with the wood shavings. With whole fish I hang each one from a small "S" hook made from a wire coat hanger and inserted through the mandible of the fish. Since the objective of smoking is both to flavor and to cure the flesh, you should spread open the body cavity with a toothpick somewhere near the vent. Although the meat has already been brine-cured, it is important for it to dry thoroughly as well as take on the unique smoky flavor. After you have burned 2 cups of wood shavings, the meat is probably smoky enough. Test for dryness with a fork, pricking the largest fish. I allow 3 hours at 110°F for thoroughly cured fish.—*S.G.B. Tennant Jr., May 1984*

PICKLED FISH

1 lb. smelts

6 oz. (about 1 cup) salt

1 qt. water

1 qt. distilled white vinegar

1 tsp. sugar

Your choice of pickling spices:

   Chili peppers, cayenne, allspice,

   nutmeg cinnamon, cardamom,

   coriander, black peppercorns,

   mustard seed, cloves

4 to 6 white onions, sliced

Fish high in oil content make the best pickled fish: herring, salmon, mackerel, shad, saltwater smelt, tuna and whitefish. The main ingredients in the pickling process are vinegar, water, salt and spices. Use white distilled vinegar of 4 to 6 percent acidity. Avoid using hard water for pickling, since the minerals in it cloud the pickling solution and give it an undesirable taste. Use fresh, whole spices instead of powdered—a mixture (your own or bought ready-made) that includes some or all of the following: chili peppers, cayenne, allspice, nutmeg, cinnamon, cardamom, coriander, black peppercorns, mustard seed and cloves. Use glass dishes (metal reacts with the vinegar). The simplest way to pickle fish is to brine the fillets for 7 days. Sprinkle iodized salt over the fillets in a ratio of ⅓ salt per pound of fish. Store in a cool (45° to 55°F) dark place. Then soak them in slowly running, cold, fresh water for a couple of hours—until the fish has a barely salted taste. Cut the fish into bite-size pieces. Next, combine equal parts distilled vinegar and water. Add a small amount of sugar to take some of the edge off the vinegar and to give a sweet-sour effect to the liquid. Wrap a few tablespoons of spices in cheesecloth and suspend the bag in the vinegar mixture while bringing it to a boil. Simmer for 10 minutes. Pack sterilized pint jars by alternating layers of fish pieces and slices of white onion. Sprinkle in a few pinches of spices as you fill the jars. Pour the hot vinegar over the fish and close the jars. Let the fish marinate a few days before serving. It will keep for weeks in the refrigerator. This recipe is very basic and is just a foundation upon which to experiment and develop your own pickling recipes. You can substitute dry white wine or burgundy for up to 25 percent of the vinegar. Otherwise, keep the vinegar concentration at least 3 percent (half 6-percent vinegar and half water).—*Stuart E. Mork, June 1987*

SMELT ARE TASTY WHEN PROPERLY PREPARED

How to prepare the silvery little fish known as smelt may be a problem for some housewives, but it's not a problem for Dr. John Van Oosten of the Great Lakes fisheries investigations for the United States Bureau of Fisheries. Here is what the good Doc submits as suggestions for cooking these fine little fish, which have become so abundant of recent years in many waters adjacent to the Great Lakes and in the big waters, themselves. "A gourmet has his smelt fried crisp and eats bones and all," declares Van Oosten. "Smelt are considered most palatable when rolled in flour, corn meal or cracker meal and fried in plenty of fat. Some prefer to mix a little brown sugar with the cornmeal. Butter or a mixture of $1/4$ butter and $3/4$ vegetable shortening or bacon grease imparts an excellent flavor. The fish should be fried until golden brown." Smelt also can be baked. One method consists of rolling the smelt in flour and placing them in a shallow pan. The fish are covered with slices of bacon, seasoned with salt and pepper, and baked in a moderately hot oven until brown. A second method consists of placing slices of bacon, tomatoes, chopped green peppers and minced onions between layers of smelt in a deep baking dish or casserole. The top should be sprinkled with cracker crumbs and dotted with butter. After the mixture has been baked thoroughly, it should be browned in a very hot oven and served immediately. Smoke smelt by soaking in a moderately strong salt brine for 24 hours, rinse in fresh water and smoke over a smoldering fire of hardwood for several hours. Pickled smelt make a very palatable appetizer. The fish are soaked in a strong salt solution for several days; then they are soaked in several changes of fresh water for 24 hours. After draining, the fish are packed in a stone crock together with slices of raw onion and lemon, bay leaves, whole black pepper, mustard seed and a little salt. For each 2 pounds of fish heat $1 1/8$ quarts of mild vinegar to the boiling point. Pour the hot vinegar over the fish and condiments in the crock and cover securely. Let the fish stand in a cool place for several days before using.

Cal Johnson
May 1940

PIKE PÂTÉ DUBONNET

3 cups pike fillets, skinned, boned
    and roughly cubed (about
    1 ½ lbs.)
½ cup heavy cream
2 anchovy fillets without capers
2 eggs, lightly beaten
4 scallions, chopped with
    1 inch of green
2 tbsps. butter
2 cups fresh cooked asparagus,
    chopped and fibers discarded

(or 20 oz. of well drained,
    canned asparagus spears)
4 tbsps. Dubonnet Blanc
2 tsps. fresh basil, chopped,
    or 1 tsp. dried
1 tbsp. fresh dill, chopped,
    or 1 tsp. dried
2 tsps. salt
1 ½ tsps. coriander, dried
1 tsp. fresh-ground white pepper
¾ tsp. ground cayenne pepper

The pike should be boned and cubed for measuring, then chilled. Simmer the cream in a saucepan and add the anchovies, stirring. Remove the saucepan from the heat and stir until the anchovies are dissolved. Pour the cream and anchovies over the pike cubes, add the eggs and whirl the ingredients in a food processor for 10 to 15 seconds. Remove the mixture to a bowl and refrigerate. Soften the chopped scallions in the 2 tablespoons of butter, taking care not to brown them. Remove to the cleaned processor bowl and combine with the asparagus, Dubonnet, herbs and spices, and whirl vigorously. Fold this into the chilled fish mixture and combine the two until they are mixed. Butter the inside of a 6-cup pâté or terrine mold (or loaf pan) as well as the tops and bottoms of 2 wax paper sheets cut to fit inside the bottom of the mold. Place 1 sheet of the wax paper on the bottom of the mold, then add the combined mixture. Distribute it carefully to all corners, and smooth the top, level with the pan. Cover with the second sheet of wax paper, and seal tightly with a lid or heavy aluminum foil. Heat the oven to 350°F. Place the mold in a roasting pan surrounded by 1 inch of hot water and cook for 1 hour, or until the mixture reaches an internal temperature of 150°F. Remove and allow the pâté to cool for 30 minutes. Remove the lid and press the pâté with about 2 pounds of weight into a mold; refrigerate overnight. Unmold and serve.—*S.G.B. Tennant Jr., July 1984*

PIKE À LA
IZAAK WALTON

Clean the pike through the gills, cutting as little as possible into the belly. Reserve the liver and shred it, adding a minute amount of dried thyme, sweet marjoram and savory. Add to 1 pound of butter, a few anchovy fillets and as many pickled oysters as you wish. Since you most likely won't have pickled oysters, buy a jar of the smoked oysters available at most good delicatessens. Add the shredded liver to the butter, anchovies and oysters. Note: 1 pound of butter is given as an arbitrary measurement—use more or less, gauging by the size of the fish. Stuff the fish, and sew up the gill as securely as you can to retain the butter mixture inside when it starts to melt. Don't scale the fish, just wipe it clean. Thrust the rotisserie spit through it lengthwise. Split several green sticks of birch or other "sweet" wood, and truss these lengthwise on the body with a fairly heavy cord—this is to keep the meat from falling off the spit as the fish cooks. Then roast it slowly, basting it frequently as the spit turns with a good claret wine, as well as crushed anchovies and melted butter mixed together. Use the drippings that fall into the pan for basting, too. Rub the serving dish severely with garlic, place the pike on the dish, cut the cord and remove the splints, pour over the fish the sauce from the drip pan, adding more butter if needed, and squeeze over it the juice of several oranges. To serve, lay back the skin and remove the flesh.

Bill Wolf
July 1956

Pike

CÔTELETTES DE BROCHETTE PURÉE DE CHAMPIGNONS

For this you must prepare in advance the following: A mushroom purée, a chou paste, pike forcemeat and béchamel sauce. The recipes for these will be given as we go along. The chou paste and béchamel sauce are used in the forcemeat. The forcemeat, in turn, is employed to make cutlets, which are poached and then sautéed and served with a mushroom purée.

CHOU PASTE
Pinch of salt
6 tbsps. butter
1 ½ cups water
1 cup flour
6 eggs
PIKE FORCEMEAT CUTLETS
1 lb. pike fillets
Chou paste
½ lb. butter, plus several tbsps.
    for sautéing cutlets
Salt, pepper and a pinch
    of ground nutmeg
4 egg yolks, beaten
4 tbsps. cream

2 whole eggs, slightly beaten
Bread crumbs
BÉCHAMEL SAUCE
8 tbsps. butter
⅔ cup flour
6 cups milk, boiling
Pinch of pepper
Pinch of nutmeg
½ tsp. salt
1 onion, peeled and whole
1 clove
Pinch of thyme
Several sprigs of parsley
1 bay leaf
Melted butter
2 eggs, beaten

PURÉE DE CHAMPIGNONS

1 lb. fresh mushrooms
4 tbsps. butter
1 ½ cups béchamel sauce
4 tbsps. cream
Salt, pepper and nutmeg

Clean 1 pound of fresh mushrooms and grind. Sauté this in 2 tablespoons of butter. Measure 1 ½ cups of the béchamel sauce, add the cream, and reduce over heat until it simmers down by about ⅔. Mix the mushroom purée with this sauce, season with salt, pepper and grated nutmeg, let it simmer for 5 minutes, take off the fire and stir in the remaining butter.

Bill Wolf
July 1956

Put the pike fillets through the meat grinder several times, then work in a mortar to produce the smoothest paste possible. Next add the flesh to an ordinary chou paste, which serves the purpose of binding the fish together for the poaching and frying that will follow.

TO MAKE THE CHOU PASTE: Add a pinch of salt and the butter to 1 ½ cups of water in a pan,

QUENELLES DE BROCHETTE

Form the quenelles of pike forcemeat with a tablespoon, or make them into little rolls. Put in a buttered skillet. Cover with boiling salted water and poach until firm. Drain on paper and serve with any fish sauce you like, which might be the béchamel or the mushroom purée. Your guests will never know the care and effort that went into the forcemeat and your only reward will be the pleasure of accomplishment and watching the end-product consumed and enjoyed. That's all a good cook gets out of cooking. The fish is the thing, the culinary triumph.

Bill Wolf
July 1956

and bring to a boil. Remove from the heat and add the flour. Return to a high flame and stir constantly until it no longer sticks to the spoon. Remove it from the fire again and, one by one, stir in the 6 eggs. Take 11 ounces of this chou paste, put it in a mixing bowl and mash into it a bit at a time the pound of ground pike flesh, ½-pound of butter, several tablespoons of cold béchamel sauce, and seasonings of salt, pepper and a bit of ground nutmeg.

TO MAKE THE BÉCHAMEL SAUCE: Melt the butter, add the flour, stir and cook briefly—a few seconds until the raw flour taste is eliminated. Add the boiled milk, gradually at first, stirring all the while over heat. Season with a pinch of pepper, a pinch of nutmeg, and ½ a teaspoon of salt. Bring to a boil slowly, then add the whole peeled onion, stuck with a clove, then the thyme, fresh parsley, and bay leaf. Let this boil gently for 20 minutes or so, stirring frequently, then strain it through a fine sieve into a bowl and pour melted butter over it.

Now you are ready to form the cutlets. To the cold forcemeat add 4 beaten egg yolks and 4 tablespoons of cream. The actual steps in making cutlets from the forcemeat you have prepared are: 1) Form into cutlets, using about 3 ounces for each one. Keep your hands floured. Put the cutlets into a buttered skillet. 2) Cover with salted boiling water and poach gently until firm to the touch; about 10 minutes. 3) Lift out the cutlets, drain them, plunge them into cold water and take them out immediately. Wipe dry. 4) Beat 2 eggs to coat each cutlet completely, then roll it in bread crumbs. Let the breaded cutlets dry for ½ an hour. 5) Sauté the cutlets in foaming hot butter until golden brown. 6) Arrange on a hot plate, forming a circle. Into the middle, pour the *purée de champignons* and serve immediately.—*Bill Wolf, July 1956*

Pike

PIKE IN THE ITALIAN MANNER

3 lbs. pike
1 tbsp. chopped parsley
1 tsp. pepper
1 carrot, diced
1 onion, minced
1 garlic clove, crushed
1 carrot, sliced
1 tbsp. olive oil
½ tsp. salt
3 cups good dry red wine
¼ cup butter
1 tbsp. flour

KING LUDWIG'S FAVORITE RECIPE

King Ludwig II of Bavaria is known as the Crazy King who almost bankrupted Bavaria by building castles in the Alps. In addition, he loved to eat game and fish. His favorite recipe was for pike Hechtenkraut. A pike was baked and then chilled and cut into small pieces. Sauerkraut was cooked with browned onions and butter. A dish was lined with bread crumbs. Alternating layers of fish and sauerkraut were laid in the dish, topped with more bread crumbs and more butter, then browned in the oven.

Almanac
July 1990

Make a marinade from the parsley, pepper, diced carrot, minced onion, crushed garlic clove, sliced carrot, olive oil, salt and red wine. In this, marinate for at least two hours 3 pounds of pike cut into serving size pieces. Then poach (simmer) the fish in the marinade for 15 to 20 minutes. Lift out the fish pieces gently and keep warm while you strain the vegetables from the sauce and cook the strained liquid another 5 minutes. Melt the butter and blend in the flour. Add this to the sauce to thicken it slightly. Put the fish back in the sauce and serve hot.—*Bill Wolf, July 1956*

TROPHY WALLEYE STEW

5 lbs. trophy walleye fillets, cut into large chunks
¼ lb. butter
4 tbsps. flour
2 cups small white onions, peeled
2 cups dry red wine
2 cups chicken stock (or fish fumet)
Salt and pepper to taste
1 cup fresh okra, chopped
(optional, for sharper taste; canned or frozen may be substituted) or assorted fresh vegetables to taste
1 cup fresh corn
1 bouquet garni (cheesecloth pouch filled with 1 tbsp. each fresh parsley and thyme, 1 bay leaf and 1 garlic clove, split)
Croutons

Melt ½ the butter in a small saucepan. Add the flour and stir constantly over low heat until the mixture browns, forming a roux. Add the remaining butter and the onions and stir for 10 minutes. Remove the roux to a larger stew pot, add the wine and stock (or fumet) and bring the sauce to a boil. Reduce the heat and simmer for 30 minutes. Add salt and pepper and stir. Add the bouquet garni and vegetables, stirring for a few minutes. Add the fish chunks and cook over medium-high heat, uncovered, for an additional 30 minutes or so. Add wine or stock as necessary to maintain a heavy sauce consistency and also to avoid scorching. Remove the bouquet garni and ladle the stew into individual platters or shallow bowls, sprinkling each with browned croutons. Serve with lemon wedges. Serves 8.—*S.G.B. Tennant Jr., March 1984*

W a l l e y e

WALLEYE ROE

2 lbs. walleye roe
1 cup flour
1 cup cornflakes, ground
1 tsp. salt

1 tsp. fresh black pepper, ground
2 tbsps. butter
2 tbsps. lemon juice
3 tbsps. chopped parsley
½ tsp. dried tarragon

Wash the roe sacs in cold water immediately before cooking. The force of the tap may tear the membrane, so a bowl of cold water is suggested. Remove and pat dry thoroughly, then remove the gristly thick membrane that lies between the two sacs. The sacs should then be separated and pricked gently with a knife point, as you would pierce a sausage casing. Mix the flour, cornflakes, salt and pepper, and dust gently over the roe sacs. The roe should then be set aside for ¼ of an hour. Use enough butter to coat the skillet and warm it till it froths. Poach the roe about 5 minutes a side, or long enough to brown it thoroughly. It should be cooked well inside, and the best way to do this is to cook it over low heat. When done, remove the roe. To the skillet add more butter if necessary, then the lemon juice, parsley and tarragon. Stir briskly. Pour this sauce over the individual roe servings and garnish with lemon wedges.—*S.G.B. Tennant Jr., March 1984*

SAVOR THIS DELICACY

If you take a trophy walleye this spring, save the roe. Roe won't freeze, and it won't keep, but sautéed fresh it is one of the great delicacies that nature has to offer. There is nothing objectionable about taking fish during the spawn where lawful. As long as a positive population balance is maintained, sportsmen will have access to a seasonal treat that's almost better than the prize money. Just down the river from Fairfield, Arkansas is a little place where they poach the roe in clarified butter. I have borrowed their recipe.

S.G.B. Tennant Jr.
March 1984

CREAMED WALLEYE

Ever try walleyed pike creamed? With this recipe, for which I thank the Lake Breezes Resort at Three Lakes, Wisconsin, you'll need 2 to 4 walleyes weighing about 1 1/2 pounds each. Salt and pepper them, put in a shallow pan with plenty of butter and a little water, and bake. About 15 minutes before they are done, pour about 1/2 a cup of cream over them. Do not cover at any time and serve as soon as taken from oven. Incidentally, baked fish must be strictly fresh or it will fall to pieces.

Duncan Hines, with Bradford Angier
March 1959

FISHY FIESTA— SEVICHE

1 lb. walleye fillets
6 limes, juiced
1 jar salsa
Crackers

Cut the fillets into strips 1/4-inch thick. For each pound of fish, squeeze the juice from 6 limes (lemons may be substituted). Put the fish into a deep, nonmetallic bowl and pour the lime juice over it. Marinate the fish for 6 to 8 hours in a refrigerator or an ice chest. Mix in a can of salsa and eat with crackers.—*A.D. Livingston, August 1994*

Walleye

KEY LIME BARBECUE

Most barbecue sauces have a tomato base. This one, which comes from the Florida Keys, is quite different. This sauce is very good with such freshwater species as walleye and bass, or such saltwater species as grouper and dolphin.

2 or 3 walleye, about 2 pounds each
½ cup butter
2 cups brown sugar
1 cup fresh lime juice
½ cup soy sauce
Salt to taste

Skin and fillet the fish. To make a marinade and basting sauce, melt the butter and brown sugar in a saucepan, then stir in the lime juice and soy sauce. Let the sauce cool. Put the fillets into a glass or nonmetallic container and pour the sauce over them. Marinate the fish for 1 hour. When you're ready to begin cooking, build a charcoal fire (or heat the gas grill) and let it burn down to a moderate heat. Grease the grid so the fillets won't stick; if you prefer, use a hinged basket. Remove the fish from the marinade, then warm the liquid for basting. Grill the fish for 5 minutes, basting once. Turn, baste, sprinkle on a little salt if you want, and cook for 3 or 4 minutes, or until the fish flakes easily when tested with a fork.—*A.D. Livingston, July 1991*

WIRE-BASKET COOKING

Add hickory chips to the charcoal if you want a smoked flavor. Also, a larger whole fish of 4 pounds or so can be used. It's best grilled in a fish-shaped wire basket. Put the grid 8 inches or so above the fire and cook for a much longer time. It helps to baste the fish often and to turn it several times during cooking.

A.D. Livingston
July 1991

BAKED ROCK

Mrs. Randolph Harrison has been a friend of mine for many years, the wife of a fishing-boat captain and lodge proprietor at Tilghman, Maryland, famed for the table she sets with seafood from Chesapeake Bay. Like so many good cooks, Lola Harrison knows the arts and blandishments of subtle seasoning, but frequently relies upon absolute simplicity, as in her "baked rock." Although I believe she could make a real rock tender, the name refers to rockfish, or striped bass. It can be used with any similar fish of like size. Take a striped bass of 3 1/2 to 5 pounds, wash it quickly and drain it. Put it in a baking pan, cover it with at least 1/2 a pound of bacon in strips. Pour over it 1 1/2 cans of tomatoes, or the equivalent in fresh chopped tomatoes in summer. Add lots of rings from sliced onions, and season well with salt and pepper. Then bake 2 1/2 hours in a moderate oven, basting frequently with the liquor that will start forming in the bottom of the pan. The vegetables and bit of fat from the bacon will gradually blend together into the most delicious sauce. Serve by transferring the fish to a heated platter and pour the sauce over it. Try this same recipe with young channel bass, with large bluefish, California white sea bass, or any fish large enough to lend itself to baking.

Bill Wolf
April 1956

STRIPED BASS BAKED

5-lb. striped bass
8 tbsps. butter
1 onion, chopped fine
1 celery stalk, chopped
1 cup mushrooms, sliced
5 slices stale bread
Salt and pepper to taste
Parsley, chopped
Oil

Make the stuffing first by melting the butter in a large skillet. Sauté the chopped onion, celery and mushrooms. Break about 5 slices of stale bread into small pieces. Place these in the skillet, add salt, pepper and chopped parsley. Turn off the heat and mix thoroughly. Stuff the body cavity of the fish with the dressing. Wipe the fish on the outside with vegetable oil and place it on a rack in a roasting pan also coated with oil. Bake for about 45 minutes in a 325°F oven.—*Charles R. Meyer, May 1959*

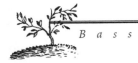

Bass

GRILLED FISH STEAKS

Here's a recipe that can be used with striped bass or any large fish of good flavor. The steaks should be cut to a uniform thickness. (In my vocabulary, a fish steak is a cross-section of the fish containing a segment of the backbone.) I recommend a thickness of about 1 inch.

Fish steaks	*White pepper*
Lemons	*Butter or margarine*
Garlic salt	*Mild paprika*
	Salt (optional)

Moisten each steak on both sides with freshly squeezed lemon juice, then sprinkle lightly with garlic salt and white pepper. After seasoning, stack the fish steaks atop one another and let them sit for several hours in the refrigerator. When you are ready to cook, build a charcoal fire in your grill and position the rack about 4 inches from the hot coals. Take the steaks out of the refrigerator. When the coals are almost ready, melt about ⅛-inch of butter or margarine in the bottom of a skillet. Using tongs, flip-flop each steak in the butter, hold it up to drain quickly, then put it on the grill. Keep the butter warm in the skillet, adding more if you need to. After 4 minutes, dip each steak in butter again and grill the reverse side for 4 minutes. Then sprinkle the steaks (both sides) lightly with white pepper and rather heavily with a mild paprika. Then grill each side for another minute or 2 until they are done.—*A.D. Livingston, July 1991*

CAMP VARIATION

When you cook breakfast, leave the bacon drippings in the frying pan—if you catch a fish large enough to cut into steaks, you'll be all set for supper. Warm the bacon grease, flip-flop the steaks in it, sprinkle both sides with lemon-pepper seasoning, and grill over campfire coals for a few minutes each side. Remember, however, that coals from a campfire are usually much hotter than charcoal, so watch what you're doing, unless you like the flavor of burnt fish.

A.D. Livingston
July 1991

TARTAR SAUCE

You have never eaten tartar sauce until you have made your own. That which comes in jars, or even that served in the best seafood houses, is an unworthy substitute for fresh sauce. For each cup of finest-quality mayonnaise, prepare and add these ingredients: 1 tablespoon heaped high with finely minced onions, 1 equally generous tablespoon of chopped olives, 2 tablespoons of India relish or chopped pickles, 1 handful of chopped parsley and 1 heaping teaspoon of prepared mustard. You can add 1 teaspoon of rinsed, chopped capers if you like their nice saltiness.

Bill Wolf
April 1956

STRIPER NUGGETS WITH SAUCE

1 lb. striped bass fillet, skinned
4 cups oil
2 eggs, lightly beaten
1 cup bread crumbs
½ tsp. garlic powder
1 tsp. parsley flakes
1 tbsp. grated Parmesan cheese
¼ tsp. salt
¼ tsp. pepper
DILL MUSTARD SAUCE
1 cup Dijon mustard
1 cup sour cream
3 tbsps. dillweed

Combine the sauce ingredients and keep it cool until needed. Heat the oil to 375°F in a deep fryer or saucepan. Trim the fish into 1 ½-inch cubes. Beat the eggs lightly. Mix the bread crumbs with the garlic, parsley, cheese, salt and pepper. Dip the fish cubes into the egg, then into the seasoned bread crumbs. Fry a few pieces at a time to a deep, golden brown. Drain on paper towels. Keep warm and serve with dill-mustard sauce. Serves up to 4.—*Annette and Louis Bignami, May 1989*

Turkey

ROASTED WILD TURKEY

12- to 13-lb. wild turkey

A fresh wild turkey should be browned initially at 450°F, then continued at 350°F until done. Foil should be used if the breast begins to brown unduly.—*S.G.B. Tennant Jr., November 1985*

ALABAMA CORN BREAD STUFFING

4 cups corn bread, made without sugar
3 cups wild rice, cooked
1 cup turkey drippings or chicken stock
1 cup pork sausage, cooked
1 tbsp. butter
2 medium onions, chopped
4 celery stalks with leaves, chopped
1/2 cup parsley, chopped
1 tsp. each salt and black pepper
1 tsp. chili pequine (or crushed red pepper)
1/2 tsp. rubbed sage
1/4 tsp. each thyme and rosemary
2 eggs, hard-boiled, chopped

M ake the corn bread the day before. Soak the wild rice overnight, then boil for 5 minutes in stock, adding enough water to prevent sticking; drain and retain a 1/2 cup of the stock. Sauté the sausage until it's brown, then remove and chop. Sauté the onions and celery in the sausage drippings until softened, adding butter if needed. Mix all the ingredients, seasonings and eggs in a casserole; adjust the seasoning, adding the 1/2 cup of stock. Cover the casserole with foil and bake at 350°F for 30 minutes. To produce an attractive crust, remove the cover for the last 10 minutes. Allow 1 cup per serving. This makes about 12 cups, enough to stuff a 13-pound bird if you prefer.

S.G.B. Tennant Jr.
November 1985

PUMPKIN BRIOCHE

1 cup cooked pumpkin
   (or equal canned)
1 cup dark brown sugar
1 pack active dry yeast
3 tbsps. water
3 1/2 cups flour
3/4 tsp. salt
1/2 tsp. cinnamon and nutmeg
1/4 tsp. ground cloves
4 eggs
1/2 lb. butter, melted and cooled
Egg wash (1 beaten egg, 1 tbsp. water, pinch of salt)

Warm the pumpkin in a double boiler over low heat. Mix the sugar, yeast and water. Allow the yeast to activate, then stir the mixture into the pumpkin. In a food processor mix the flour, salt and spices, then add the pumpkin mixture and eggs and blend thoroughly. Slowly pour in the butter, blending. Scrape the dough into an oiled mixing bowl, cover and let rise for 3 hours, until tripled. Punch down, cover tightly and refrigerate overnight. Butter muffin tins for 24 rolls. Turn the dough onto a floured board and divide into 24 pieces. Press the dough into the tins, making a cut across each piece. Cover and let rise again. Heat the oven to 425°F. Brush the tops with egg wash. Bake for 5 minutes, reduce to 350°F and bake for 3 to 5 minutes more.

S.G.B. Tennant Jr.
November 1985

TURKEY GIBLET GRAVY

Turkey neck and giblets
1 onion, quartered
1 celery stalk with leaves
1 carrot
1 rutabaga, peeled and sliced
Salt and pepper to taste

Sauté the neck and giblets in a saucepan with butter until tender. Remove to a pot, cover with stock, bring to a boil, and simmer for 20 minutes. Remove the gizzards and simmer the neck until the meat flakes. Pick over the meat. Add it to the giblets, chop finely, and set aside. Add enough of the giblet broth to cover the vegetables; add salt and pepper. Reserve the remaining broth. Simmer the veggies until soft, then purée in a food processor. Skim the fat from the turkey roasting pan, retaining the meat juices. Over medium heat, add the reserved broth, stirring, and scraping the pan to incorporate the browned bits into the gravy. Add the vegetable purée to achieve the consistency desired. Add the chopped giblets and meat to warm before serving.—*S.G.B. Tennant Jr., November 1985*

Turkey

CAJUN FRIED TURKEY

1 medium turkey (about 12 lbs.)
1 catfish propane cooker
1 injector

1 Zatarain's Crab Boil or
   Trappey's Cajun Shake
1 large pot peanut oil (24-qt.)
1 deep-fry thermometer

Remove the turkey innards. Place the turkey on a cookie sheet for drainage. Inject as many areas of the turkey as possible with 16 ounces of liquid marinade (Zatarain's Crab Boil or Trappey's Cajun Shake). Liberally sprinkle the outside of the turkey with Cajun Shake. Have your peanut oil heated to 350°F. Plan ahead, because it takes time to heat. Hang the deep-fry thermometer over the side of the pot with a bent coat hanger for easy reading of the oil temperature. Place the turkey into the strainer basket, and slowly lower the basket into the oil with something long enough to keep you a safe distance away. There's quite a reaction when the cold turkey hits the hot oil. Be careful! The oil temperature will drop, so increase the flame a bit to bring it slowly back up to 350°F. Cook the turkey 3 ½ minutes per pound at 350°F. To remove the turkey, carefully find the basket handle with a coat hanger, then slip the lifting rod back under the handle to remove the basket. Let the excess oil drip into the pot. It helps if two people do this, so one person can slide the cookie sheet back under the turkey. HELPFUL HINTS: Before filling the pot with oil, fill it with water and lower the packaged turkey into the pot. This lets you find the right level for the oil and avoid overflow. A 40-quart pot filled to 24 quarts is usually about right.—*True Redd, Winter 1995*

COFFEE, TEA OR ME?

Jonathan Hutchinson, in his "Archives of Surgery," says he has long been in the habit of prescribing coffee as a medicine. He regards it as a remedy unique in sustaining the nervous energy in certain cases. Tea and coffee seem to be alike in many respects, but the writer notes what many sportsmen will confirm: that it is far better to drink coffee than tea when shooting. Tea, if strong, will induce a sort of nervousness which is very prejudicial to steady shooting. Under its influence one is apt to shoot too quickly; whereas coffee steadies the hand and quiets the nerves.

J.W. Fowler
October
1898

IN THE PINK

Over the years I have become somewhat of an anti-charcoal man, leaving that outdoor grill work to the eager amateurs and the weary weekend specialists with the laugh-aprons. Few of the "cookout, backyard barbecue brigade" know that you must have a quiet fire, actually no fire at all, but flame-empty coals, to cook steak, chops, chicken or even hotdogs and hamburgers properly. And you should see these types with game. After the fire gets going in a merry blaze, the briquettes going like a home afire, our charcoal chef mixes up the gin-and-tonics, brings out a nice, fat porterhouse cut of moose and plops it on the grill and the flames lick up around it, blackening it in seconds. Often someone will dash into the house for a glass of water to quell the flame and then throw it on, bringing the ashes from the flared-up fire all over the noble cut of meat. Then more gin-and-tonic, another flame up and another water session. If the porterhouse doesn't come to the table raw, it is overcooked and bitter from the combination of ashes and charcoal crust. All very sad and a shameful way to treat a good steak, bird or chop, be it moose, venison or Angus, Rhode Island red or Mongolian pheasant.

Jack Denton Scott
August 1963

WILD TURKEY AND ORANGE BURGERS

¼ *lb. cooked wild turkey meat, cold*
    (left over from the roast)
1 lb. cooked ham, cold
1 small onion, minced and
    sautéed in butter
1 egg, beaten
1 tbsp. cointreau or triple sec
2 thick slices white bread, crumbled
Grated rind of 1 orange
1 tsp. rosemary
4 tbsps. butter, softened
Salt and pepper to taste

Mince the meats together in a bowl. Beat the egg and liqueur, add the bread, and mash together with a fork. Add to the meat, along with the onion, grated rind and seasonings. Beat the softened butter into the mixture and form into patties. Broil the patties for about 10 minutes per side. Reserve the pan drippings, add a dash of white wine and a splash of heavy cream, and stir. Pour this sauce over the patties on toasted buns. Serve with mustard mayonnaise and a chicory salad.—*Jane Tennant, January 1987*

Turkey

ELEGANT BRIMBLE JERKY

Breasts from 1 turkey
MARINADE
2 cups apple cider
¼ cup brown sugar
¼ cup salt

1 tsp. orange peel, grated
1 tsp. ground cloves
1 tsp. ground ginger
Grated rind of ½ a grapefruit
Juice of ½ a grapefruit
Dash of cointreau

The breasts should be sliced in horizontal sheets. It is easiest to slice meat when it is lightly frozen. The cuts should be thin, long and with the grain. Remove all the fat that you can, as it will not keep and will spoil the jerky. Marinate the strips in a glass container overnight. Pat the strips dry and arrange them side by side on oven roasting racks, without overlap. Cook at minimum heat, say 150°F, for 6 hours. Leave the oven door ajar to allow moisture to escape. Store the jerky in a cool, airtight container. Alternate drying techniques include a "hard cure" in an electric smoker for 12 hours. For sweeter jerky, baste with molasses or honey and water just before drying. When drying outdoors, the meat—whether laid on rocks and turned every few hours, or hung from a rack on the porch—must be protected from moisture and creatures at all times. A cool fire keeps the flies at bay, sometimes. You can vary the marinade given here by adding more sugar, salt or juniper berries to taste.—*S.G.B Tennant Jr., September 1983*

TOO MANY TURKEYS

I have my doubts that jerky could ever truly be accurately termed "elegant." Colonel Whelen refers to jerky as "a provision against a meatless time." A sort of last resort. But this cointreau-laced marinade must give the turkey breasts an exquisite flavor and could easily be used on skinned turkey (and then roasted) for a very elegant occasion. Indeed, save the Elegant Brimble Jerky for a time when you are far from meatless and have so many turkeys you've nothing better to do but jerk...the correct thing to do with too many turkeys.—R.C.G.

SMOKED TURKEY

For turkeys to be consumed shortly after smoking, which is our main interest, a 2-day cure in 80°F brine is all that's necessary. If it's a big gobbler, say 16 pounds or more, allow 3 days, and in the 20-pound class continue for 4 days. After brining, the turkey should be rinsed in tap water to remove all residual salt and left to drain for several hours. Set the bird on end or the body cavity will collect most of the fluid. The turkey should then be rubbed with butter or vegetable oil to prevent the skin from cracking and to help reduce shrinkage while in the smokehouse. To begin the smoking process, place your bird on an oiled rack in the kiln and get the temperature up to 130°F. Maintain this for 4 hours. A slow start will minimize moisture loss. Next, add more wood chunks and gradually raise the house temperature to 180°F during the following 2 hours. Any nonresinous wood may be used, but hickory is the most common. Add more wood and briquettes and continue for another 8 to 10 hours at 200°F to 225°F. Check the bird with your meat thermometer. At an internal temperature of 145°F the gobbler is both cooked and smoked.

A.J. McClane
November 1978

BRINE

12-lb. wild turkey
1 ½ lbs. coarse kosher salt
½ lb. brown sugar
1 gallon water
Anise
Sage
Mace
Ginger
Rosemary
Onion powder
Nutmeg
Bay leaf

To make an 80 percent brine solution, dilute ½ a pound of coarse salt and ½ a pound of brown sugar to each gallon of water. Various seasonings can be added such as anise, sage, mace, ginger, rosemary, onion powder, nutmeg or bay leaf. When preparing the brine, or actually curing the meat, never use a metal container unless it's enameled. The brine must be completely diluted and kept at a cool temperature, preferably in the 38°F to 40°F range.—*A.J. McClane, November 1978*

Redfish

REDFISH SEVICHE

2 cups fresh lemon juice

2 cups fresh lime juice

4 tomatoes, peeled, seeded, chopped

2 tbsps. olive oil

4 tbsps. fresh cilantro (or parsley),
	chopped

6 chili serranos or jalapeño en
	escabeche (canned), chopped

2 tsps. salt

1 garlic clove, chopped

1 tsp. cracked black pepper

2 purple onions, sliced into
	thin rings

3 lbs. fresh redfish fillets, cross-
	sliced into ½-inch strips

After spending the day being parboiled in tepid water, nobody feels like doing a big kitchen number in the evening. Seviche is the answer—raw fish marinated in citrus juices, oil and seasonings. Most fresh-caught marine fish make good seviche, but techniques and even the spelling of the word vary. Redfish need at least 5 hours in the marinade to come up to flavor. The flesh will turn from opaque to a solid, marble-white color. Left too long, any fish becomes vinegary and hard. Frozen fish will not compare. Mix ingredients the night before and refrigerate in large glass jars with leak-proof lids. Fill them about ⅔ full and don't forget to take them with you the next day. Fillet the first few fish in the morning and drop them into the jars. Stir or shake occasionally during the day when you open the cooler for whatever reason, and you have an effortless evening salad, prepared while you were out fishing. Drain off the juice and serve the fish and onions on a bed of lettuce, with a split avocado and lemon wedges. Serves 4.—*S.G.B. Tennant Jr., March 1985*

GRUB FOR A HOT CLIMATE

When I was exploring and mapping Panama, away from all the sources of supply for two to three weeks, packing everything on our backs, the grub we packed consisted mainly of oatmeal, bacon, self-rising flour, salt, sugar, powdered milk and lard. In addition, each man carried a can or two of corned beef or other meat, and also in the party we had several cans of jam. The grub was supplemented almost every day by birds, small animals or fish. You should select to pack food that gives energy and fills the stomach.

Colonel Townsend Whelen
July 1952

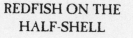

REDFISH ON THE HALF-SHELL

My husband, Ed, once went on an assignment in absentia of Rebecca for redfish. He fished with a guide from Texas named Chuck Naiser, who taught us a new method for cooking redfish. It goes like this:

1 redfish fillet, skin
    and scales left on
½ cup oyster sauce
Sprinkle of cayenne pepper
Sprinkle of dill
Salt
Mesquite

Paint the redfish with oyster sauce and sprinkle with cayenne, dill and salt. Do this while the grill heats. Place the fish on the grill with the skin side down. Cover and cook until done (about 25 minutes) and don't turn the fish over. It can easily be lifted from the skin with a fork.—R.C.G.

PENSACOLA FISH CHOWDER

4-lb. redfish (or 2 fish 2½ lbs. each)	2 tsps. Worcestershire sauce
Salt	8 black peppercorns
Ground white pepper	2 tbsps. fresh parsley, minced
2 large baking potatoes, cubed	2 pinches dried basil
1 large yellow onion, chopped	2 pinches dried oregano
2 large garlic cloves, chopped	2 large bay leaves
6 scallions, chopped	2 lemons
⅔ cup celery leaves, chopped	⅔ cup dry red wine
2 medium fresh tomatoes, diced	2 slices bacon or 4 tbsps. bacon drippings
1 medium green pepper, chopped	4 tbsps. flour
¾ cup tomato paste	4 cups canned tomatoes

When you dress the fish, put the heads in cheesecloth and tie. Cut the fish into steaks. Peel and cube the potatoes. Peel and chop the onion and garlic. Chop the scallions, including some of the greens, the celery leaves, fresh tomatoes and green pepper. Put these last ingredients in a large bowl with the tomato paste, Worcestershire sauce, peppercorns, herbs, ½ a lemon and ⅓ cup of wine. Crisp and crumble the bacon. Set aside. Sprinkle flour into the fat, stirring. Add the onions, garlic and canned tomatoes. Heat and stir. Add boiling water to fill the pot. Add the chopped ingredients, seasonings and bacon crumbs. Drop the bag of fish heads into the chowder. Boil, cover and simmer for about 2 hours. Remove the heads. Add the potatoes and cook for a few minutes. Add the fish steaks and cook until the potatoes and fish are done. Add the remaining wine. Slice the remaining lemons and put a slice in each bowl, with black pepper.—*A.J. McClane, June 1980*

Summer

SUMMERTIME, AS THE SONG SAYS, is when the living is easy. The fishing is, too (well, except for that picky August trout fishing), and it's not just easy-going; it seems easier to do. Most certainly it's hot and the atmosphere languid; clothes are minimal and shoes lost to the back of the closet. To go fishing, it's simply a walk to the lake or a troll in the boat....It's cruising.

"The whole of nature, as has been said, is a conjugation of the verb 'to eat,' in the active and passive."

—William Ralph Inge, Outspoken Essays: Second Series, *1892*

Summer, more than any other time of year, seems to have this kind of potpourri quality to the fishing. You have to be ready for surprises. You cast out your spinner bait and yes, it might catch the bass you were looking for or it might be bream on the end of the line. And for me, since I'm often ocean fishing in the summer, it could be a bluefish or a dogfish or a mackerel or that really ugly thing I caught once, a squawking sea robin. Your purpose is only surreptitiously to catch a specific species of fish; the aim is as much to be out there and to catch a good-eating fish, or lots of fish, or a big fish. For me it's all of the above. I confess to having a meat-fishing dominion to my soul; in another time and place I was probably a grizzly bear, or a horse, or a pig or possibly all three. And in the summer I feel dismissed from much of the moral obligation of catch and release. I do put back trout (there always seems so few trout); and yes, of course, I'll put back a small-size striped bass, per the law. But the abundant ocean and easy summer at least allows me the possibility to catch enough fish for dinner.

And as for cooking the fish, summer's surprises actually have an advantage: they demand flexibility. Since you usually don't know the size, the quantity or even the species of the main course until after you're back standing on the dock, you must learn to improvise with the ingredients, the proportions and the cooking time. It demands imaginative use of what's on hand; it requires that the cook be creative. As the great Pierre Franey says, "One of the most important things in learning to cook—and knowing how to cook—is flexibility."

The summer I learned to make pastry dough, my cooking instructor was appalled to return home one evening to find on her doorstep a sad, gray little pile of pastry pieces. Clearly left by some frustrated student who preferred no further explanation, only the vague innuendo of the misshapen blob left as a kind of threatening hex. It's hard to make pastry roll out properly in the heat of the summer, especially without the aid of a cool marble tablet; but as my instructor explained, if your apple tart fails because the pastry won't roll to size, make an apple *tarte tartin*. Or, in a fisherman's language, if it's too hot to bake and there's barely enough, make a seviche hors d'oeuvre.

The summer season is for a shrug of the shoulders, a grin, an "oh, la di da," and for eating lots of fish.

MIXED-CATCH FRIED FISH

Have three plates ready. In the first, put flour seasoned with salt and pepper. In the second, beaten eggs diluted with 1 tablespoon of milk to each egg. In the third, a mixture of seasoned flour and bread crumbs. Roll each fish, or other seafood, in the seasoned flour first, then in the egg, then in the flour-and-bread-crumb mixture. Fry in deep fat or in a pan, in fat of your own choice. Lard is the cheapest, butter one of the most expensive and vegetable fat the most digestible. Don't chill the fat by putting too much fish in at one time. Fry briefly.

Bill Wolf
April 1956

MANHATTAN-STYLE FISH CHOWDER

FISH STOCK
Head and bones of 2 filleted fish
4 qts. water
1 whole garlic head
2 to 3 carrots and celery stalks
1 onion
CHOWDER
2 fish fillets, cut into 1-inch cubes
¼ lb. salt pork, cut into ½-inch cubes

28-oz. can crushed tomatoes
3 carrots, grated
3 potatoes, grated
1 parsnip, grated
3 celery stalks, finely chopped
3 cloves garlic, crushed
2 tsps. thyme
Crushed red pepper flakes to taste
Salt and pepper to taste

To make a stock, fillet the fish and boil the head and bones in 4 quarts of water. Add the garlic, carrots and onion (all unpeeled), plus a few celery stalks. Cover and simmer for 30 minutes to 4 hours. Strain the stock through cheesecloth and return it to the pot, adding enough water to make 1 gallon. Bring the stock to a boil. Add the salt pork, vegetables and seasonings. Bring to a boil again. Cover, reduce the heat and let the stock simmer for 1 hour or so. Add the cubed fish. Simmer for another 20 minutes. Serves about 8.—*Fred Everson, September 1993*

Fish

BOURRIDE

1-lb. fillet of red snapper,
  rockfish or black bass, skinned
1-lb. fillet of sea bass,
  cod or walleye, skinned
1-lb. fillet of striped bass or yellow
  or white perch, skinned
1-lb. fillet of halibut, white sea bass,
  whitefish or any trout, skinned
1 large onion, sliced into rings
1 large carrot, sliced

4 fennel ribs, sliced
2 leeks, julienned
2 tbsps. parsley, chopped
1 bay leaf
1 tbsp. salt
2 cups dry white wine
2 cups fish stock or plain water
4 egg yolks
2 cups aioli sauce

Cut each fillet into pieces. Place
in a large pot. Add the onion, carrot, fennel, leeks, parsley, bay
leaf and salt. Mix the wine and stock and pour in. If necessary, add more liquid to cover the fish. Bring to a boil, reduce the heat and simmer for 12 minutes; remove from the
heat. Remove fish to a large serving bowl and add just enough
liquid to keep the fish moist. Beat the egg yolks; add 1 cup of
the aioli sauce and turn into a large saucepan. Strain the
remaining liquid into the egg-and-aioli mixture. Simmer
until thick; do not let it boil. Strain it into the second serving bowl. Place potatoes around the fish, spoon a little of the
sauce over it, and sprinkle it with parsley. Serve the rest of
the sauce and remaining aioli in separate bowls. Accompany
with toasted slices of French bread.—*A.J. McClane, June 1980*

AIOLI SAUCE

8 to 10 garlic cloves
2 egg yolks
1 tsp. salt
Dash of white pepper
2 cups olive oil

Peel the garlic cloves
and push through a gar-
lic press into the container of
an electric blender. Add the
egg yolks, salt and pepper.
Blend at the lowest speed for
a few minutes. Drop by drop,
slowly add the olive oil, and
blend. The sauce will be very
thick. Makes about 2 cups.

A.J. McClane
June 1980

SWEET-AND-SOUR MARINADE

½ cup salad oil
¼ cup tarragon vinegar
½ tsp. ground ginger
3 tbsps. soy sauce
1 tbsp. sugar
¼ tsp. garlic powder
2 tbsps. sherry

Combine all of the ingredients in a blender and mix at medium speed for 1 minute. Pour over the fish. Use this marinade later as a baste during barbecuing. Sauces are usually spooned on fish after it has been grilled. They add color and flavor as well as moisture.

Erling Stuart
July 1983

FISH BALLS

1 ½ cups flaked fish
1 ½ cups mashed potatoes
2 tbsps. butter
¼ tsp. pepper
¼ tsp. salt
1 egg, beaten
1 cup buttermilk pancake mix

Bake the fillets in a covered glass baking dish at 400°F for 15 minutes, or until the flesh flakes. Mix the flaked fish with the potatoes, butter, pepper, salt and egg, and form into one-inch balls. Coat with the pancake flour. Fry in shallow, hot fat. Serve with tartar or shrimp sauce.—*Almanac, January 1992*

F i s h

WHITE WINE COURT BOUILLON

8 cups water

4 cups dry white wine

2 onions, chopped

2 celery ribs with leaves, chopped

2 carrots, chunked

4 tbsps. chopped parsley

1 sprig fresh thyme,
     or ½ tsp. dried

2 bay leaves, broken up

1 garlic clove

8 peppercorns, cracked

1 tbsp. salt

12 thin lemon slices

CAPER SAUCE

4 tbsps. butter
4 tbsps. flour
2 cups strained court bouillon from poached fish
6 tbsps. capers with juice

Over low heat, make a roux with the butter and flour; add enough liquid, stirring as you add it, to give the consistency of white sauce. Stir in the capers. Makes 2 ½ cups.

A.J. McClane
February 1980

Combine all the ingredients in a large kettle and bring to a boil. Reduce the heat and simmer for 40 minutes. Strain the broth through a sieve into your fish poacher. With the back of a spoon, press down on the vegetables to extract all their juices into the broth. This makes about 2 quarts, which is a minimal amount. Double or triple the recipe according to fish size, adding a little water, if necessary, to cover. After you make the court bouillon, measure the fish at its thickest point to determine cooking time and carefully wrap it in cheesecloth. Place it on the poacher rack and lower it into the broth, which is just lukewarm by now. Bring the liquid to a slow simmer. Put the lid on the poacher. Cook the fish according to the estimated time, then remove the pan from the stove and leave the fish in the broth for another 10 minutes. Transfer the fish to your work counter and open the cheesecloth. Remove the skin from one side of the fish by lifting it free with a small sharp knife and peeling it loose by hand. Remove the eye: This can be replaced later with a sliced olive or cherry tomato. The layer of dark-colored meat, which lies just under the skin and is prominent in some species, can be removed after the fish has set. When you have skinned one side of the fish, roll it onto a heated serving platter and skin the other side. Garnish the platter with suitable citrus, vegetables and fresh herbs. Serve with a bowl of sauce; one of the most simple and versatile is caper sauce. At this point, many amateurs pour the broth down the sink. This is a total waste. Assuming that you came home with more than one fish and have other uses for the rest of the catch, that broth can be converted into a rich fish stock or fumet that makes a wonderful base for sauces, soups and chowders. It can be used in any recipe in place of water. All you have to do is add some fish heads and bones to the leftover broth and simmer over low heat for another ½ hour. The heads of any kind of fish may be used, but some species are meatier (as seen in the adductor muscles or "cheeks" of cod and salmon, for example) and contain more cartilage, making the stock more gelatinous. Equally rich are grouper, Pacific rockfish, snapper and striped bass. I throw in fins and skins also (make sure the skin has been scaled) then strain out all the trimmings after cooking. The Chinese classic is shark fin. (In reality, shark fin soup is a gelatinous stock derived from the radial cartilages which support the fins and, like grouper heads, they have long been the "secret" ingredient of many famous fish and bivalve chowders.) Fish stock is easy to make and keep on hand, frozen in pint or quart-sized plastic containers. As in a court bouillon, there's no exact formula for making a fumet. I usually follow the ratio of 12 cups of broth to each 2 pounds of trimmings. To expedite the cooking of large heads, they should be split lengthwise and, regardless of size, the gills should always be removed.—*A.J. McClane, February 1980*

Fish

SAUCE ROUILLE

1 red bell pepper, or canned
    pimento
4 garlic cloves
½ to 1 cup fresh bread crumbs
¼ cup olive oil

Roast the pepper until the skin is blackened; rub off the skin, trim out the ribs and seeds, then chop. Peel and mash the garlic; add the pepper pieces and continue to mash until well mixed. Soak the bread crumbs in water and squeeze dry. Add the olive oil to the mash, 1 tablespoon at a time, then add as much of the crumbs as needed to make a thick sauce. When diluted with fish broth, it should have the texture of thick cream.

A.J. McClane
June 1980

BOUILLABAISSE—1980

12 lbs. assorted fish,
    crustaceans and mollusks
1 cup olive oil, plus 2 tbsps. for bread
7 lbs. onions, shredded
1 garlic clove, peeled
1 ½ lbs. fresh tomatoes, peeled
Bouquet garni (thyme, bay leaf,
    parsley stems, peel of 1 orange)

7 celery ribs, chopped
5 ½ oz. fresh fennel
Coarse salt and white pepper
    to taste
6 tbsps. tomato concentrate
½ oz. saffron
French bread (baguette)
⅔ cup grated Parmesan cheese
1 ½ cups sauce rouille

Dress the fish and cut it into appropriate pieces. Pour 1 cup of the olive oil into a deep kettle, then add the onion shreds. Simmer over low heat, stirring, for 15 minutes. Mash the garlic with the flat side of a knife; quarter the tomatoes. Add these and the celery to the kettle. Tie the bouquet garni and the fennel ribs together with string. Add it to the pot and simmer for 15 minutes. Layer the shellfish and fish chunks in the kettle on top of the vegetable mixture. Add boiling water to reach 2 inches above the fish. Season with salt and white pepper. Add the tomato concentrate and saffron. Simmer the stew for 25 minutes. Remove the kettle from the heat. Remove the fish and arrange it on a warm platter. Reduce the broth in the kettle by ⅓; it will thicken. Cut the bread, sprinkle it with olive oil and grated cheese and brown it in the oven. Thin the *sauce rouille* with the broth, stir in some grated cheese and pour it over the platter of seafood. Serve the soup over toast in individual bowls, adding seafood as desired.—*A.J. McClane, June 1980*

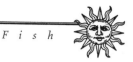

BOUILLABAISSE—1956

6 lbs. fish
½ cup olive oil
2 onions, chopped
2 leeks, chopped
2 tomatoes, peeled and crushed
½ cup parsley, chopped
Pinch of saffron
1 bay leaf
4 cloves garlic, crushed
Pinch of summer savory
Salt and pepper to taste

When you have a mixed catch, try a bouillabaisse. You will have to add a few things to your fish catch, such as lobster tails and eels, but this is a good way to stir up a fine chowder or stew. Take 6 pounds of mixed fish—sea bass, haddock, red gurnard, grouper, whiting, small eels, spiny lobster (lobster tail) and small tomcods. The kinds will vary depending upon where you fish, but mix them up. We will assume they have been cleaned, scaled if they need it, and cut up into pieces, if large. Put the fish into a kettle with the olive oil, onions, leeks and seeded tomatoes; a handful of chopped parsley; a pinch of saffron, which can be secured at your drug store, since grocery stores seldom carry such a savory ingredient; 1 bay leaf or 2; crushed garlic cloves; and a pinch of summer savory; plus salt and pepper to taste. Add enough cold water to cover everything and let it cook for about 15 minutes after coming to a boil. That's it. All that remains is the serving. Cut some slices of plain French bread and place them on a hot platter. Pour the broth over the bread. Serve the fish on a separate hot platter, decorating it with the pieces of lobster tail. Give each diner some of the bread and broth, and some of the pieces of fish.—*Bill Wolf, April 1956*

Fish

TURKISH FISH SOUP

In A Book of Middle Eastern Food by Claudia Roden, I found a recipe for a delicious fish soup, using fish heads, that I have adapted for the Crock-Pot.

THE STOCK
Fish heads, bones and tails
1 qt. water
4 tbsps. wine vinegar
Salt and pepper to taste
1 tsp. turmeric
2 large onions
3 garlic cloves, crushed

2 tbsps. parsley, finely chopped
LATER ADDITIONS
1 tbsp. butter
1 qt. boiling water
1 lb. boneless fish fillets
  or fingers
Yolks of 3 medium eggs
Juice of 1 large lemon
Ground cinnamon to taste

Pour the water and vinegar into the Crock-Pot and turn it on low heat. Add the salt, pepper and turmeric. Spread a piece of cheesecloth and pile the fish heads, bones and tails, onions, garlic and parsley in the middle, pull up the corners and tie. Put the bag into the pot, cover tightly and cook on low for 8 hours. Lift the bag, let it drain into the pot, then dispose. Turn the pot to high and stir 1 tablespoon of butter into the broth. Add 1 quart of boiling water and the fish fillets. Let them poach for 20 minutes. While the fish is poaching, beat the egg yolks in a small bowl. Whisk in the lemon juice and ½ a cup of stock from the pot. Add this mixture to the pot and heat almost to boiling. Stir well, but make sure the fish holds together. Put the fish into bowls and ladle the soup over it. Sprinkle lightly with cinnamon.—*A.D. Livingston, September 1989*

ORIENTAL MARINADE

2 scallions or green onions
2 thin slices of fresh
    ginger root
1 garlic clove
⅓ cup soy sauce
⅓ cup salad oil
⅓ cup sherry
2 tsps. sugar
Freshly ground pepper
    to taste

Mince the scallions, ginger and garlic. Combine the liquids and add sugar and pepper. Mix in the minced items. Makes just over 1 cup of marinade.

Erling Stuart
July 1983

TOMATO SAUCE

3 tbsps. olive oil
1 medium onion, chopped
3 garlic cloves, minced
1-lb. 2-oz. can whole tomatoes, chopped
8-oz. can tomato sauce
1 cup dry red wine
1 ½ tsps. dry sweet basil leaves
1 ½ tbsps. tarragon leaves
1 tbsp. dry parsley flakes
½ tsp. each salt and pepper

Heat the oil in a large saucepan over medium-high heat. Add the onions and garlic and sauté until brown. Add the chopped tomatoes (a blender works well) and tomato sauce. Add the wine and seasonings and bring to a boil; lower the heat and cook for 2 to 3 hours. Stir occasionally. Serve over pasta or rice.

Annette and Louis Bignami
January 1988

NINO'S FISH BALLS

6 slices of day-old French bread
2 cups poached or
    baked fish flakes
1 egg
1 ½ tsps. parsley flakes
1 tsp. Italian seasonings

1 tsp. basil leaves
1 tbsp. grated Parmesan cheese
¼ tsp. salt
½ tsp. pepper
1 tbsp. olive oil
1 tbsp. bread crumbs (if needed)
4 tbsps. vegetable oil

Cover the bread with water for 10 minutes. Remove, discard the crust, and squeeze out water until the bread is fairly dry, then crumble it to make ¾ of a cup. Mix the fish with the bread, egg, dry ingredients and olive oil. Form the mixture into golf-ball size rounds. If it is too soft to form a ball, add more soaked bread or bread crumbs. Heat the vegetable oil in a skillet on medium-high heat. Fry the fish balls, turning them to brown them evenly, until a crust forms. Remove and drain them. Place the balls into the meatless tomato sauce during the last ½ hour of cooking. Makes 10 to 12 balls. Note: The fish mixture can be formed and fried as fish cakes. These are delicious alone and make wonderful sandwiches with tartar sauce or your favorite spread. You can freeze cooked fish balls or cakes on cookie sheets, then bag them and store them in the freezer until needed.—*Annette and Louis Bagnami, January 1988*

COURT BOUILLON AND FISH CHEEKS

Here's an excellent recipe for those parts of a fish that are normally wasted: the tail, bones and head. The finished court bouillon could best be described as fish gravy. Use it to moisten dry, flaky fish flesh. Ladled over rice, court bouillon turns otherwise tasteless grain into a piquant complement to your main dish. There's a bonus for cooks, too. When the bouillon is done, they have first crack at the fish cheeks, an oyster-like plug of solid meat lodged just below the eye. It rates right up there with Beluga caviar and goose liver paté as a rare and delicious hors d'oeuvre. Here's the recipe.

2 qts. water
2 tsps. salt
½ cup vinegar or lemon juice
2 bay leaves
½ tsp. coriander

3 or 4 cloves
½ cup chopped celery
1 large onion, diced
½ cup carrots
2 sprigs parsley
6 peppercorns

Bring to a boil 2 quarts of water in a large pan. Add the remaining ingredients and fish parts. Bring back to a boil and allow the fish to simmer for a ½ hour or more, or until the fish is tender. Strain the mixture. If the liquid is too thin for your taste, it can be thickened with flour.—*Almanac, January 1977*

MIXED-CATCH FILLETS WITH RAREBIT SAUCE

I came upon this recipe in a booklet called "The State of Maine's Best Seafood Recipes," assuredly one of the best and best-illustrated booklets ever published on the subject. (Unfortunately, it is no longer available. It has been much cribbed from and plagiarized by writers on cooking without their ever crediting the source. The recipes are prize-winning ones submitted by Maine women in a competition, and they are the best that a region famous for its seafood has to offer.) It is as simple as this: You put fillets of fish in a buttered baking pan (even an iron skillet, if you wish), pour over them a Welsh rarebit sauce, and bake in the oven. That's all. The Welsh rarebit is a bit more delicate than that served as such, being made with milk instead of beer, and lacking Worcestershire sauce, but the cheese is the perfect complement for fish. The original recipe called for a whole haddock, skinned and boned, but I have used it for the fillets of many kinds of fish. Place about 3 pounds of fillets in the buttered baking dish. Then, in a double boiler, melt 1 cup of cheddar cheese which has been cut into small pieces. You can use white or yellow

cheddar, but make sure it is sharp enough to have some bite, and use yellow if you like the pretty color of the finished product, as I do. Add 1 cup of milk to the cheese, and heat slowly until it is a smooth mixture. Stir these ingredients into ½ a cup of cold milk: 1 heaping teaspoon of dry mustard, 2 heaping tablespoons of flour, ½ teaspoon of salt and a dash of pepper. When blended smooth, pour into the cheese mixture and stir over heat until everything thickens. This sauce is poured over the fillets. Sprinkle with paprika for a touch of color, and bake at 375°F for about 30 minutes, or until the mixture is bubbling and starting to turn gently golden on top. Serve in the baking dish.

Bill Wolf
April 1956

F i s h

NUTTY FISH

2 lbs. fish fillets
1 cup chunky-style peanut butter
¼ cup (2 oz.) brown sugar
¼ cup Teriyaki or soy sauce
¼ cup lemon juice
½ tsp. liquid hot pepper sauce
½ tsp. nutmeg
1 tsp. garlic, minced
1 medium onion

To start, mix the chunky peanut butter, brown sugar, Teriyaki or soy sauce, lemon juice, hot pepper sauce, nutmeg and minced garlic. Place a single layer of washed and dried fillets in a shallow foil-lined baking pan (using foil speeds cleanup). Spread the peanut butter mixture evenly over the dish, topping it with thinly sliced onion. Bake at 350°F until the fish flakes easily when tested. Serves 6.—*Almanac, April 1993*

OLD-FASHIONED BARBECUE SAUCE

¼ cup onions, chopped
2 tbsps. brown sugar
½ cup water
1 cup ketchup
¼ cup lemon juice
2 tbsps. vinegar
1 tbsp. Worcestershire sauce
1 tsp. chili powder
½ tsp. salt
¼ tsp. pepper
¼ tsp. paprika

Sauté the onions in vegetable oil or margarine until they are brown. Combine the liquid ingredients and add the onions and spices. Simmer the sauce for 15 or 20 minutes so it thickens.

Erling Stuart
July 1983

BACKPACKER'S BASIC FRIED FISH LIKE MOMMA THOUGHT SHE COULD MAKE

Keep some seasoned flour in a plastic bag: 1 cup all-purpose flour, 1 teaspoon salt, ¼ teaspoon pepper, ½ teaspoon paprika (and ¼ teaspoon ginger if the feeling of being a gourmet is overwhelming). Roll the fish in this seasoned flour. Pour a small amount of oil (packed, of course, in a little plastic bottle that hasn't yet leaked) into the skillet. When the oil is hot, place the fish in the pan and cook until flaky—usually no more than 3 minutes a side.

John Eckberg and
David Lowery
May 1993

BUTTER AND ALMOND SAUCE

1 fish, grilled
1 cup butter
2 egg yolks
½ tsp. dry mustard

1 tbsp. lemon juice
Dash of cayenne
1 tbsp. hot water
1 tbsp. dry sherry
½ cup slivered almonds

Toast the slivered almonds in a dry frying pan over medium heat. Set them aside. Next, heat the butter in a saucepan until it has melted and turned a golden brown. Remove from the heat and cool to lukewarm. Put the egg yolks in a mixing bowl and beat in the mustard, lemon juice and a dash of cayenne. Add the melted butter to the egg mixture, beating constantly. As the sauce begins to thicken, beat in the hot water and sherry. If the sauce becomes too stiff, add a little more hot water. Fold in ¾ of the almonds. Pour the sauce over the fish. Sprinkle the remainder of the almonds over the fish.—*Erling Stuart, July 1983*

 *Fish*

SEVICHE

My first experience with seviche—marinated raw fish—was on a sailboat off southern California. We were barely coasting along before a very light summer breeze, trolling a handline to catch anything that might hit. What hit was a small bonito. Someone had had the foresight to bring the ingredients for a marinade, and by the time the sun went over the yardarm we were ready for seviche and cocktails. This is a dish that originated in Peru, but it has counterparts in various cultures around the world. Basically, it is marinating fish in citrus juice, and the acid does the "cooking." You can use any firm-fleshed white fish, such as sole, pompano, red snapper, lingcod, rock cod, sea bass, striped bass, shrimp, scallops, lobster or crab.

2 lbs. skinned, filleted fish, cut into bite-sized pieces
Juice of 4 to 5 fresh limes (about 2 cups)
½ cup finely chopped onion
2 tomatoes, chopped
Dash of cayenne pepper
⅛ tsp. oregano
Salt and pepper to taste

Mix all the ingredients in a glass bowl. Cover the dish and marinate the fish in the refrigerator for at least 3 hours. Be sure the lime juice covers all the fish. Serve with tortilla chips and cold beer.—*Stuart E. Mork, June 1987*

FISH FACTS

Did you know that the common puffers, such as blowfish, despised by all anglers, are delicacies? The strip of meat along the backbone is sold in seafood restaurants under a variety of fancy names, including chicken of the sea, sea squab, fish fingers and the like. Usually they are breaded and fried. Likewise, did you know that beer is the perfect partner for a fish fry, while white wine goes well with most other ways of preparing fish? That lemon quarters should be served with fish? That good, young, fresh flounder can be prepared by any of the recipes advocated for imported, expensive English sole, and will come close to equaling the import? That the only thing which will spoil fish is a poor cook, because the fish is naturally good, and requires only a minimum of heat and attention to reach perfection.

Bill Wolf
April 1956

BLACK BASS IN WHITE WINE

Take about 3 pounds of bass fillets and place them in a buttered baking dish, season lightly with salt and pepper, and add a heaping tablespoon of chopped scallions. Shallots should be used instead of scallions, if available. Pour in dry white wine until it barely shows around the fillets. Dot the top liberally with butter, cover with aluminum foil and put into a 350°F oven for 10 to 12 minutes. Thicken the sauce in the pan by adding to it 1 tablespoon of butter with flour. Stir this in and bake another 10 minutes. Serve in the dish, sprinkled liberally with minced onions and parsley.

Bill Wolf
May 1956

FILLET OF BASS NORMANDY

1 recipe court bouillon
  (see p. 230 or use your own
  recipe)
6 bass fillets
6 oz. sweet cider
3 egg yolks beaten with 1 tbsp.
  heavy cream

6 fresh mushrooms,
  sliced and sautéed in butter
18 small shrimp (shelled,
  deveined, lightly boiled)
8 mussels, optional (cleaned,
  steamed, removed from shells)

First make a court bouillon by putting the washed heads and trimmings of the filleted bass in a saucepan with 1 pint of water; 2 garlic cloves; 2 small white onions, halved; 3 ribs of celery; 1 small bay leaf; 3 sprigs of parsley; 1 teaspoon of salt. Boil for 20 minutes, add a pint of dry white wine and cook for another 10 minutes. Then strain. Butter a baking dish that can be brought to the table, arrange the fillets in it and cover them with the court bouillon. Place in a 350°F oven and poach the fish for no more than 10 minutes. Remove the dish from the oven and carefully drain off the court bouillon into another pan. Meanwhile keep the fish in the baking dish warm. Place the bouillon pan over the heat and stir in the cider; when it simmers, stir in the beaten egg yolks and cream. Check consistency by dipping in a spoon. If it becomes coated, the sauce is ready. Add the cooked mushrooms, shrimp and mussels, blending well. Pour this sauce over the bass fillets and place in a broiler. Serve when lightly browned. My favorite accompaniment for this is a white Burgundy. Serves 6.—*Jack Denton Scott, May 1968*

B a s s

BLACK BASS CHAUD-FROID

2 black bass, 2 to 3 lbs. each, whole,
*   gutted and scaled, fins intact*
Salt and pepper
1 cup champagne
Chicken broth
Bouquet garni (1 thyme sprig,
*   parsley, bay leaf, tarragon)*
1 cup poaching liquid
1 envelope unflavored gelatin
1 cup mayonnaise

Sprinkle the bass with salt. Place it in a skillet or poacher. Add the champagne and chicken broth to cover the bass. Add the bouquet garni. Cover and simmer for 25 to 30 minutes, then let cool. Remove the bass and peel off the skin. Place the bass on a rack set over a shallow pan and chill. In a saucepan, mix the gelatin and 1 cup of strained broth. Stir over low heat until the gelatin dissolves. Beat in the mayonnaise. Chill the mixture until it thickens slightly. Spoon the gelatin over the bass, coating it completely. Chill until the gelatin is firm, then coat again until smooth. Refrigerate until serving time.—*A.J. McClane, May 1979*

POACHED (BOILED) BASS

This is only cooking fish in a liquid until it is tender, whereupon it is served with a sauce or used in the preparation of salads or other fish dishes. Poached fish requires further treatment to be appetizing. The simplest way to poach a bass is this: Wrap 3 to 4 pounds of fillets or pieces of fish in cheesecloth (to keep from flaking apart when cooked) and place it in 2 quarts of boiling water that contains 3 tablespoons of salt and 6 tablespoons of vinegar. Poach gently until done, about 10 to 12 minutes, and lift out carefully. Use a spatula to lift the fish to a serving plate, and pour over it a hot sauce of your own preference. A very simple sauce is made thus: Stir 4 tablespoons of flour into ¼ cup melted butter over low flame until it makes a paste, then gradually add 1 pint of warm milk, stirring constantly until a smooth cream sauce is produced. Season this with salt and pepper to taste, add some finely chopped hard-cooked eggs, minced onion, grated cheese or whatever your fancy dictates. Thin with more warm milk if you wish.

Bill Wolf
May 1956

THE FRAGILITY OF FISH

I don't quite agree with the fish lovers of the East, especially the Orient, who "cook" their fish by simply marinating it overnight in fresh lime juice or soy sauce and spices. But I do agree with the "fish people" of the East and of Europe that the most common mistake made in fish cookery is overcooking. Fish have fragile connective tissues and need gentle, carefully watched cooking. Over-cooked fish is hard and taste-less. I guess the only time you can be gentle with a big buster of a bass is in that peri-od just before you put him on the table.

Jack Denton Scott
May 1968

BASS WITH WHITE GRAPES

4 bass fillets
1 cup white wine
4 tbsps. butter (for sautéing)
4 tbsps. butter (for sauce)
1 tbsp. flour
1 ½ cups milk
8 ¾-oz. can seedless white grapes

Rinse and dry the fillets. Poach them in the white wine for 5 minutes, then remove. Melt the first 4 tablespoons of butter in a saucepan and sauté the bass for 10 minutes, turning them and making sure they don't get overcooked. Lift the fillets out whole to a warm plate. In another sauce-pan, melt the second 4 tablespoons of butter and slowly stir in the flour, making a smooth, golden paste. Warm the milk and add slowly, stirring in a little at a time to prevent lump-ing. Cook, stirring, until the white sauce is smooth and well blended. If it is too thick, add more milk. It should have a velvety consistency. Now place the fillets in 4 ramekins, cover with the white sauce and arrange an equal quantity of grape around each fillet. Brown in a broiler and serve immediate-ly. Buttered green beans and white wine go well. Serves 4.—*Jack Denton Scott, May 1968*

Bass

BLACK BASS
IN CIDER ASPIC

1 lb. bass fillets, skinned

1 cup dry white wine
    (or dry apple cider)

1 cup fish stock (for marinade)

2 tbsps. parsley, chopped

2 tsps. salt

⅛ tsp. black pepper, cracked

1 qt. fish stock (for aspic)

2 ½ envelopes dry gelatin

5 lemons, diced

3 eggs, hard-boiled

4 oz. canned pimentos,
    drained and minced

4 tbsps. green peppercorns,
    drained

2 shallots, peeled and minced

2 tsps. fresh tarragon, minced

2 tsps. fresh chervil (or parsley)

Cut the bass into lengthwise strips and marinate in a baking dish with the cider, stock, parsley, salt and pepper for 1 hour. Make an aspic from 1 quart of fish stock, adding 2½ envelopes of gelatin. Bring to a simmer. Place in the refrigerator, stirring occasionally. Place the baking dish, marinade and bass over direct heat and bring to a simmer, poaching the bass for 3 minutes. Drain the fish and pat it dry. Peel the lemons and dice. A chilled 2 quart glass terrine should be ready as the aspic reaches the point of setting. Have the egg, the strips of bass, bits of lemon, pimento and peppercorns laid out. Mix the shallots, tarragon and chervil together. Ladle the aspic into the mold to form a base, then sprinkle the shallot mixture, the eggs, lemons, pimentos and peppercorns, then a few strips of bass, lengthwise. Return to the refrigerator until the layer has set, then repeat the procedure, finishing with a layer of aspic. Cover and refrigerate overnight. Serve from the terrine.—*S.G.B. Tennant Jr., June 1986*

SAUCE GERLETTE

1 ¼ lbs. firm, ripe tomatoes

6 tbsps. fromage blanc
    (5 tbsps. low-fat ricotta
    mashed with 1 tbsp.
    low-fat yogurt)

1 tbsp. crème fraîche (2 tsps.
    each sour cream and
    sweet cream)

1 tsp. parsley, minced

½ tsp. tarragon, minced

1 tbsp. tomato sauce

2 tsps. cognac

Lemon juice

2 tsps. salt

White pepper

Peel, seed and quarter the tomatoes (about 1 lb. canned) and set aside. Whip together the fromage blanc and crème fraîche, adding the herbs, tomato sauce, cognac and lemon to taste. Stir again, adding the tomatoes, salt and a bare pinch of white pepper. Chill. Serve a dollop with each slice of bass in aspic.

S.G.B. Tennant Jr.
June 1986

BAG YOUR BASS

2 lbs. bass, skinned
1 large bell pepper
1 large onion
1 garlic clove, minced
1 cup butter, melted
1 tsp. salt
1/4 tsp. pepper
Sweet paprika, for garnish
(optional)

Set the oven to 375°F. Slice the onion and pepper into rings and mix with the minced garlic. Dip the fillets in melted butter. Sprinkle the salt and pepper onto the fillets. Place a plastic baking bag on a pan and put the onions, pepper rings and garlic in the bag. Place the fillets on top, pouring on melted butter. Close the bag and punch holes in the top. Bake for 20 minutes. Remove the fillets from the oven and transfer to serving plates.

A.D. Livingston
December 1990

SUNSHINE BASS EN PAPILLOTE

4 lbs. sunshine bass fillets,
    skinned (red vein removed)
1/2 lb. mushrooms, sliced
4 tbsps. butter
2 tbsps. olive oil
4 tbsps. chopped shallots
    (or onions)
1 cup tomatoes, chopped
    and lightly boiled in
    2 tbsps. water
Salt and pepper to taste
1 tsp. honey
1/4 cup white wine
1 tbsp. lemon juice
1 cup whole black olives
1 cup shrimp, peeled and cooked

Heavily greased white paper is most picturesque for *en papillote* cooking, but you may substitute aluminum foil or manufactured oven bags. Salt and pepper the fillets and brown them in 2 tablespoons of butter and 2 tablespoons of oil over high heat. Remove the fillets to the parchment and cover them to keep them warm. In the saucepan, cook the mushrooms and shallots in 2 more tablespoons of butter until the liquid evaporates. Add the tomatoes, salt and pepper to taste; add the honey and continue cooking for 2 minutes while stirring. Pour this glaze over the fillets. In the same saucepan, simmer the wine, lemon juice, olives and shellfish over low heat for 5 minutes, scraping the sides; then pour it over the fillets. Seal the paper or oven bag (be sure to perforate the oven bag); if using aluminum foil, twist up the edges, folding 3 times, to make an airtight seal. Place the envelope in a baking pan and bake at 400°F for 10 minutes. Remove to a serving platter, split open the envelope, and serve the bass.—*S.G.B. Tennant Jr., May 1985*

BASS COPENHAGEN

4 bass fillets
¼ lb. butter
2 eggs, beaten
3 cups fine, white bread crumbs
Salt and pepper to taste
1 large lemon, quartered

Rinse and dry the fillets. Melt the butter in a saucepan and remove from the heat. Dip each fillet into the beaten egg, then roll it in bread crumbs until completely covered. When all the fillets have been coated with crumbs and seasoned with salt and pepper, place the butter back on the heat. When it is foaming, cook the bass over moderately high flame until it is crusty on each side—no longer than 15 minutes; 10 is better. Serve on hot plates with a wedge of lemon and tiny boiled potatoes drenched in hot butter. Serves 4.

—*Jack Denton Scott, May 1968*

BASS AT ITS BEST

I had advice from my Danish fisherman friend before we ate. "Don't eat the blasted egg and bread crumbs," he said. "Eat the fish! Underneath. The enemy of fish is dryness. They like moisture. Got to be juicy. That cover of egg and bread just protects them from being fried out and dried out." I took his advice, and the morsels of fish that I ate after peeling off the crusty coating were supreme—fish at its simplest and best, with just a squirt of lemon juice. I must admit that my friend also taught me how to use a lemon correctly with fish. Take your fork in your right hand, lemon in the left. Hold the lemon over the fish, insert the fork in the lemon, squeeze the lemon. Out comes juice without effort—controlled, not squirting all over the place.

Jack Denton Scott
May 1968

RANGE SAUCE

2 tbsps. butter
1 small onion, grated
1 cup flour
2 cups orange juice
¼ cup orange liqueur
Slivered rind of 1 orange
1 tsp. dry mustard
Salt and pepper to taste

While the bass are baking, melt the butter in a saucepan and simmer with the onion for 2 or 3 minutes. Stir in the flour. Gradually stir in the orange juice and liqueur. Add the slivered rind and dry mustard. Stir over medium heat until the sauce thickens and bubbles. Season to taste with salt and pepper. Serves 4.

A.J. McClane
May 1979

HERB BAKED BLACK BASS

2 black bass, 2 to 3 lbs. each,
    whole, gutted and scaled,
    fins intact
Salt and pepper to taste

⅓ cup melted butter
Grated rind of 1 lemon
1 tbsp. each fresh tarragon,
    oregano, sage, parsley,
    chopped (or 1 tsp. each dried)

Oil the bottom of a shallow baking pan and both sides of the bass. Cook in a moderate oven (350°F) for 15 minutes, until the skin loosens. Remove from the oven and peel off the skin. Pluck out the fins, except the tail, removing the basal bones. Mix the butter with lemon rind and herbs. Brush the herbed butter over the bass. Bake another 20 to 25 minutes.—*A.J. McClane, May 1979*

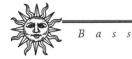

Bass

BASS AND SHALLOTS

8 shallots

6 tbsps. butter

Peanut oil (or a good cooking oil)

4 bass fillets

Salt and black pepper to taste

1 cup buttered, white bread crumbs

2 tbsps. minced Italian parsley

4 tbsps. finely chopped Italian ham
        (prosciutto), cooked until crisp,
        drained, kept warm

Cut the shallots into paper-thin slices and cook in melted butter until soft. Lightly rub a shallow enameled baking dish with the peanut oil. Arrange the fillets in the dish, season with salt and pepper, layer with the cooked shallots and sprinkle with the buttered bread crumbs. Bake uncovered at 425°F for 10 minutes. Serve in separate hot ramekins with parsley and crisp Italian ham pieces sprinkled atop. A jug of white wine, a loaf of bread and—wow! Serves 6.—*Jack Denton Scott, May 1968*

BASS BILL OF FARE

I've been a bit miffed with sporting magazines: They tell you in great and repetitive detail just how to plan a fishing trip, inform you where to go, describe the best technique to catch the fish and even reach into those personal fields, advising you what underwear and boots to wear and what socks go best with certain waders. Lordy, they even have gadgets they recommend for taking the temperature of the water, and they advise on the personalities of various species of fish at certain seasons of the year. But how seldom they tell us what to do with a fish once you have it out of water! Too often the weary fisherman clumps into his house and either quickly freezes them or perpetrates a holocaust in the kitchen. This essay (like others) has been prepared with the thought that fish will receive better treatment than any have been getting.

Jack Denton Scott
May 1968

BASS AND CASHEWS

¼ lb. butter
9 tbsps. slivered cashew nuts
6 bass fillets
8 tbsps. dry vermouth

Melt the butter in a skillet and sauté the bass fillets, 4 minutes to a side; remove to a hot plate. Brown the cashews in the butter in which the bass cooked and spread 1½ tablespoons over each fillet. Then pour the vermouth into the skillet and stir with a wooden spoon, scraping the pan and blending the vermouth well with the butter and cashew residue. Simmer for 5 minutes. Then pour 1 tablespoon of the mixture over each fillet and serve immediately. Baked potatoes are great with this. So is a frosty glass of ale.

Jack Denton Scott
May 1968

BASS AND BUTTER

6 bass fillets
½ lb. butter
Salt and pepper to taste
1 large lemon
4 tbsps. finely minced Italian parsley

The French call this *sauté meunière*, believing that butter and fish are the perfect pair. I can't argue the point. Season the fillets with salt and pepper, melt all but 2 tablespoons of the butter and sauté the fish for about 10 minutes, turning the fillets so they are cooked and both sides get the butter bath. The exact cooking time depends upon the size of the fish—large fish, naturally, taking a bit longer. But the principle, as the old Danish fisherman hammered at me, is to keep the flesh moist. Before removing the fillets from the saucepan, squeeze the juice of the lemon over the fish and sprinkle on the parsley. Warm the remaining butter and place a small bit of it in the center of each of the fillets as you serve them on hot plates. Serves 6.—*Jack Denton Scott, May 1968*

BLACKENED BASS

6 to 7 ½ lbs. bass fillets
2 tsps. paprika
¼ tsp. dried basil leaves
¼ tsp. thyme
3 bay leaves, crumbled
½ tsp. garlic powder
2 tbsps. salt
¼ tsp. pepper
¼ tsp. cayenne pepper
¼ tsp. white pepper
¼ stick butter

Pat the fillets dry and chill for 1 hour in the refrigerator. Combine the remaining ingredients, except the butter, in a bowl. Sprinkle the seasonings on both sides of each fillet and place on wax paper. Melt the butter in a separate pan. Heat a cast-iron skillet (or Dutch oven) until the bottom is gray-hot. Dip the fillets in the melted butter and immediately drop them into the skillet. Cook just 30 to 40 seconds, or until dark brown; then flip and cook the other side 30 to 40 seconds. Serve topped with any left-over melted butter.—*Annette and Louis Bignami, May 1989*

BASS IN THE FRYING PAN

This is the way the fish is most frequently encountered when eaten outdoors (and often the best way to handle it in the home). Small whole fish, fillets or small cuts of larger fish can be cooked very well in the skillet. No further preparation is necessary than to salt and pepper the fish, drop it in hot butter, bacon drippings or other cooking fat, and fry it 3 minutes on one side, 3 minutes on the other. However, if you like breading, mix 1 cup of fine-ground yellow cornmeal with 1 cup of flour, 1 ½ teaspoons of salt, and ½ a teaspoon of pepper. Put it in a pint jar (it will just about fit) and carry it in your food box. Dip the fish in milk or water, roll the moistened fish in the mixture and let it dry for a while before plunging it into the hot fat. This drying period makes the breading stick better. Variations: Roll the fish in mayonnaise, then in a cornmeal/flour mixture; or, at home, dip the fish in seasoned flour, then in an egg slightly beaten, then in bread crumbs and flour mixed in equal portions, and seasoned with salt and pepper. Under no circumstances allow fried fish to stand in the fat after cooking is done, or else they will soak up grease like a sponge.

Bill Wolf
May 1956

BASS COOKING IN GENERAL

The instructions are the same for all fish: Don't overcook, no matter what method is used. Don't actually boil the fish if the recipe calls for "boiling," but poach it gently. Bass are classed as lean fish, as are most freshwater species, and are inclined to be dry and flaky if not cooked right. Remember, in frying, baking and broiling the flavor is best retained by subjecting the fish at first to a very severe heat which seals in the savoriness. The heat can be reduced later, except in frying which is over with so quickly that lowering the heat is inadvisable.

Bill Wolf
May 1956

MUY FUERTE BASS

16 bass fillets, 4 inches
1 tsp. salt
2 tbsps. lime juice
2 lbs. fresh tomatoes
1 medium onion, finely sliced
2 garlic cloves, sliced
¼ cup olive oil
1 large bay leaf
½ tsp. oregano
12 green olives, pitted and halved
    (pimentos optional)
2 tbsps. capers
2 jalapeño peppers, cut in strips
½ tsp. salt

Salt the fillets and rub them with lime juice. Set aside for 2 hours in a shallow dish. Skin, seed and chop the tomatoes. Heat the oil and sauté the onion and garlic; do not burn them. Add the tomatoes, spices and olives, shaking the skillet over a brisk flame for about 10 minutes. Add the rest of the ingredients and spoon a few tablespoons of sauce into a casserole, then arrange a layer of fillets and continue alternating. Bake at 325°F for about 40 minutes, covered, never allowing the fish to dry out. Serve with rice and fried bananas. Serves 4 hungry anglers.—*S.G.B. Tennant Jr., August 1983*

MEXICAN BLACK BASS WITH SALSA CRUDE AND CHEESE

2 black bass, 2 to 2 ½ lbs. each, whole,
    gutted and scaled, fins intact
¼ cup olive oil
2 garlic cloves, chopped
1 small onion, chopped
4 large ripe tomatoes, chopped
1 can (4 oz.) sweet green chilies,
    drained and finely chopped
Salt and pepper to taste
¼ cup melted butter
3 cups grated Monterey Jack cheese

In a saucepan, heat the olive oil and sauté the garlic and onion for 5 minutes. Add the tomatoes and chilies and simmer, stirring occasionally, for 20 minutes. Oil the bottom of a shallow baking pan and both sides of the bass. Cook in a moderate oven (350°F) for 15 minutes, until the skin loosens. Remove from the oven and peel off the skin. Pluck out the fins, except the tail, removing the basal bones. Spoon the sauce, seasoned with salt and pepper, over the bass. Sprinkle with cheese and bake for another 20 minutes. Serve on a platter garnished with peppers and onion rings. Serves 4.

—A.J. McClane, May 1979

BLACK BASS IN LIGHT BEER

Beer is a natural companion for fried fish when used as a beverage, but beer also can be used in cooking. In the following recipe, you will note that beer forms a part of a court-bouillon, just as wine, vinegar or lemon does. Take 1 quart of light beer and reduce to 3 cups by drinking 8 ounces of it! Put the 3 cups of beer and 3 or 4 pounds of bass, either in fillets or cut into serving-size pieces, in a pan with 1 tablespoon of lemon juice, 1 bay leaf, 6 whole peppercorns that have been slightly crushed or ¼ teaspoon ground pepper, 2 onions and 1 celery stalk, both chopped. Bring this to a boil, reduce the heat and simmer until the fish is done—about 20 minutes. Lift out the fish gently, so it doesn't break up, and put it on a hot platter to stay warm while you thicken the beer broth with 1 tablespoon of butter and 1 tablespoon of flour worked together and stirred in, along with 1 tablespoon of brown sugar. This must be stirred constantly while cooking several minutes. Strain, pour over the warm fish, and serve.

Bill Wolf
May 1956

BLACK BASS DUMPLINGS WITH CUCUMBER SAUCE

1 ½ lbs. black bass fillets,
*   skinned*
2 eggs, plus 2 egg whites
1 ½ cups heavy cream
1 tsp. salt
1 tsp. mace
2 cups chicken broth
2 cups dry white wine
CUCUMBER SAUCE
¼ cup butter

1 large cucumber, peeled, seeded
*   and diced*
1 cup flour
1 cup poaching liquid
1 cup heavy cream (room
*   temperature)*
2 egg yolks
2 tbsps. chopped fresh dill or
*   2 tsps. dried dill weed*
Salt and white pepper to taste

Cut the fillets into pieces. Place the bass, eggs and egg whites in a blender or food processor and whirl until smooth, adding the cream, salt and mace while the machine is on. Turn the mixture into a bowl; cover and chill it for several hours. Pour the chicken broth and wine into a large skillet. Bring to a simmer. Shape rounded tablespoons of the bass mixture and place them carefully into the simmering liquid. Cook for 10 minutes or until the dumplings are firm; remove them with a slotted spoon. Arrange on a platter and keep them warm. In a saucepan, melt the butter and sauté the cucumber for 3 to 4 minutes. Blend in the flour. Gradually add 1 cup of the poaching liquid. In a bowl, whisk the cream and yolks until smooth, then stir into the saucepan. Add the dill. Continue stirring over medium heat until the sauce thickens. Season with salt and pepper. Spoon the sauce over the dumplings and serve garnished with cucumber slices.—*A.J. McClane, May 1979*

MUSKOKEE
BASS STEW

⅓ cup corn oil

3 onions, finely chopped

3 garlic cloves, chopped

4 slices smoked bacon, diced

1 green pepper, chopped

½ lb. mushrooms, sliced

1 ½ cups chopped
   celery and leaves

4 large tomatoes, diced

½ tsp. each oregano and sage
   or 6 branches fresh oregano
   and 3 clusters fresh sage

1 bay leaf

1 can (13 ¾ oz.) chicken broth

1 cup dry white wine

1 cup tomato purée

1 ½ lbs black bass fillets, skinned

Salt and coarse black pepper

I n a large saucepan, heat the oil and sauté the onions, garlic, bacon, green pepper, mushrooms and celery for 5 to 10 minutes or until lightly browned. Add the tomatoes, herbs, bay leaf, chicken broth, wine and tomato purée. Cover and simmer for 15 to 20 minutes, until the vegetables are tender. Cut the bass fillets into bite-size pieces and add them to the stew. Cover and simmer for another 15 minutes. Remove the herbs (if fresh are used) and bay leaf. Season to taste with salt and pepper. Serve in large bowls with slices of crusty bread. Serves 6.—*A.J. McClane, May 1979*

FROZEN FISH

Item: Fish should not be frozen. Item: They should be eaten fresh and as quickly as possible once they have been taken from their natural habitat. But if you have a large catch and must freeze some, try it this way: Save your empty waxed cardboard milk cartons, in both quart and gallon sizes; place your cleaned fish in them; fill with water and freeze. Soon the fish will be completely encased in ice, which will slow down the dehydrating process. But even with this method, don't keep them frozen too long. One month is enough. Freezing breaks down the tissues and also destroys the flavor of fish by taking much of the moisture from it. I've found the following method especially good for frozen fish.

2 pkgs. frozen chopped spinach
Salt and pepper to taste
6 tbsps. butter
1 ½ cups dry white wine
2 small white onions, halved
2 sprigs Italian parsley
6 bass fillets
2 ½ tbsps. flour
½ cup heavy cream
Juice of ½ a lemon
3 tbsps. grated Parmesan or Romano cheese

Cook the spinach, without water (it has enough natural moisture), until tender; drain very well. Sprinkle with salt and pepper and stir in 3 tablespoons of butter. Butter a shallow baking dish and spread the spinach on it; keep it warm. Bring the wine, onions and parsley to a rolling boil, lower the heat to the simmering point, add the fillets and cook for 7 minutes. Remove the fillets and cook the wine for 5 minutes longer, then strain it. Melt 3 tablespoons of butter in the top of a double boiler and slowly stir in the flour, blending it to a smooth golden paste; keep stirring and add the warm, strained wine, small amounts at a time. The sauce should be creamy and smooth, not lumpy. Now stir in the cream and the lemon juice. Arrange the fillets on the spinach in the baking dish, pour the sauce over them, then sprinkle on the grated cheese. Bake in a 450°F oven until evenly browned. I like hot toasted garlic bread with this and a beaker of cold beer. Serves 6.

Jack Denton Scott
May 1968

BASS CHOWDER

4 or 5 lbs. bass (undressed weight)

3 strips smoke-cured bacon

1 large onion, chopped

3 garlic cloves, minced

1 tbsp. parsley, chopped

16-oz. can tomatoes, chopped

2 bay leaves

Salt and pepper to taste

Scale and dress the bass whole. Cut out the top and bottom fins. Be sure all the bones come out with the fins. Fry the bacon until crisp, then drain. In drippings, sauté the onion for 3 or 4 minutes, then add the garlic and parsley. Simmer on low heat for a few minutes. Meanwhile, put the dressed fish into a Dutch oven (or a similar pot), cover with water and add bay leaves. Bring to a light boil, lower the heat and simmer for 10 minutes, or until the fish flakes easily. Remove and drain the fish. While the fish are cooling, pour all the liquid out of the pot, straining out 2 cups. (Add water if necessary.) Discard the bay leaves. Put the 2 cups of liquid back into the pot, then add the contents of the skillet and the crumbled bacon. Add the tomatoes (with their liquid) to the pot. Put it over low heat and stir in a little salt and pepper. Flake the meat off the backbones, watching carefully for bones around the rib cage, and add it to the pot. Simmer for a few minutes, but do not bring to a hard boil. Add more salt and pepper to taste, if needed, and stir lightly with a large spoon. Serve the chowder steaming hot in bowls, along with a loaf of New Orleans or San Francisco-style French bread, or with Saltines. Serves 4 or 5.—*A.D. Livingston (author of the* Complete Fish and Game Cookbook, *Stackpole Books), April 1995*

DANIEL WEBSTER'S
FISH CHOWDER

Sometimes an angling party will bring home a large catch, and will want to feed a lot of persons at a "sea food" party. In that case a chowder is indicated, and I would like to pass on one that is at least 100 years old, and, I can promise, as good today as when first tried. It is entirely different from most chowders. Before proceeding, it should be pointed out that the recipe requires 25 large oysters, which are not too hard to obtain, even far inland during summer in this day of frozen foods; but, just in case they shouldn't be available in the warm months when bass are ordinarily caught, put your bass in the freezing compartment and keep them there until oysters come back in season in the fall. And so, to work: Cut up a pound of salt pork into small pieces and put it into a large kettle that can be closed tightly later in the cooking. Chop up 2 large onions while the heat under the kettle dries out the salt pork. Before the fat is completely dried out, put in the onions and sauté them until light yellow. Skim off the salt pork pieces. Add 1 quart of boiled potatoes, put through a ricer or mashed, to the pot. Put in 1 ½ pounds of soda crackers, broken up (the original recipe called for sea biscuit, which is rather hard to come by nowadays). Season with ½ a teaspoon dried thyme and ½ a teaspoon dried summer savory, both of which are available in most large grocery stores. Season to taste with black pepper, but don't use too light a hand. Pour in ½ a bottle of ketchup, or slice up ½ a dozen large tomatoes and add them. Grate ½ a nutmeg into the pot, or use its equivalent in ground nutmeg (about a generous ½ teaspoon), add ½ a dozen whole cloves, and a ¼ teaspoon of allspice. Now then, put in 6 pounds of bass cut in slices and the 25 large oysters. Pour 1 bottle of port or claret into the kettle, and add enough water to cover, about 1 inch. Stir the mixture and put over a slow flame. After it comes to a high heat, simmer gently for 1 hour. Keep covered tightly at all times, except when stirring it. Stir gently to avoid breaking up the pieces of fish as they become tender.

Bill Wolf
May 1956

BLACK BASS CRÊPES

CRÊPES
4 eggs
½ tsp. curry powder
½ tsp. salt
1 cup milk
1 cup unsifted flour
FILLING
2 lbs. black bass fillets, skinned
Salt and white pepper to taste

1 cup dry white wine
½ cup butter
½ cup flour
Poaching liquid with enough
    half-and-half added to
    make 4 cups
1 package frozen, chopped
    broccoli, cooked and drained
⅓ cup grated Parmesan cheese

In a bowl combine all the crêpe ingredients and beat until smooth. Let the batter stand for 1 hour. Make 18 crêpes as follows: Spoon about 2 tablespoon of batter into a heated, lightly buttered 7-inch skillet and coat the bottom with a thin layer. Brown on one side, then turn out onto a piece of foil. Butter the pan again and repeat until the batter is used. FILLING: Sprinkle the bass fillets with salt and pepper. Place in a large skillet and add the wine. Cover and simmer for 20 to 25 minutes. Let the bass cool in the liquid. Break the meat into bite-size pieces. Reserve the poaching liquid. In a saucepan, melt the butter and stir in the flour. Add the liquid and half-and-half, stirring over low heat until the sauce thickens and bubbles. Season with salt and white pepper. Place ½ of this sauce in a bowl and add the bass pieces and broccoli; spoon 3 tablespoons into each crêpe and roll it. Place the crêpes side by side, seams down, in a lightly greased casserole. Spoon the remaining sauce over them and sprinkle with cheese. Bake in a moderate oven (350°F) for 35 minutes.—*A.J. McClane, May 1979*

PREP BASS FOR COOKING

Clean the bass as soon as possible. Wipe the body cavity dry and sprinkle with lemon juice, which both adds flavor and "firms" the flesh. Now for that "muddy taste." It is seldom in the flesh, but in the outer and inner skin. If the fish is skinned or filleted carefully, much of the objectionable taste is removed. Whole fish should be scaled, of course. Scaling is easier when they are in the round; that is, before the entrails are removed. If water must be used in the cleaning, dry the fillets or whole fish carefully with a cloth. Water makes the flesh mushy.

Bill Wolf
May 1956

BLACK BASS PUDDING WITH SAUTERNE SAUCE

1 black bass, 2 to 2 ½ lbs,
    whole, gutted and scaled,
    fins intact
Salt
Sauterne
¼ cup butter
2 tbsps. each green pepper,
    pimento, celery, leaves and
    chives, all chopped
4 cups plain croutons

3 eggs, well beaten
1 tsp. each Worcestershire sauce
    and salt
2 cups half-and-half
Fine dry bread crumbs
SAUTERNE SAUCE
½ cup butter
½ cup flour
1 cup poaching liquid
1 ¼ cups heavy cream
Salt and white pepper to taste

Sprinkle the bass with salt. Place it in a skillet and add the sauterne to half cover the fish. Simmer, covered, for 20 minutes. Let the bass cool in the liquid. Remove the fish and reserve 1 cup of the liquid. Skin and bone the bass. Break the meat into small pieces. Sauté the green pepper, pimento, celery leaves and chives. Scrape them into a bowl and stir in the bass and the croutons. Beat the eggs with Worcestershire sauce, salt and half-and-half. Stir it into a bowl. Let it stand for 15 minutes. Butter two 3-cup fish molds; sprinkle the inside with dry bread crumbs. Fill the molds with the bass mixture and bake at 350°F for 45 minutes. Loosen the edges of the pudding and unmold onto a serving platter. Top with sauterne sauce. To MAKE SAUTERNE SAUCE: Melt the butter in a saucepan and stir in the flour. Slowly stir in the reserved poaching liquid and cream. Stir until the sauce thickens and bubbles. Season with salt and white pepper.—*A.J. McClane, May 1979*

Bass

BLACK BASS CUSTARD

1 ½ lbs. black bass fillets, skinned

2 tbsps. butter

¼ cup parsley, chopped

½ cup celery and leaves,
    finely chopped

1 small onion, chopped

3 cups soft bread crumbs

1 qt. milk

4 eggs

2 tsps. salt

¼ tsp. pepper

2 cups (8 oz.) sharp cheddar
    cheese, grated

⅓ cup chopped pimento

Cut the bass fillets into 1-inch-wide strips. In a skillet, heat the butter and sauté the parsley, celery and onion for 5 minutes. Add the bass fillets and continue to cook for 5 minutes. Remove from the heat and cool. In a bowl, mix the bread crumbs with the milk and eggs, beating them until well blended. Stir in the salt, pepper and contents of the skillet. Fold in half the cheese and pimento. Pour the mixture into a greased baking pan (8 inches square and 2 inches deep should be right). Sprinkle with the remaining cheese. Bake in a moderate oven (350°F) for 40 to 45 minutes or until lightly browned and firm to the touch at the center. Serve garnished with red and green pepper rings. Serves 4, or 6 as an appetizer.—*A.J. McClane, May 1979*

BROILED BASS

Outdoors, bass can be broiled quite simply by spitting the seasoned pieces on a stick of green wood and holding the fish over good live coals, skin side down, 5 to 8 minutes until it is nicely browned. At this point it is reversed and broiled flesh side down for a like period. At home, soak the fish 5 minutes in a solution of 1 cup of water in which 2 tablespoons of salt have been dissolved, or 1 tablespoon or 2 of lemon juice or vinegar has been added. Drain the fish well and brush with melted butter or cooking oil. Put it under the broiler, cook until browned, then reverse. Baste often.

Bill Wolf
May 1956

SOUR CREAM WITH DILL SAUCE

1 cup sour cream
1 tsp. dried dill
1 tbsp. red wine vinegar
¼ tsp. sugar
1 tsp. salt

Combine all of the ingredients and refrigerate for at least an hour. You may substitute fresh dill for dried dillweed. Serve the sauce at room temperature.

Erling Stuart
July 1983

BLACK BASS MUSHROOM PIE

1 ½ cups (6 oz.) grated Gruyère cheese

1 tbsp. flour

1 unbaked 9-inch pie shell with high fluted edge

2 tbsps. butter

1 lb. black bass fillets, skinned

1 can (6 oz.) sliced mushrooms, drained

4 eggs, beaten

2 cups half-and-half

¼ tsp. each dried oregano and thyme

2 tsps. salt

Mix the cheese and flour and spread it evenly in the bottom of a pie shell. Melt the butter in a skillet. Cut the bass fillets into 1-inch-wide strips and sauté for about 5 minutes. Place the fish and mushrooms in the pie shell. In a bowl, beat the eggs with the half-and-half, herbs and salt. Pour this mixture into the pie shell. Bake in a moderate oven (350°F) for 45 to 50 minutes, or until the pie is puffed and browned. Cool 10 minutes before cutting into wedges. Serve garnished with a sprig of fresh oregano, or a speckling of dried oregano and tiny whole mushrooms. Serves 6.—*A.J. McClane, May 1979*

Bass

BLACK BASS FONDUE

3 egg yolks

1 cup beer

1 cup unsifted flour

1 tsp. salt

1 tsp. paprika

Dash of garlic powder

3 egg whites, stiffly beaten

2 to 3 lbs. black bass fillets,
    skinned

Deep fat or peanut oil
    heated to 360°F

In a bowl, mix the egg yolks, beer, flour, paprika and garlic powder. When ready to serve, fold in the egg whites. Cut the fillets into bite-size pieces. Spear them on fondue forks and dip into the batter. Drop them into hot oil and fry for 5 to 6 minutes, or until the pieces are golden brown and crisp. Serve with one or several of the sauces listed at right. Serves 4 to 6.—*A.J. McClane, May 1979*

BLACK BASS FONDUE SAUCES

HOT SAUCE

Mix ½ cup chili sauce with 2 tablespoons of frozen-concentrated orange juice and 1 tablespoon of white horseradish.

TARTAR SAUCE

Mix ¾ cup of mayonnaise with 1 tablespoon of lemon juice, 1 tablespoon of drained capers and ¼ cup of well-drained pickle relish.

CURRY SAUCE

Mix ⅓ cup of mayonnaise with ⅓ cup of sour cream, 1 teaspoon of curry powder and ⅓ cup of shredded, peeled green apple. Add salt to taste.

A.J. McClane, May 1979

HOW TO ROAST A BASS

For simplicity, you can't beat this recipe for roasting a large bass. You have caught a big one that will weigh about 4 pounds after it has been scaled, cleaned and the head has been removed. Wipe it thoroughly with a damp cloth, sprinkle lemon juice and salt and pepper it well inside and out, make several lengthwise slashes into the skin on its sides (this prevents skin from curling off too much). Put the fish in a roasting pan, pour 1/2 a cup of melted butter over it and roast for 1/2 an hour or a bit more in a 350°F oven, basting often with the butter in the pan. Serve on a hot platter.

Bill Wolf
May 1956

BASS WITH BREAD

There's more than bread and bass to this one, but when I had it in Spain, the item I remembered was the bread. It was prepared with a local salt-water fish, but I've done it a dozen times with smallmouth bass and can say without fear of successful contradiction that bass are better.

4 bass fillets
4 small white onions, finely chopped
4 tbsps. butter

2 tbsps. olive oil
1 cup boiling water
Salt and pepper to taste
12 slices French bread

Sauté the onions in 2 tablespoons of butter and 1 of olive oil until they are soft. Stir in the water and salt and pepper. Place the bass fillets in a baking dish and cover with the onion broth. Cover the baking dish and simmer in a 300°F oven for 30 minutes. The key word here is "simmer." Do not overcook or cook too briskly, or the dish will break up. While the fillets are cooking, sauté the slices of bread in the remaining 2 tablespoons of butter and 1 of olive oil, turning so that both sides are brown and crisp. If necessary, use more butter and oil. Place 3 slices of bread on a warm plate for each person, arrange 1 fillet over them and cover with the broth from the baking dish. I give this added flavor by sprinkling minced parsley or freshly grated Parmesan cheese over it. Cold white wine is a must; a salad of tomatoes and hearts of Boston lettuce goes well. Serves 4.—*Jack Denton Scott, May 1968*

Bass

MAGIC BASS

3- to 4-lb. whole bass
¼ lb. bacon, sliced
1 cup onions, chopped
1 cup red wine
1 cup fish or chicken stock
2 cups fresh mushrooms, sliced

1 medium tomato, chopped
1 tbsp. thyme leaves
1 tbsp. oregano leaves
1 tbsp. butter
1 tbsp. flour
Salt and pepper to taste

FRESH FISH

If you must buy fish to prepare these recipes, try to get whole fish. Check that the eyes are bright and full, flesh firm and the smell fresh.

Annette and Louis Bignami
May 1989

Scale the bass and remove the head and tail. Dice the bacon into ¼-inch pieces. Place an ovenproof casserole or Dutch oven over medium heat and fry the bacon until it's brown and crisp. Drain the fat, keeping 1 tablespoon. Add the onions and sauté until transparent; add the bass, wine, fish stock, mushrooms, tomato, thyme and oregano. Cover and bake 30 to 45 minutes in a 350°F oven, or cook over medium flame on a campfire or campstove. The dish is done when the thickest portion of the bass flakes with a fork. Remove the bass and keep it warm. Mix the butter and flour and roll it into a ball. Blend this butter ball into the liquid in the casserole and cook over medium heat until the sauce thickens, about 2 to 3 minutes. Salt and pepper to taste. Serve over the bass. Mashed potatoes and a green vegetable complete this meal. Serves 4 to 6.—*Annette and Louis Bignami, May 1989*

THE PLEASURE OF THE CATCH

W hat did we eat? Well, fish in the first place. For the first time in our lives we had more fresh trout than it was possible for us to consume. As for the pickerel, found in the little lakes just back from the shore, we caught these "pirates" just for the pleasure of catching. Many a string was dragged into camp, only to be thrown away and become food for the gulls. The pickerel bit on any old thing, but the best luck was with a piece of bacon rind crudely cut in the shape of a fish.

Ellen Erg
April 1905

FISH FILLETS IN CURRY

2 ½ lbs. muskie or
pickerel fillets
3 tbsps. butter
1 cup celery, diced
1 cup onion, thinly sliced
¾ cup milk
1 tsp. salt
1 tsp. curry powder
Dash of pepper

P lace the fillets in a greased glass baking dish. Sauté the celery and onions for 5 minutes in the butter. Stir in the salt, curry powder and pepper. Remove from the heat and add the milk under brisk stirring. Return to a low flame, stirring constantly until the sauce is smooth and fairly thick. Pour it over the fish; place the baking dish in a 350°F oven for 30 minutes.—*Harry Botsford, February 1953*

Salmon

POACHED SALMON

COURT BOUILLON

1 medium onion, roughly sliced	2 bay leaves
2 carrots, roughly sliced	10 black peppercorns
2 celery stalks with leaves,	½ tsp. dried thyme
roughly sliced	2 cloves
2 parsley sprigs with stems	1 tbsp. salt
1 branch fresh dill (optional)	2 cups dry white wine
	2 quarts (8 cups) water

Combine all of the ingredients in a saucepan. Bring them to a boil, immediately lower the heat, then simmer for 25 minutes. Let the liquid cool and strain it into a cooking pot; makes about 2 quarts. Before cooking the fish, measure it at its thickest point. Simmer it 10 minutes for each inch of thickness, or about 35 minutes for a 3 ½-inch-thick fish. Thickness rather than weight determines timing, since a long flat piece of fish weighing 3 pounds will cook much more quickly than a chunky piece of the same weight. You can put the fish in the water just as it is, or you can play it safe, as I do, and wrap it in cheesecloth. It's easier to take out of the broth that way and sure not to fall apart. Put the fish in the cooled bouillon and add enough cold water to cover it. If the fish is too big to cover with liquid, you'll have to turn it over halfway through the cooking. Start timing the cooking when the water comes to a boil. Then lower the heat to simmer. Once the cooking time is up, turn off the heat and leave the fish in the broth to cool uncovered until you're ready to decorate it the next day. Don't refrigerate it unless the weather is very hot.—*Fayal Greene, May 1977*

COOK IT FROZEN

A note on frozen fish: Cook it still frozen if possible, but double the cooking time. If for some reason you have to defrost the fish, let it defrost in the refrigerator and try to cook it before all the frost is out of it.

Fayal Greene
May 1977

BERING SEA HASH

This is a most satisfying one-dish meal devised by that breed of hardy men who once fished the waters of the Bering Sea. They simply boiled the bejabers out of potatoes and onions, and when these were soft, tossed in a hunk of fat salmon belly. When the fish was done, any extra water was poured off and the whole mess whipped and stirred into a most savory goo. Most of the sailboat veterans of the Bering Sea are now old men, permanently on the beach, but they nostalgically whip up a meal using canned salmon. Try 2 large potatoes, 2 large onions and a 1-pound can of salmon. Add butter or margarine, depending on the oiliness of the fish. The only condiment you need to make it extra special is plenty of fresh, coarse-ground black pepper. If you have any imagination at all, you can play endless variations on this basic kitchen theme.

Terry Pettus
May 1960

KING SALMON À LA MARIANI

6 salmon fillets
Seasoned flour for dredging
3 garlic cloves, diced
1 large onion, diced
1 carrot, diced
2 tbsps. butter
2 tbsps olive oil
1 ½ cups red wine
⅓ cup fish or chicken broth
Salt and pepper

Dice the garlic, onion and carrot and set aside. Heat the butter and olive oil in a nonstick pan. When the butter and oil sizzle, quickly sear the fillets on each side, then remove them from the pan. Turn the heat down to medium and add the garlic, onion and carrot. Sauté until they begin to brown slightly. Add the wine, reduce, and deglaze the pan. Then add the broth and reduce by half. Add the salmon and cook until the interior flesh is just past translucence; about 3 to 5 minutes. Season with salt and pepper, remove from the heat and serve up with the sauce, buttered boiled potatoes and chopped parsley.—*John Mariani, May 1995*

Salmon

GREEN MAYONNAISE FOR SALMON

GREEN HERBS

6 scallions

Leaves of ¼-lb. fresh spinach or
    ½-package defrosted,
    drained, chopped spinach

½ cup watercress leaves,
    tightly packed

½ cup parsley leaves,
    tightly packed

1 tbsp. fresh or dried tarragon

2 tbsps. fresh or dried dill leaves

MAYONNAISE

4 egg yolks

2 tbsps. lemon juice

2 tsps. dry mustard

½ tsp. salt

¼ tsp. white pepper

2 ½ cups oil
    (partially olive, if possible)

1 tbsp. or more lemon juice

Cut off the roots and wilted leaves of the scallions, then chop the white and remaining green parts coarsely. Have a pot of boiling water ready. Add the greens in the above order and let simmer for 1 minute after the dill is added. Drain into a sieve and run cold water through it. Press out as much water as possible, then pat dry with paper towels. This seems a bit complicated, but the slight harshness of the fresh vegetables must be removed, along with any excess water, or else the mayonnaise will become acid or watery. Beat the first 5 ingredients of the mayonnaise together until well mixed. Continuing to stir, start adding the oil, drop by drop, without stopping until the sauce has begun to thicken. Then start pouring the oil in a thin stream, stopping occasionally. As the mayonnaise gets very thick, add a few drops of lemon juice, then more oil. When all the oil has been used, add the greens, which have been very finely chopped or puréed in a food mill. Taste and add salt and lemon juice if needed. Refrigerate. Making mayonnaise is not as hard as people think. Have the egg yolks at room temperature, pour the oil in literally drop by drop, and just be sure not to stop beating until the thickening starts. It's a matter of a minute or so at most. If by some chance your mayonnaise should refuse to thicken, all is not lost. Start with another egg yolk at room temperature, and beat in about ¼ of the unthickened sauce drop by drop. It should be good and thick, and you can beat in the rest of the sauce a little faster.—*Fayal Greene, May 1977*

HOW TO SERVE SALMON

In warm weather, wait until the last possible moment before decorating the salmon to be sure that the fish and the mayonnaise are in perfect shape. In cooler weather, you can decorate the fish a couple of hours in advance. A salmon in the center of an outdoor buffet is a beautiful thing, but remember to keep it in the shade. If you can't find any shade, serve the food indoors and let the guests eat it outdoors. You'll need something to serve the fish on. Lay the fish on a platter or tray, removing the cheesecloth carefully. If the fish is in 2 pieces, fit them together as closely as possible. Carefully remove the skin between the base of the head and the tail. If the eye bothers you, cover it with a large caper or a slice of black olive. French cooks commonly place the black olive on top of a slice of hard-boiled white to give the fish a lively expression. Coat the exposed flesh with mayonnaise. Spread the mayonnaise carefully so that it covers the salmon, but don't lay it on so thick that it overpowers the fish when served. Next, slice unpeeled cucumbers very thinly. Lay the cucumber slices in neat overlapping rows starting at the tail, so that they cover the mayonnaise. The idea is to make them look like stylized scales. Now sprinkle the cucumbers lightly with very finely chopped parsley or dill leaves. Once the fish is decorated, it's time to prepare the platter. Bunches of parsley, watercress and dill, interspersed with whole lemons, make a very pretty picture, but I prefer to eat the decorations. Choose the best vegetables you can find and arrange them by colors and shapes the way you think looks best. Intersperse the vegetables with bunches of parsley, quarters of lemon and hard-boiled egg, and whatever else you think will look beautiful. The key word is lavish. A whole salmon deserves nothing less. To serve the fish, start cutting it in the middle and lift slices off the top. Usually you'll serve only the top half of the salmon for first helpings. If people are still hungry, take the fish back to the kitchen and remove the skeleton. An easy way to do this is to clip it off with a knife or scissors below the head and above the tail. Spoon a little more mayonnaise over the salmon and return it to the table.

Fayal Greene
May 1977

BAKED JOSEPHINE

Baked Josephine probably originated as a shoreside dish among fishermen and cannery workers. It is not a workaday meal but has always had a somewhat rakish and festive air.

4- to 5-lb. salmon,
    whole and scaled
2 garlic cloves, sliced
2 large onions, finely chopped
28-oz. can whole tomatoes
1 oz. dry mustard
Salt and pepper to taste

Take a well-scaled fish and inflict deep gashes about 2 inches apart in every direction. Into these insert thick slices of garlic; use your own judgment on the garlic. A mound of finely chopped onions and canned tomatoes is used to stuff the cavity and cover the fish. Then sprinkle with dry mustard, the best that is available, in addition to the salt and pepper. There is no danger of the fish drying out, so cook it uncovered in a hot or medium oven. When the onions are tender, the fish is done. Serve sauce over steamed rice.—*Terry Pettus, May 1960*

WHITE RICE SALAD

1 ½ lbs. (3 cups) enriched long-grain rice, uncooked
6 cups water
3 tbsps. salad oil
3 tsps. salt
2 8-oz. cans water chestnuts
2 tsps. salt
3 tbsps. fresh or dried dill leaves
½ tsp. white pepper
½ cup wine vinegar
1 ½ cups salad oil (could be partly olive)
2 cloves garlic, pressed

For firm, well-separated rice, bring the water to a boil with the oil and salt. Pour in the rice. When the water returns to a boil, stir the rice with a fork, cover the pot, lower the heat and simmer for about 14 minutes. If, after simmering, all the water hasn't been absorbed, cover and continue to cook for another 2 minutes. When done, uncover and fluff the rice with a fork. Slice the water chestnuts very thin and mix them with the rice in a serving bowl. Make the dressing in a 2-cup measure. Put salt, dill and pepper in the bottom, fill with vinegar to the ½-cup mark and mix well. Add the oil to the 2-cup mark and mix again. Press in the garlic. Finally, toss the salad, cover it and refrigerate overnight. Serves 12.

Fayal Greene
May 1977

SORREL OR ARUGULA PESTO

3 cups sorrel or arugula leaves
¼ cup parsley
½ tsp. sea salt
3 tbsps. olive oil
1 garlic clove

Peel and slightly crush the garlic clove, then add it to 1 quart of boiling water. Blanch the sorrel leaves in the boiling water very briefly, then drain. Combine the blanched leaves and all the other ingredients in a blender or food processor and give it a few zips. Top char, salmon steaks or large trout fillets with spoonfuls of this pesto.

Jerome Robinson,
from *When Fishermen Cook Fish* by Rebecca Gray, 1996

NOVA SCOTIA SALMON

1 whole salmon fillet, skin left on
1 cup plain yogurt
4 tbsps. fresh dill
2 cups white wine
1 tbsp. rosemary
Juice of 1 lemon, plus several lemon slices
Salt and pepper
Fresh dill or parsley sprigs for garnishing (optional)

Rinse the fillets in cold water and pat dry. Wrap them individually in wax paper and store them in the refrigerator until needed. First make the sauce by combining the yogurt, ground pepper and 2 tablespoons of the dill and let it sit in the refrigerator for several hours. Make a large charcoal fire and let it burn down to hot coals or turn on a gas grill to ¾ high. Out of tinfoil make a "boat" and lay the fillet skin-side down in it. Pour the white wine over the fish and add the remaining dill, rosemary, lemon juice, lemon slices, and salt and pepper. The sides of the boat should be high enough to come easily together; crimp them closed. Add a second layer of tinfoil to the boat and place it on the grill. Baste the fish with the juices every few minutes. Poach the salmon for approximately 20 minutes, then check for doneness. When cooked, the fish should easily pull away from the skin. Remove the fish with a spatula to a heated platter and garnish with fresh dill or parsley sprigs. Serve immediately with the dill-yogurt sauce on the side.—*Charles Gaines, from* When Fishermen Cook Fish *by Rebecca Gray, 1996*

Swordfish

TERRY McDONELL'S SWORDFISH

2 to 4 swordfish steaks, thickly cut (1 inch to 2 inches)
¼ cup Worcestershire sauce
½ cup green olive oil
2 garlic cloves, finely chopped
1 tbsp. lemon juice
1 tbsp. chives, chopped
Tabasco
Salt (garlic salt if you like a lot of garlic)
Pepper

In a bowl combine the Worcestershire sauce, olive oil, garlic, lemon juice, chives and Tabasco sauce to taste (remembering that Tabasco intensity increases over time) and make any adjustments. Place the swordfish steaks (1 per person) in a small shallow baking dish and pour the marinade over them. Let them sit for approximately 1 hour while you have a cocktail and get the charcoal hot. Turn the steaks at least once. Paint the grill with some of the marinade and lay the steaks on. Salt and pepper the steaks as they cook. Cook rare.

—*Terry McDonell, from* When Fishermen Cook Fish *by Rebecca Gray, 1996*

COOKS IN THE KITCHEN

Only a few of the recipes in this book did not appear in Sports Afield: the salmon recipe by Charles Gaines on page 271, the redfish recipe of mine on page 223, and this swordfish recipe from Terry McDonell. I forced Charles and Terry into the pages of Eat Like a Wild Man for a couple of reasons. Charles Gaines writes frequently for Sports Afield but has never contributed a recipe, and he certainly should have. He is a superb cook; and in the cooking of salmon he is highly experienced, living as he does on Nova Scotia's northern coast for half the year. So I thought it imperative to include one of Charles's salmon recipes.

As editor-in-chief and publisher of Sports Afield, Terry McDonell has that great editor's ability to be pervasive but oh-so-subtle. His influence has much to do with what Sports Afield is all about.

And my redfish recipe? I guess it's just hard to keep a cook out of the kitchen.

—R.C.G.

MUSTARD SAUCE

3 tbsps. prepared mustard
1 tbsp. sugar
1 tbsp. white vinegar
Salt and pepper to taste
5 tbsps. vegetable oil
Fresh dill, finely chopped onions or chopped
    hard-cooked egg yolks

Add the vegetable oil to the mustard, sugar, vinegar, salt and pepper drop by drop, stirring with a wooden spoon. Just before serving, add either the fresh dill, the onions or the egg yolks.

Stuart E. Mork
June 1987

GRAVLAX

Gravlax is a Swedish method of serving uncooked, cured fish. The name comes from the Scandinavian word lax, *which means salmon. King salmon and sockeye make the best* gravlax *simply because of their deep red color.*

3 lbs. fresh salmon,
    filleted and boned
1 large bunch fresh dill
2 tsps. vegetable oil
4 tbsps. salt
4 tbsps. white sugar
2 tsps. crushed black pepper

Place the salmon fillets skin side down over a thick bed of the dill in a shallow dish. Brush the meat side of the fillets with the oil and gently rub in the mixed salt and sugar. Sprinkle the pepper over the fish. If there is more than one fillet, place one on top of the other, flesh touching flesh; either way, cover with a generous layer of dill and place a piece of plastic wrap over the top. Let the fish marinate in the refrigerator for 2 to 3 days. Turn the fillets from time to time so they marinate evenly. Scrape off the dill and cut the fish diagonally to form long, thin slices. Garnish with fresh dill and lemon wedges. Serve with rye bread and a cold mustard sauce.—*Stuart E. Mork, June 1987*

SASHIMI ON THE ROCKS

1 fillet from an arctic char,
*   salmon, brook trout or lake trout*
Pinch of salt or a few drops of lemon juice

The finest sashimi is made from a fish that has just been caught. Simply fillet the fish, removing all small bones. Then slice, 1/8" thick in a slanting stroke across the grain. Eat raw fish with a pinch of salt or a few dribbles of lemon juice.—*Jerome Robinson, from* When Fishermen Cook Fish *by Rebecca Gray*

THE COLONEL'S CUP

1 scoop lemon sherbet
1 tbsp. vodka

Put the sherbet in the prettiest glass you can find—preferably one with a stem. Spoon the vodka over and serve. That's all there is to it. You might also want to pass thin, crisp cookies to go with the sherbet.

Fayal Greene
May 1977

274

LEVI BATES'S SALMON PATTIES

Fortunately, there are those plying their trade in far places, who by their work proclaim that grub cooked over the campfire can be wholesome and delicious. Such a woods chef was Levi Bates, whose campfires burned for 75 years in the wilderness headwaters of Maine's Fish River chain. Levi was a guide by profession but his instincts were those of Escoffier. His biscuits were light as a Fanwing Royal Coachman and his crisp broiled trout would melt in the mouth like snowflakes. But it is for his salmon cakes that I remember him best. The recipe called for canned salmon but this makeshift was unnecessary in Levi's bailiwick. As it was, the supply exceeded the demand. Our salmon were landlocks, fighting, silvery fish that came leaping to net, and we had eaten them broiled, fried and boiled for a week. I was beginning to tire of them and then one night on the shores of Big Machias Lake, Levi stirred up his salmon cakes. First, he removed the bones from a boiled salmon until he had about 2 ½ cups of pink, flaky meat. To this he added 3 tablespoons of condensed milk, 2 beaten eggs, 1 teaspoon of dried onion and a little pepper and salt. Then he formed the mixture into patties and dropped them into a kettle of smoking fat to fry until they were crispy brown.

Ted Janes
April 1957

BAKED SALMON FILLETS

1 salmon fillet, cut into
    ½-pound portions
1 lemon
1 tbsp. butter per ½-pound salmon
½ cup mayonnaise
½ cup sour cream
4 green onions, chopped
½ cup cheddar cheese
Paprika

Place the ½-pound fillets in a shallow, ungreased baking dish. Next, cut the lemon into wedges and squeeze a wedge over each fillet, following with a tablespoon of melted butter. Bake the fillets at 400°F for 10 minutes. Top them with a sour cream sauce consisting of mayonnaise, sour cream and the chopped green onions. Sprinkle the fish with shredded cheddar cheese and paprika. Bake for another 10 to 15 minutes, or until the fish is firm and the cheddar cheese begins to brown. Remove the fillets carefully from the pan with a thin metal spatula, leaving the skin stuck to the bottom.—*Fred Everson, March 1995*

SALMON AND SHAD

1 fish
8 oz. salt
1 gallon water

Cut the fins and tails from the cleaned headless fish. Without filleting or boning the fish, cut across the backbone so that the pieces are about ½ an inch shorter than the jar. Prepare a brine with 8 ounces of salt to 1 gallon of water, and soak the fish in the solution for 1 hour. A gallon of brine is sufficient for soaking 20 pounds of fish. Do not reuse the brine. Drain the liquid from the fish as it is packed, and do not add water. Close the jars and process the pints for 1 hour and 50 minutes at 10 pounds pressure (240°F). As a general rule, 25 pounds of fish (live weight) will yield approximately 12 pint jars of canned fish. Another method for storing salmon and shad is to prepare the fish as described above and to pack them directly into the jars without brining them. Add 1 teaspoon of salt to each jar and fill it with boiling water. After closing the jars, process them for 1 hour and 50 minutes at 10 pounds of pressure (240°F) in the container.—*Erling Stuart, April 1983*

CANNING SALMON

Pack the fish firmly in pint jars, leaving 1 inch of space at the top. Add 1½ teaspoons of salt to each jar. You may also pour 2 tablespoons of heated vegetable oil over the top before closing the lid. Process the jars for 2 hours at 10 pounds pressure (240°F).

Erling Stuart
April 1983

FANCIER BASIC FRIED FISH LIKE MOMMA THOUGHT SHE COULD MAKE

An excellent recipe for those rip-snorting bluegill and smallmouth bass pulled from the picturesque Shenandoah River in northern Virginia. You might be camped illegally on someone's private pasture. It got too dark too soon and you forgot to bring a flashlight. Not to worry. This will save the day. A bound batter may be used if powdered eggs and powdered milk have been packed. Mix the two with sufficient water, and dry the fish after filleting. First, dip each fillet into the seasoned flour, pat off the excess, then dip it into the batter. Allow excess batter to drip away, then dip the fillet back into the seasoned flour. Allow the fish to dry 10 minutes before frying in hot oil. Sip a glass of the wine you brought for cooking— you are, after all, cooking—and watch the river flow. Think about the Civil War and the 600,000-plus who died. Drink to 'em, in fact. After the fish is cooked (about 6 minutes, 3 a side), squeeze the juice from at least ½ a lemon and spill maybe ¼ cup of wine into the pan and jack up the heat. Cook for no more than 1 minute. If it's black, you cooked it too long.

John Eckberg and David Lowery
May 1993

PANFISH CAKES

4 to 6 panfish
½ cup cornmeal
1 egg
½ cup milk
Oil for deep-fat frying

Clean the crappies, bluegills or other panfish. Remove the meat from the skeleton and put the meat in a mixing bowl. Add ½ a cup of cornmeal and mix together. Make patties from the mixture, but don't press too hard; the cornmeal will hold the fish together. It usually takes 2 or 3 palm-size panfish to make 1 patty. Make a batter with the eggs and milk and dip the patties in this. Deep-fry them until golden. Serve on sandwich bread or between hamburger buns, or forget the bread and eat the patties plain. Serve with spinach salad for a "finer touch."—*Steve Ellis, June 1976*

Crappie

KENTUCKY SIMMERED CRAPPIE

1 lb. crappie fillets

4 tbsps. butter or margarine

Pinch each of salt and garlic powder

1 large onion or 8 scallions, thinly sliced or chopped

1 tsp. lemon pepper

Small bunch fresh parsley, shredded

½ cup Kentucky bourbon, slightly diluted with water

In a cast-iron skillet, melt the butter and add the salt, garlic powder and onion. Sauté over low heat for 4 minutes. Add the crappie fillets and lemon pepper, then sauté 5 more minutes, adding the shredded parsley leaves while stirring. Add the bourbon and simmer, covered, for 10 minutes. Serves 2.—*Cordy Swinton, February 1994*

CAMP ROLLS

1 cup warm water
1 package dry active yeast
2 tbsps. sugar
2 ½ cups flour
1 tsp. salt
1 egg
2 tbsps. shortening or
    vegetable oil, melted

In a pot, dissolve the yeast in water with the sugar. Stir in ½ the flour. Add the salt and beat the mixture with a spoon until smooth. Add the egg and shortening. Beat in the rest of the flour until smooth. Cover the pot and let the dough rise until double in size, about 30 minutes. Stir down the dough, spoon it into a greased Dutch oven, and let rise until double in size again, about 30 minutes. Bake until brown, about 20 to 25 minutes.

J. Wayne Fears
October 1985

FISH ON THE GRILL

Murphy won't give out the location of the fishing hole that provides basketfuls of large bluegills, but here is his secret on how to cook them.

Bluegills or other good panfish	1 cup light cooking oil
Tabasco sauce	¼ cup vinegar
Salt	¼ cup fresh lemon juice
	¼ cup Worcestershire sauce

Scale the fish and cut the heads off. When you slit the belly, cut past the vent a little toward the tail, exposing some meat. Wash the fish, then put a drop or two of Tabasco sauce in the cavity and onto each side. Spread this around the fish with your finger, then sprinkle the fish lightly inside and outside with salt. Build a charcoal fire in the grill and have the grid about 4 or 5 inches from the heat. In a basting pot, heat the cooking oil, vinegar, lemon juice and Worcestershire sauce. Keep the sauce warm and handy to the grill. When your fire is ready, spray the basket with Pam or brush it with cooking oil. Arrange the fish in the basket. The tails can overlap a bit if necessary, but the thick parts of the fish should barely touch. Use 2 or more baskets if you've got lots of fish. Adjust the basket to keep the fish tight, and lock it shut. Baste both sides and grill for about 5 minutes, for larger bluegills, 4 minutes for smaller fare. Baste the sides and turn several times. When the fish are done, the meat will start pulling away from the backbone. If in doubt, reach through the grid with a fork. If the meat flakes off easily, the fish are done. Open the basket carefully and remove the fish with a spatula.—*A.D. Livingston, July 1991*

Catfish

GROVER'S DREDGE

2 lbs. catfish fillets
4 eggs, beaten
1 cup flour
1 *cup* masa harina
    (rough cornmeal)
2 tbsps. pepper, freshly ground
2 tsps. garlic powder
1 tbsp. salt

Preheat some vegetable oil in a heavy skillet as you mix the flour, cornmeal and seasonings. The fillets should be cut no greater than ¾-inch thick. Draw them quickly through a shallow bowl containing the egg, turning them to cover both sides. Roll the fillets in the flour mixture and drop them immediately into the grease. Turn them occasionally to avoid burning. Cook until the flour is thoroughly browned, then serve. Serves 4.—*S.G.B. Tennant Jr., April 1984*

IN THE PINK

Gentle is the word when handling fish—all fish. If you broil them, handle them carefully and cook them quickly, so that they come to your plate juicy, not dry and tasteless. If you poach them (the preferred European way) in wine or broth, also do this quickly. If you sauté them in butter (not fry in deep grease!), turn them often and make sure they are off the heat before that fragile connective tissue breaks up and the fire ruins the fish. Exothermic heat acts here, too, and your fish should be removed from the fire while they are still solid and one piece, not breaking apart and shot through with grease and overcooking. Minutes, even seconds, is the time gauge with fish.

Jack Denton Scott
August 1963

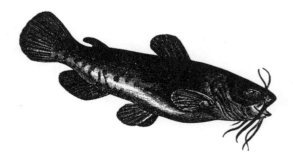

POISSONCHAT BLEU ARKANSAS (BACK-PACKER'S ARKANSAS BLUE CATFISH)

Should you hook a catfish while casting at sunset for smallmouth at Lake Ouachita near the dock at Crystal Springs Resort, then here's what you do: Kill the catfish, clean it and nail it to a board. Scrub the mud vein from the neck along the length of the spine. Be careful. Get all the mud from the fish's meat. Take your time. Use the board for leverage. Boil 1 quart of broth. Take the fish off the board, throw it away, boil the board and serve with mustard and beer.

John Eckberg and
David Lowery
May 1993

CAJUN-STYLE CATFISH

6 cleaned catfish (patted dry)
¼ cup prepared mustard
1 egg, beaten
1 tsp. hot pepper sauce
¼ cup dry bread crumbs
½ cup yellow cornmeal
¼ cup flour

½ tsp. salt
¼ tsp. garlic powder
¼ tsp. pepper
¼ tsp. paprika
1 inch vegetable oil in skillet,
    heated to 350°F

Combine the mustard, egg and pepper sauce. Then combine the bread crumbs, cornmeal, flour, salt, garlic, pepper and paprika. Mix well. Dip the fish in the mustard mixture and then in the cornmeal mixture. Fry in hot oil until golden and crispy. Drain on paper towels and serve hot with green onions and sliced tomatoes.—*Robert Hendrix, December 1993*

W i l d
V e g e t a b l e s

FORAGING FOR WILD VEGETABLES is so comparable to hunting and fishing, it would have been nearly unthinkable to include recipes here for the meat and fish and not the greens. Stalking the wild asparagus is a little less aggressive than hunting but not nearly as contemplative as fishing can be. Yet the pleasure of the search, the requirement of knowledge in the natural world, understanding the uniqueness of the resource and being involved in the bounty of each season—all of these elements are analagous.

One last word about wild veggies. Part of what makes them terrific is that they are so momentarily and delicately ripe; this should be taken advantage of. A fiddlehead can be pale and sweet green in the morning and by afternoon be full of chaff and unfurling into a fern. Alice Waters, the great Chez Pannise chef, said of garden vegetables, "time is part of their essence; one moment they are perfectly ripe, and then they'll change and you have to conceive a different way to cook and eat them. Then they'll change again and be gone and another year passes." It's true of the wild ones, too.

"Most vigitaryans I iver see looked enough like their food to be classed as cannybals."

—Finley Peter Dunne, "Casual Observations," Mr. Dooley's Philosophy, *1900*

BORDEN'S WILD RICE

6 cups wild rice, soaked (1 lb. dry)
4 cups fresh mushrooms, thinly sliced
¼ lb. butter
1 tsp. tarragon leaves
½ cup scallions, greens and whites, chopped
2 cups ham, cooked and julienned
Salt and substantial freshly cracked black pepper
1 bottle Burgundy

Rice should be washed several times and soaked overnight. Sauté the mushrooms in butter until they're tender, then add the tarragon, scallions, ham, salt and pepper and continue to cook until the scallions soften. Add the mixture to the drained rice in a large pot and stir thoroughly. Add enough wine to cover the rice, then form a lid over the pot with foil, punching a silver-dollar-sized hole in the center. Bake in the oven at 350°F for 1 hour, or until the wine has cooked out and the rice is al dente. Makes 12 cups.

—*S.G.B. Tennant Jr., January 1986*

WILD RICE PUDDING

3 cups wild rice, rinsed

½ cup dried currants

⅓ cup dark rum

2 cups whole milk

3 cups whipping cream

½ tsp. ground nutmeg

1 tsp. ground cinnamon

½ cup brown sugar, firmly packed

4 tbsps. unsalted butter

4 tsps. finely grated lemon zest

6 eggs, beaten

Cook the rice in boiling water for 10 minutes; drain it in a sieve, then rinse it under cold water. Drain it again. In a small bowl, pour the rum over the currants and set aside. In a saucepan, heat the milk, 2 cups of the cream and the spices until hot but not boiling. Stir in the wild rice. Simmer, covered, stirring occasionally, for about 30 minutes. Be sure you don't overcook it. Remove from the heat. Preheat the oven to 325°F. Stir the brown sugar, butter, lemon zest and currant mixture into the hot rice mixture. Combine 1 cup of the rice mixture with the beaten eggs, then stir in the remaining rice. Pour it into a buttered 1 ½-quart casserole. Set the dish in a larger pan, then pour hot water into the larger pan to a depth of 1 ½ inches. Bake at 325°F for 45 to 50 minutes. Place on a wire rack until cool; unmold. While the pudding bakes, whip the remaining cup of cream; add a little dark rum if desired. Serve it over the warm pudding. Serves 6 to 8.—*Kit and George Harrison, August 1988*

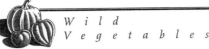

WILD RICE WILLOWMERE

1 cup wild rice, rinsed

4 cups chicken stock or chicken broth

3 tbsps. butter

1 medium onion, chopped; or ¾ cup green onions,
*   thinly sliced, including some tops*

½ lb. fresh mushrooms, sliced

¼ cup dry sherry

¼ cup parsley, chopped

½ cup slivered almonds, chopped pecans or hazelnuts (optional)

Salt and pepper to taste

In a bowl, cover the rice with boiling water and set it aside for 30 minutes. Drain the rice and cover it again with boiling water; set it aside until the water cools, then drain it again. Bring the chicken broth or stock to a boil in a large saucepan or pot; stir in the wild rice. Simmer, uncovered, for about 40 minutes, until the liquid is absorbed. In the mean-time, sauté the onion and mushrooms in butter until the onions are golden. Remove them from the heat; add sherry, parsley and, if desired, nuts, and stir them into the cooked wild rice until the mixture is well blended. Season to taste with salt and pepper. This dish may be prepared ahead to this point and stored, covered, in the refrigerator for up to a day. Excellent with poultry or any wild game. Serves 4 to 6.

—*Kit and George Harrison, August 1988*

WILD RICE BREAD

4 tbsps. unsalted butter

¼ cup honey

2 eggs, slightly beaten

1 ⅓ cups cooked wild rice (see "Basic Wild Rice")

½ cup pecans or hickory nuts, chopped

1 ¼ cups whole-wheat flour

1 tsp. baking powder

1 tsp. salt

¼ tsp. ground mace

¼ tsp. ground cloves

¾ cup whole milk

P reheat the oven to 325°F. In a large bowl, cream the butter and honey. Add the eggs and beat until smooth. Stir in the rice and pecans. In a small bowl, combine the flour, baking powder, salt and spices. Add these dry ingredients, about ⅓ at a time, to the egg mixture, alternating with the milk and mixing each time until everything is just combined. Pour the dough into a well-greased standard loaf pan. Bake 55 to 60 minutes, until a toothpick inserted to the center of the loaf comes out clean. Cool the loaf on a rack for about 10 minutes, then remove it from the pan. Cool it completely before serving. Serve with softened cream cheese or butter. Serve at lunch or dinner. Makes 1 loaf.—*Kit and George Harrison, August 1988*

BASIC WILD RICE

In a sieve, rinse 1 cup of wild rice under cold water. Drain. Put the rice in a bowl and cover it with cold water; let it soak for about 1 hour and drain. Bring 1 quart of salted water to a boil. Stir in the rice. Cover, lower the heat, and simmer the rice, stirring occasionally, for 40 to 55 minutes. Remove the cover and continue to simmer the rice for 5 minutes longer. Drain off any liquid. Makes 3 cups of rice.—*Kit and George Harrison, August 1988*

DANDELION COFFEE

Clean the dandelion roots thoroughly by scrubbing them with a brush. Dry them, then roast them gently in a 200°F oven till coffee-colored, or till crisp and a deep brown on the inside—about 4 hours. Store in a tightly capped jar and grind coarsely just before brewing. Use about the same proportions as you would for regular coffee.—*J.A. Pollard, April 1987*

MEDICINAL TEA

Dandelion roots will make a strong tea reputedly suitable for curing scurvy or eczema. Boil together 1 quart of water and about 2 ounces of cleaned and scraped root until reduced to 1 pint. Drink a small glassful every 3 hours.—*J.A. Pollard, April 1987*

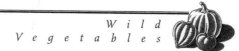

SALAD GREENS

Springtime dandelion crowns make a satisfactory salad green, though most people use the entire early plant. The crown is the part that remains blanched, mostly underground between the root and leaves. It's easy to collect if you follow these basic instructions: When digging a mess of greens, avoid roadways or any area where herbicides or pesticides have been sprayed. Choose large single or double plants with tender green leaves and small, tightly closed buds. When the buds are large, the leaves are less sweet; when the buds bloom, the leaves are bitterness personified. Tiny plants that seem to sit atop one another, forming a cushion, take forever to untangle and are often not worth the effort of collecting and cleaning them. A special two-tined fork for dandelion digging works wonders, but any kitchen paring knife will do. Shove your digger through the root, severing it far enough down to avoid disconnecting the leaves. Right there in the outdoors (rather than the kitchen), clean each plant. Using your knife, scrape off the brown leaflike material at the base. Trim the root close to where the leaves begin. Shake off dirt, insects or worms. Keep the cleaned plants in a brown paper bag as you proceed. You'll need a large bagful if you're going to collect enough for 6 people, because the greens shrink. Once you're in camp or back home, wash the greens till the water runs clear. This may take as many as 6 rinses. Years ago, cooks placed dandelion greens in a kettle with boiling water and a piece of pork. Served with vinegar, salt and pepper, they were delicious but also full of fat, and most of the nutrients were lost in the cooking water.—*J.A. Pollard, April 1987*

STEAMED DANDELION GREENS

Place freshly washed greens in a large steamer kettle. Steam them for 20 to 40 minutes, depending on their age, turning them with a fork. They must be al dente to be good. The amount of moisture left from washing should be enough for steaming, but check periodically, so they don't burn. When they're done, place them on a hot platter, cut them into wedges, and dress them with any vinaigrette (freshly squeezed lemon juice, virgin olive oil, sea salt, freshly ground black pepper and any herb you fancy). Or serve them with a natural soy sauce and lemon juice.—*J.A. Pollard, April 1987*

DANDELION CROWNS

Steamed greens are classic, but the aforementioned crown is a delicacy. Slice it off at the root low enough that it won't fall apart, and slice it again just where the leaves start to turn green. Wash the crowns well. To cook them, pop them into a fair amount of water and simmer perhaps 5 minutes, or until tender. Drain and serve with a natural soy sauce, olive oil and lemon juice.—*J.A. Pollard, April 1987*

DANDELION BEER

This was long favored by English foundry workers: Dig
a ½-pound of young, whole dandelion plants, including the
roots. Wash them well and remove the small hairy roots
without breaking the taproot. Place them in a pan with ½ an
ounce of bruised ginger root and the juice and rind (no pith)
of 1 lemon and 1 gallon of water. Boil 10 minutes. Place 1
pound of sugar and 1 ounce of cream of tartar into a large
crock. Strain the liquid and pour it into the crock for fer-
menting. Stir it until the sugar has dissolved. When the liquid is lukewarm, add 1 ounce of wine-maker's yeast and the
lemon juice. Cover the crock with a cloth and allow the mix
to rest in a warm room for 3 days, then strain and bottle it
in screw-capped beer bottles; store them on their sides. This
beer will be ready in about 1 week—when it hisses as the
top is loosened. It doesn't keep long.—*J.A. Pollard, April 1987*

SALADE DE PISSENLIT

The French devised this marvelous salad, wonderful
with any rich meat dish. Pick young tender leaves before the
buds grow, wash them well, and pat them dry. Dress them
with a basic vinaigrette of ⅔ virgin olive oil and ⅓ freshly
squeezed lemon juice and a bit of sea salt. Garnish with finely chopped chives, parsley, minced garlic and chopped hard-
boiled eggs.—*J.A. Pollard, April 1987*

Wild Vegetables

SALADE DE PISSENLIT AU LARD

This is a classic dish: dandelions dressed with a hot, oily dressing. Gather the leaves and treat as above. In a skillet fry 3 pieces of bacon. When they're crisp, remove and drain them. Add 2 tablespoons of cider vinegar to the hot fat and, as it boils up, pour them over the leaves. Add a little black pepper and eat them at once. At blossom time, the leaves turn bitter, but there is a way to trick them into sweetness. Cover a healthy plant with a bucket and let it bleach. As the chlorophyll disappears, so does the bitterness. You can use bleached dandelions in salads and in cooked dishes. Frost also helps the leaves to lose their bitterness. During Indian summer, the plants may sprout new leaves.—*J.A. Pollard, April 1987*

SAUTÉED DANDELION BUDS

In the morning of a nice day, collect as many young buds as you think you can eat. Ignore the very old ones. Wash the buds well and drain them thoroughly. Sprinkle on a little sea salt and some freshly ground black pepper. Warm a cast-iron skillet over moderate heat and bring ¼ cup of clarified butter to a foam. Sauté your buds in it, a few at a time, until they burst into bloom, or nearly so. Serve hot.—*J.A. Pollard, April 1987*

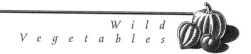

DANDELION FRITTERS

The blossoms can become culinary masterpieces. Just before dining, pick as many fresh blossoms as you can eat (perhaps 2 cups for this recipe). Remove any stems quickly. Wash and drain the blossoms well (also quickly, or they'll close up). Pat them dry. Place a wok on its ring over high temperature to warm it. Pour in about 2 inches of peanut oil and heat to 350°F. Beat together ½ a cup of milk, 2 tablespoons of yeast and 2 eggs. Sift in 1 cup of whole-wheat pastry flour, 2 teaspoons of baking powder (the kind that excludes aluminum salts—found in health food stores) and a pinch of sea salt. Whisk till very smooth. Dip the blossoms into batter and fry until golden. Drain and eat quickly.—*J.A. Pollard, April 1987*

DANDELION WINE

Made with golden petals, dandelion wine is like a sherry when suitably aged. It's worth making. Pick dandelion blossoms—fully open and bright yellow—on a sunny day after the dew has left them. They close on rainy days; they also close up shortly after picking, so work fast. Spread them out on a sheet of paper to get rid of insects if you think they are present. Take care to discard every pinch of bitter stem and green leaves, as they spoil fermentation and taste. To do so, hold the green stem part in one hand and the petals by digging into the middle with your thumbnail. Place 2 quarts of firmly packed dandelion petals into a 6-quart glass or stainless-steel mixing bowl. Pour in 1 gallon of boiling water. Stir. Cover and leave 2 or 3 days, stirring daily. Transfer to a large pot and add the peeled rinds of 2 lemons and 2 oranges—no white pith. Reserve the juice. Bring to a boil and simmer 10 minutes. Place 3 pounds of white sugar in a crock. Strain the boiled mixture through fine cheesecloth. When lukewarm, add the juice of 2 lemons and 2 oranges, plus 1 ounce of wine-making yeast. Allow the mixture to ferment in a warm room for 2 to 3 weeks. By the end of this the petals will have completely dissolved, leaving a brass-colored sweet liquid. Strain it into a big pot or bowl using a colander with several thicknesses of muslin or fine cheesecloth over it. Pour this clear liquid through a nonmetal funnel into a glass fermentation jar and seal it with an air lock. Store in a warm room 2 to 3 weeks, at an even temperature if possible. Place in a cool spot for 2 weeks longer, or until no bubbles rise to the surface when the jar is moved. At this point you will notice a little sediment on the bottom of the jar. This is spent yeast and must be removed. Do this by siphoning—it's called racking—the wine into a clean jar using about 4 feet of ½-inch-diameter rubber or plastic tubing. Be sure the tube is above the sediment. Insert the air lock tightly closed and leave the jar in a cool place. Siphon again as more sediment forms, and again, if necessary, till the wine remains clear for a week or so. This clearing may take as long as 4 months. Wash some wine bottles, dry them in a warm oven, and cool them with a plug of cotton wool in the top to keep it sterilized. By siphoning, fill the bottles to within 1 inch of the top. Soften new, straight-sided corks in boiling water and insert them with a cork-flogger, a gadget that blows the corks home without a lot of fuss; they're inexpensive. Store the bottles on their sides in a cool, dark place. Age them a year or more.—*J.A. Pollard, April 1987*

SALAD ON THE HOOF—WATERCRESS

Typically, watercress is a small to medium plant, seldom over a foot high, and it's a hydrophyte, or "water-lover." Sometimes you find it growing entirely underwater, sometimes partly in and partly out, sometimes on land but in very wet soil. It has a whitish, succulent root, many hair roots and rootlet nodules up and down the stem. Its flower, in spring and summer, has four petals, arranged in the form of a cross, hence the family name of Cruciferae. But the most easily identifiable feature of this group is the rosette of leaves at the top of the plant. Take a look at some cultivated cress in your grocery store and you won't fail to recognize this crown rosette when you see it afield. They're not only tender and tasty but they're packed with trace minerals. Once you start looking for it, you'll find watercress nearly everywhere the habitat is at all suitable—in streams, ponds, marshlands, wet meadows, spring pools—and the best varieties are available throughout the winter, unless the water freezes all the way to the bottom. It grows in thick mats and islands, and very abundantly; patches covering a quarter of an acre are not uncommon. It occurs all over the United States and most of Canada, in settled country and wild, in highland and lowland—few, indeed, are the places where you can't find it readily. This matter of freshness is really vital with leafy greens. It's one big reason the greens you gather outdoors and eat at once are generally incomparably higher in food values than the grocery-store item. You know the old saying about fish— "from hook to kettle." Well, you can double that for leafy

greens. Some believe they lose as much as 30 percent of their value if not eaten within an hour of picking, and some of the fragile properties are entirely lost in a couple of hours. Considering that store greens are usually many hours (or even days) old, you can see that a salad of wild greens has a food value that can't be bought at any price. When I prepare water-cress myself, I merely cut it up, roots and all, and use a salad dressing of my own making. This dressing is about as simple as you can make, but it tastes good. You can whip up a batch in 2 minutes, it lasts indefinitely, goes well with almost any greens and it isn't all hopped up with strong spices and flavoring. The ingredients are: 1) 2 parts malt or tarragon vinegar diluted with 1 part water; 2) brown sugar; 3) a sprinkle of salt; 4) a sparing amount of clear, light salad oil or its equivalent. Proportion the sugar and vinegar to fit your individual taste.
—*William Byron Mowery, August 1957*

FREE VITAMIN C—ROSE HIPS

Three rose hips, the nutritional experts say, have as much vitamin C as an orange. We don't pay much attention to these gratuitous vitamins in the United States and Canada. But in England during World War II, some 5 million pounds of rose hips were gathered from the roadsides and put up to take the place of then scarce citrus fruits. Dried and powdered, rose hips are sold in Scandinavian countries for use in soups, for mixing with milk or water to make hot and cold drinks or for sprinkling over cereals. You get the good from this cousin of the apple,

one of the many members of the rose family, whether you
eat it straight off the bush, cut up in salad, baked in cake or
bannock, or boiled into jam or jelly. Matter of fact, plain
dried rose hips are well worth carrying in a pocket for a
midday snack. To prepare them, just cut each in half. Remove
the central core of seeds. Dry the remaining shell-like skin
and pulp quickly, in a cool oven or in a kettle suspended
above the fringes of a small campfire. What I like to do with
rose hips is turn them into syrup. Snip the bud ends from a
freshly gathered batch. Then cover the fruit with water and
boil rapidly until soft. Strain off the juice. Return the pulp
to the kettle, add enough water to cover, and make a second
extraction. For every 2 cups of juice you end up with, add 1
cup of sugar. Boil until thick. Pour the syrup into sterilized
bottles. That's all. Poured over steaming sourdough hotcakes
blue-black winter mornings when the northern lights are
ablaze, this syrup never lasts long.—*Bradford Angier, April 1961*

Index

aioli sauce, 228
antelope
    baked, 52
    in fondue, 74
    marinade for, 128
    meatballs, 54
    quality of, 32, 47, 61
    in stew, 47
apples
    baked, 178
    pureed, 88
arugula, 271
aspic, 173, 244
barbecue sauce, 78, 90, 212, 238
bass
    baked, 245, 247-248, 251, 255,
    263-264
    broiled, 260
    in chowder, 256
    cooking tips for, 251, 258, 259
    fried, 157, 215, 246, 250
    grilled, 212
    poached, 241-242
    sauteed, 243, 249
    in stew, 254
bat, 172
bear
    in casserole, 86
    fried steaks of, 84
    marinade for, 128
    pot roast, 85
    in sausage, 87
    soap, 86
beaver, 172
bechamel sauce, 52, 206
beer, dandelion, 291
black bass
    baked, 247, 252
    in bourride, 228
    cold-molded, 242, 244
    in crepes, 258
    in custard, 259, 260
    in dumplings, 253
    in fondue, 262
    in mushroom pie, 261
    poached, 241, 252

black duck, *See* duck
bluefish, 213
bluegill, *See* panfish
blue trout, 191
boar
    baked tenderloin of, 88
    roasted, 89, 90
    scrapple, 91
bouillabaisse, 232, 233
bouillon, 62, 195, 230-231, 236, 241,
    252, 266
bourride, 228
brain, deer, 67
brant, *See* duck
bread
    potato, 56
    wild rice, 287
brioche, pumpkin, 217
broth, *See* bouillon
buffalo fish, 158
burgers
    buns for, 49
    turkey, 219
    venison, 49-51
butt clams, *See* clams
butterfish, 158
camp cooking
    with fish, 187, 193, 197, 214,
    239, 250, 260, 275, 277
    with gamebird, 105, 115
    with liver, 64, 66
    of soup, 62
    with venison, 23-25, 33, 58, 61, 81
    of venison stew, 34, 36-37, 40, 45, 48
    See also pit cooking
canning, 163, 165, 276
canvasback, *See* duck
caribou, 23, 32, 61
catfish, 280, 281
channel bass, 213
char, arctic, 274
cherrystone clam, *See* clams
chili, venison, 56, 57
chou paste, 206
chowder
    clam, 161, 166

fish, 223, 227, 233, 256
    oyster, 257
chukar, 125 *See also* partridge
clams
    canned, 163, 165
    in chowder, 161, 166
    types of, 161
    clay-pot cooking, 116
cod, 158, 161, 228, 231
coffee, dandelion, 288
coot, *See* duck
corn bread stuffing, 216
cougar casserole, 170
court bouillon, 195, 230-231, 236,
    241, 252, 266
crab, 160, 164, 240
crackers, 162
crappie, *See* panfish
crepes, 258
croquettes, 80, 109
crow, 174, 175
curing fish, *See* fish; smoked
curing meat, *See* jerky
custard, fish, 156, 259, 260
dandelion
    beer, 291
    coffee, 288
    fritters, 293
    salad, 289, 291, 292
    sauteed, 292
    steamed, 290
    tea, 288
    wine, 293-294
deer
    brain of, 67
    crown rack of, 4
    in fondue, 74
    heart of, 65, 68
    liver of, 20, 64, 66, 69
    marinade for, 128
    quality of, 32, 61
    See also venison
dolphin, 212
dove
    baked, 135
    with curry, 133

terrine of, 134
drying meat, *See* jerky
duck
　　baked, 99, 102
　　cooking tips for, 95, 96, 101,
　　103, 107, 109
　　fried, 109
　　gumbo, 106
　　jerky, 110
　　pastries, 107
　　pressed, 93, 99, 100
　　roasted, 92, 94, 96, 97, 98, 101,
　　104, 111
　　sauteed, 93
　　tacos, 105
　　in wonton skin (potstickers), 108
　　See also gamebird; quail
dumplings, 35
　　black bass, 253
eel, 158, 233
elk
　　baked, 52
　　in burgers, 49
　　camp cooking with, 23
　　in meatballs, 54
　　quality of, 32, 61
　　in stew, 47
　　See also venison
fish
　　baked, 154-155, 213, 237, 238,
　　255, 265
　　camp cooking with, 187, 193,
　　197, 214, 239, 250, 260, 275, 277
　　chowder with, 161, 223, 227, 257
　　cooking tips for, 185, 212, 233,
　　240, 266, 280
　　in custard, 156, 168, 259, 260
　　fried, 157, 227, 229, 235, 239, 277
　　frozen, about, 255, 266
　　grilled, 212, 214, 239, 279
　　in hash, 272
　　pickled, 202, 203
　　poached, 153, 195, 199
　　in quiche, 139
　　sauteed, 169
　　in seviche, 211, 222, 240
　　smoked, 158-159, 201, 203,
　　271, 276
　　in stew, 160, 209, 228, 232,
　　233, 254
　　See also specific species
flounder, 154, 168, 169
fondue, 74, 262
forcemeat, 201, 206-207
frogs' legs, 173

fruit bat, 172
gamebirds, 110, 128, 136
　　cooking tips for, 92, 96, 101, 105, 107
　　See also specific species
geoduc clams, *See* clams
giblets, 125, 136, 217
goat, 23, 61
goose, 110, 111
　　cooking tips for, 92, 96, 101, 107
goulash, venison, 45
　　See also stew
gravlax, *See* lox
gravy
　　bear, 85
　　turkey giblet, 217
grouper, 212, 231, 233
grouse
　　baked, 131
　　with curry, 129
　　jerky, 132
　　marinade for, 128
　　pit cooked, 132
　　stew, 130
guiyas, 45
gumbo, duck, 106
haddock, 158, 233, 237
halibut, 160, 228
hardshell clams, *See* clams
hasenpfeffer, *See* rabbit
hash
　　sea, 267
　　venison, 81
heart
　　of gamebird, 110
　　of venison, 65, 68, 70
　　See also giblets
hen clam, *See* clams
herring, pickled, 202
iguana, 171
javelina, *See* boar
jerky
　　gamebird, 110, 132, 220
　　venison, 43, 51, 57, 72, 73
kidneys, venison, 70
kippered fish, 158
lingcod, 240
littleneck clam, *See* clams
liver
　　deer, 20, 64, 66, 69
　　gamebird, 110
　　See also pate
longneck clams, *See* clams
lox, 158, 273 *See also* salmon
mackerel, pickled, 202
mallard, *See* duck

marinades
　　oriental, 234
　　for rabbit, 148
　　sweet-and-sour, 229
　　use of, 16, 233
　　for venison, 16, 72, 80
　　wine as, 128
marsh rabbit (muskrat), 179
mayonnaise, 74, 168, 268
meatballs, venison, 54
meat sauce, 138
meat thermometer, use of, 15
milk, powdered, 156
mincemeat, venison, 58
moose, 32, 46, 49, 61, 128
　　burgers, 49
　　camp cooking with, 23
　　marinade for, 128
　　quality of, 32, 61
　　stew, 46
mountain sheep, 61
mouse stew, 171
mousse, fish, 168
mulligan, *See* stew
mushrooms
　　in pie, 261
　　puree of, 206-207
　　with wild rice, 284
muskie, 265
muskrat, 179
mussels, 153, 241
opossum, 180
oysters, 163, 167, 257
　　canape, 167
　　canned, 163
　　and fish chowder, 257
　　fried, 167
　　on the half shell, 163
　　soup, 162
panfish
　　cakes, 277
　　grilled, 279
　　simmered, 278
　　smoked, 158
partridge, 125, 127, 128
pasta, 52, 125
pastry crust
　　for duck pasties, 107
　　for pie, 118, 147
　　for quiche, 139
　　shell, 124
　　for venison Wellington, 11
pate
　　chicken-liver, 11
　　deer-liver, 68

pike, 204
pemmican, 73
peppers
  stuffed, 53, 55
perch, 157, 158-159, 228
pesto, 271
pheasant
  baked, 116
  cold, 115
  fried, 113
  giblets, 125
  marinade for, 128
  pie, 117
  pressure-cooked, 113
  roast, 112, 119
  salad, 115
  stew, 119
  stir-fried, 114
  with truffles, 117
  and venison pie, 118
pickerel, 265
pickling fish, 202, 203
pigeon, *See* dove
pike, 204-208
  baked, 197, 208
  cutlets, 206-207
  forcemeat, 207
  marinated, 208
  pate, 204
  roast, 205
pintails, *See* duck
pit cooking, 27, 132, 177
  See also camp cooking
pompano, 154-155, 240
pork, *See* boar
possum, 180
pot pie
  fish, 261
  gamebird, 117, 118, 124
  pastry crust for, 107, 118, 124, 147
  possum, 180
  rabbit, 143, 147
  squirrel, 177
  venison, 118
potstickers, duck, 108
pudding
  fish, 156, 259, 260
  wild rice, 285
quahaugs, *See* clams
quail
  giblets, 125
  grilled, 123
  marinade for, 123, 128
  pot pie, 124
  roasted, 121

sauteed, 120, 122, 125, 126
  See also duck; gamebird
quiche, 76, 139
rabbit
  baked, 143, 145
  broiled, 152
  in casserole, 151, 152
  deep-fried, 150
  fried, 150
  with gravy, 145
  marinated, 146
  pit cooked, 132
  pot pie, 143, 147
  shish kabob, 148
  stew, 144
  stir-fried, 149
raccoon, 181
ragout, *See* stew
rainbow trout, 201
  See also fish; trout
razorback, *See* boar
razor clams, *See* clams
redfish, 222, 223
red gunard, 233
red snapper, 228, 231, 240
rehfleisch, 71
ribs, venison, 4, 71, 78
rice, wild
  basic, 288
  bread, 287
  with mushrooms, 284
  pudding, 285
  willowmere, 286
rice pilau, 135
rice salad, 270
rissoles, 80
rock cod, 240
rockfish
  baked, 213
  in bourride, 228
  in envelope, 154-155
  for fish stock, 231
  marinated, 240
  stew, 160
  See also bass
roe, walleye, 210
rolls, 278
rose hips, 296-297
salad, 295-296
  dandelion, 289, 291, 292
  dressing for, 115, 123
  with fish, 200, 222
  with gamebird, 115, 123
  with rice, 270
salmon

baked, 154-155, 270, 275
canned, 276
cooking tips for, 268, 269
for fish stock, 231
Nova Scotia, 271
patties, 275
pickled, 202
poached, 266
sashimi, 274
smoked, 158, 276
  See also lox
sashimi, 274
sauces
  aioli, 228
  barbecue, 78, 90, 238
  bechamel, 52, 206
  caper, 74, 230
  cucumber, 253
  curry, 115, 262
  dill mustard, 215
  for fondue, 74, 262
  garlic, 74
  gerlette, 244
  Hollandaise, 198
  horseradish, 71
  hot, 262
  hot mustard, 74
  key lime, 212
  macadamia nut, 186
  Madeira, 98
  meat, 138
  Mornay, 153
  mustard, 273
  orange, 98, 111, 247
  poivrade, 94
  red, 74
  rouille, 232
  sauterne, for black bass
  pudding, 259
  Sheriff House, 188
  sour cream with dill, 261
  tartar, 215, 262
  tomato, 53, 235
  Welsh rarebit, 237
  wine, 99
sausage, 108
  bear, 87
  venison, 59, 60, 76, 136
scallops, 240
scaup, *See* duck
scrapple, boar, 91
sea bass, 228, 233, 240
sesame dressing, 115
seviche, 211, 222, 240
shad, 158, 202, 276

sherbet, 274
shish kabobs, 75, 148
shrimp
    with bass fillets, 241
    broiled, 164
    fried, 166
    grilled, 165
    in halibut stew, 160
    marinated, 240
    with Mornay sauce, 153
smallmouth bass, 277
smelt, 202, 203
smoked meats
    fish, 158-159, 201, 203
    turkey, 221
    venison, 77
snowshoe rabbit, See rabbit
soap, bear, 86
softshell clams, See clams
sole, 188, 240
sorrel, 271
soup
    camp cooking of, 62
    from court bouillon, 231
    fish, 200, 234
    oyster, 162
    venison, 61-63
spaghetti sauce, venison, 8
spareribs, venison, 79
spatzle, See dumplings
squab, See dove
squirrel, 176-179
steamers, See clams
steelhead, 139, 158, 185
    See also fish; trout
stew
    crow, 174
    fish, 160, 209, 228, 232, 233, 254
    gamebird, 119, 130, 136
    moose, 46
    mouse, 171
    rabbit, 144
    squirrel, 176, 178
    venison, 19, 26, 34-37, 39-42,
        44, 45, 47, 48
    woodcock, 137
stir-fry
    with pheasant, 114
    with rabbit, 149
    with venison, 27, 28
striped bass, 154
    baked, 213
    in bourride, 228
    in broth, 231
    marinated, 240

stuffing
    corn bread, 216
    crabmeat, 187
    for peppers, 53, 55
    for trout, 185, 187, 188, 190, 201
    venison, 55
    walnut, 190
sturgeon, smoked, 158-159
swordfish, 272
syrup, rose-hip, 297
tacos, duck, 105
tea, dandelion, 288
teal, See duck
tomcods, 233
trout
    amandine, 196
    baked, 197, 198, 199
    boiled with herbs, 189
    in bourride, 228
    broiled, 187, 195, 197
    cooking tips for, 185, 190
    fried, 157, 186, 193, 194
    poached, 191, 199
    raw, 274
    salad, 200
    sauteed, 192-193
    smoked, 158-159, 201
    soup, curried, 200
    stuffed, 185, 187, 188, 190, 201
tuna, 158, 202
turkey
    burgers, 219
    Cajun fried, 218
    giblet gravy for, 217
    jerky, 220
    roasted, 216
    smoked, 221
venison
    aging of, 8
    baked chops of, 32
    baked for Wellington, 10-11
    baked in pie, 3, 30, 80
    baked slices of, 82
    baked with pasta, 52
    barbecued, 33, 78
    boiled, 38, 71
    boiled heart of, 68
    broiled chops of, 31, 33
    broiled shish kabobs of, 75
    broiled steaks of, 82
    in burgers, 49-51
    camp cooking of stew, 34, 36-
        37, 40, 45, 48
    camp cooking with, 23-25, 32-
        33, 58, 61-62, 64, 66-67, 81

    in chili, 56-57
    cuts of, 7, 19, 30-31, 34, 39, 79
    definition of, 61
    in fondue, 74
    fried brain of, 67
    fried heart of, 65
    fried liver of, 66, 69
    fried steaks of, 20, 24-25
    in hash, 81
    in jerky, 43, 51, 57, 72, 73
    marinade for, 16, 18-19, 72
    in meatballs, 54
    in mincemeat, 58
    in pate, 68
    pilaf, 22
    pit cooking with, 27
    in pot roast, 19, 21, 71
    in quiche, 76
    roasted, 13, 17-18
    roasted haunch of, 6-7, 9
    roasted leg of, 14-15
    roasted rack (ribs) of, 4, 79
    roasted saddle of, 9, 12, 14-15
    in sausage, 59, 60, 76
    sauteed for stroganoff, 43
    sauteed heart of, 70
    sauteed kidneys of, 70
    sauteed liver of, 20, 64
    sauteed steaks of, 23
    smoked, 77
    in soup, 61-63
    spaghetti sauce, 8
    in stew, 19, 21, 26, 29, 34-37,
        39-42, 44-48
    tender, 22
vinaigrette, raspberry walnut, 123
walleye
    baked, 197, 211
    with barbecue sauce, 212
    in bourride, 228
    roe, 210
    in salsa, 211
    stew, 209
watercress salad, 295-296
waterfowl, See specific species
weakfish, 154-155
Welsh rarebit sauce, 237
whitefish, 202, 228, 240
white sea bass, 213, 228
whiting, 158, 233
wine
    dandelion, 293-295
    as marinade, 128
    mulled, 139
woodcock, 127, 137, 138